"The hot dog *Moby-Dick*."
Branson Reese

"Wonderfully
weird and wild."
BookPage

"Gonzo yet vulnerable."
Gabe Dunn

PRAISE FOR *RAW DOG*

THE *NEW YORK TIMES* BESTSELLER

"Deeply incisive
and hilariously honest."
Jack O'Brien

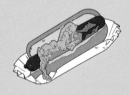

"Revealing, funny, sad,
horny, and insatiably curious."
Sarah Marshall

"You will never read a funnier
book about taking a
hot dog–themed road trip
across America."
Glamour

"Gross."
Library Journal

"A wild ride."
Robert Evans

"Wise and funny."
Andy Richter

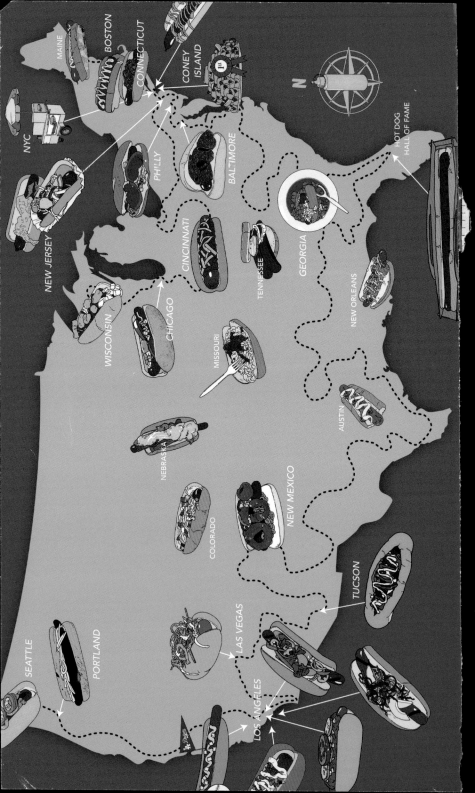

Praise for *Raw Dog*

"Somewhere between a send-up and a takedown of America's favorite sausage." —*Bon Appétit*

"Equal parts meat-processing indictment, travelogue, hot dog history, and odd facts, this book is irreverent, hilarious, entertaining, honest, and, at times, gross. Will fascinate readers interested in hot dogs, road trips, and regional recipes." —*Library Journal*

"*Raw Dog* will leave you nourished." —*BuzzFeed*

"Jamie Loftus is a wise and funny storyteller, and her enthusiasm is inspiring. There's so much about hot dogs that you need to know, and Jamie is here to teach you!"

—Andy Richter, actor and writer

"A moving, gorgeously written, and lovingly researched dive into the world of hot dogs, American nationalism, in-group scandal, and delicate human relationships. This gonzo yet vulnerable trek is meaty, fun, critical, and evocative all at once. Jamie Loftus is the hot dog generation's Joan Didion."

—Gabe Dunn, *New York Times* bestselling
coauthor of *I Hate Everyone But You*

"Jamie deftly interweaves the absurdity of the ubiquitous hot dog with the chaos of an American culture trying to suss out its post(?)-pandemic identity. Her eye for detail, sly wit, and whip-smart way with words make her one of the freshest and most insightful new comedic voices of this decade."

—Lindsay Ellis, *New York Times* bestselling author of *Axiom's End*

"Who but Jamie Loftus could've given us the hot dog *Moby-Dick*? This book is like getting shot in the chest and waking up three hours later, stronger and wiser."

—Branson Reese, *New York Times* medium-selling
author of *Hell Was Full* and creator of FX's *Swan Boy*

RAW DOG

The Naked Truth About Hot Dogs

Jamie Loftus

TOR PUBLISHING GROUP · NEW YORK

Interior illustrations and photos by Jamie Loftus
Tip-in illustrations by Faye Orlove

A Forge Book
Published by Tom Doherty Associates / Tor Publishing Group
120 Broadway
New York, NY 10271

www.torpublishinggroup.com

Forge® is a registered trademark of Macmillan Publishing Group, LLC.

The Library of Congress has cataloged the hardcover edition as follows:

Names: Loftus, Jamie, author.
Title: Raw dog : the naked truth about hot dogs / Jamie Loftus.
Description: First edition. | New York : Tor Publishing Group, [2023]
Identifiers: LCCN 2023007671 (print) | LCCN 2023007672 (ebook) |
    ISBN 9781250847744 (hardcover) | ISBN 9781250847751 (ebook)
Subjects: LCSH: Loftus, Jamie—Travel—United States. | Frankfurters—
    United States. | Fast food restaurants—United States. | Diners (Restaurants)—
    United States.
Classification: LCC TX649.L64 R39 2023 (print) | LCC TX649.L64 (ebook) |
    DDC 641.5092—dc23/eng/20230310
LC record available at https://lccn.loc.gov/2023007671
LC ebook record available at https://lccn.loc.gov/2023007672

ISBN 978-1-250-84776-8 (trade paperback)

Our books may be purchased in bulk for promotional, educational, or business use.
Please contact your local bookseller or the Macmillan Corporate and Premium Sales
Department at 1-800-221-7945, extension 5442, or by email at
MacmillanSpecialMarkets@macmillan.com.

First Forge Paperback Edition: 2025

Printed in the United States of America

0   9   8   7   6   5   4   3   2   1

For the workers who walked and the workers who stayed.

For Gram and for Papa, who made all of it possible
with love and with volume.

And for a guy named Al Freni I met at a hot dog eating
contest.

Humans can't understand something without a narrative, so we'll make one up in the absence—it's a very powerful thing.

George Shea, 2021

CONTENTS

INTRODUCTION

Welcome to the softest version of *Raw Dog* available. This is Jamie, reporting from the future—imagine me leaning out of a Jeep, screaming critical information that will save your life in the present from the world you're about to enter. Welcome to the book. If you act now you can still save yourself from knowing exactly how a hot dog is made.

A lot has changed since the first edition of this book was released, but the appetite for processed tubed meat has only increased. Three hot dog summers have passed since I wrote this book, and I'm thrilled to report it's very possible we're *just* crossing into her golden era.

Allow me to explain. A month ago, I found myself in Las Vegas wearing a hot dog jumpsuit I bedazzled during a little Mental Episode, watching the greatest sports rivalry in history conclude. I'm talking, of course, about the televised rematch between eating champions Takeru Kobayashi and Joey Chestnut.

These are men who'd lived in my head rent-free for years, ones I'd accepted would never compete against each other again. The world was too different, the harm done between the two too severe. But then, fifteen years after they'd last laid eyes on each other, something had changed and here they were, appraising the fluffiness of grocery-store hot dog buns and feeling the angry buzz of actual *competition,* for once.

This was a year after *Raw Dog* was released, a full summer after I'd traveled the country in my hot dog suit spreading the good word about a rivalry I was so sure would never be resolved. If you're reading this now, you're holding a softer version of that same book (with a few pages at the beginning) that knows the woman in the pages after can't conceive of the world this one will be released into.

So, some dispatches from the future:

• I *would* meet Joey Chestnut at the after-party for the Nathan's Famous International Hot Dog Eating Contest in 2023, and he'd ask if I was "the writer who pretended to be married to him." I'd quietly confirm I was. Elsewhere, I would loudly scream that onstage while letting an inflatable doll with Joey's face on it disembowel me.

• At the first release event for this book, I would get to talk with the Wienermobile driver from the next-to-last chapter, and he'd decide to share something he wasn't comfortable saying while still under contract with the Oscar Mayer corporation. This was, of course, that the seat where the Wienermobile drivers would fuck was in the back left of every vehicle and was called "the meat seat."

• Just a few months later, I'd get to show the photographer this book is dedicated to that I'd finished the book he didn't believe I was writing and put a copy in his hands.

• During Brat Summer (and by this I do mean *bratwurst*), I'd get to perform in front of a gigantic hot dog in Times Square that ejaculated confetti every day at noon exactly, while learning about the "absent referent" from feminist vegan Carol J. Adams, who paradoxically adores hot dogs as much as I do.

• And most important for myself and for society writ large, Joey and Kobi would face off one last time. It felt as impossible as being paid to write a whole book about hot dogs, much less a book named after something I'd done with two men named Josh in early 2017.

What I'm getting at is this: the world changes quickly and chaotically, but hot dogs are forever.

One last thing for the paperback edition—this version, the softer, more pragmatically priced one, is dedicated to my dad, too. When I was first researching *Raw Dog*, he had just been diagnosed with lung cancer, and I wrote with the certainty that he would be here, checking my work and boiling hot dogs to the gnarliest temperature possible, forever. When I wrote this book, he was okay, and as long as this book is in print without these pages at the front, he'll always be okay. But this brief portion of the soft version of my book knows the future, and that he's not with us anymore.

A softer, gentler *Raw Dog** has the pages that tell you that the pages behind this were read carefully by my dad, a career sports reporter who thought I left five words too many in every sentence. The pages behind this were marked up on an old laptop with "fragment or Jamie creative choice?" A draft that nearly made it to print included a factually correct but ultimately disgusting anecdote about my grandma, and my dad isn't here to tell me a second time to please not mention his beloved mother's diarrhea in my book in case it's the only one I ever get to write. (Sorry.)

The harder version of this book was the one I got to bring onstage with both of my parents the week it came out, not knowing we had just over a year left together. It can't know what these few pages do, that the last time my dad and I would eat together the week he died, he asked if I'd make hot dogs. The harder version of *Raw Dog* doesn't know a hot dog could be cut into such tiny pieces, but I can tell you from these pages at the front that it's the most gratifying thing I've experienced in my life as a six-foot piece of processed meat.

Thank you for buying the soft version of *Raw Dog*. I would have waited, too; twenty-eight dollars is a lot.

Jamie Loftus
October 2024

P.S. Kobi should have won the rematch, but I'd still marry Joey in a second.

---

* (I don't know how to avoid having this phrase appear in a sentence about my dead father and I'm sorry.)

RAW
DOG

Jamie's Content Warning Corner

Before we begin, a few content warnings. "But Jamie, content warnings are for babies, *I* don't need a *'content' 'warning.'*" Well, mind your business and turn the page, then.

In this book, there are occasionally frank (pun not intended but cannot access better word at this time) discussions of disordered eating, drug use, violence, and descriptions of working slaughterhouses. Much of the book isn't about these topics, but some of it is, and I've tried to give you a heads-up where those sections are in case you'd rather read ahead. Take care of yourself; it is not worth it to sacrifice your mental health over my hot dog book even though I think it's pretty good and thanks for picking it up.

These parts are important and unavoidable, but there's good news: there are also descriptions of hot dogs I loved, there's a picture of my cocker spaniel, there're passages that get extremely horny out of nowhere. There's a whole section about an intense fantasy I have where I get my shit rocked completely raw in Radiator Springs, which is the fictional town that the *Cars* franchise takes place in if you live under a rock. Depending on who you are, the Radiator Springs bit might be the worst part of all.

Next order of business—while true, all the events of this book took place some time ago! I'm fine. If you find yourself growing parasocially attached and wanting to ask if I'm fine, I am fine.

Not every hot dog place I visited is included in this book—it's been edited for length and clarity, and to protect small businesses with shitty hot dogs.

And finally—if you're standing in a big box store wondering if you should steal this book, the answer is yes.

A Word (Different from Jamie's Content Warning Corner)

For a piece of Americana that virtually everyone has been forced to eat in celebration of European colonialism, there is stunningly little written about hot dogs in detail. There are a handful of books written with a swirl of research and love, and the assumption that you would only read a book about hot dogs because you love them. I will relieve you of that assumption. I would like to be a writer who can keep a cool distance from the subject, who can wait, like sitting meat, and look over at what interests me flirtatiously until *it* comes to *me*. That is not what I am like. I want to consume and be consumed by the objects of my desire until they make me sick; I want to puke them back out and rearrange them like tea leaves. I am a terrible flirt and an excellent hot dog eater. Tell me what's interesting about you, and I will put it in my mouth, chew it up, and spit it out later on, never guaranteed to be better than I found it.

Think about how you feel about hot dogs right now, and let me know how you feel at the end. If it's exactly the same, I promise I won't write another one of these things.

My book is about hot dogs because like anyone, if you ask me a single follow-up question on the topic, I feel strongly about them. I grew up eating hot dogs boiled when my dad was left home alone with us, came of age with hot dogs sitting in a wet cardboard container at the bottom of my free-with-seventy-five-dollar-purchase tote bag "just in case," got fired for tweeting about hot dogs after a cart sponsored by StubHub failed to pay me when I handed out lukewarm bacon-wrappeds after a Bruins game in 2013. The tweet said something akin to, say it with me, "fuck hot dogs."

It's my understanding that the best makers of and writers about food tell you a story—my grandmother who was trapped in a mine for fifteen years used to make me this soup; my husband turned into a mermaid and left me for a grad student who made a mean sourdough; learning how to make ramen at my apartment is self-care, praxis, body positivity, a radical political act, and pottery class. Food is a connector to one's culture in the same way language can be—something that can launch you back onto a ratty couch during a commercial break where someone's offering you either drugs or a Barbie doll depending on the year you're airdropped into. The feelings some foods hold rattle in your skull, sink into your bones, and release into your toilet.

So I'm going to tell you a story, and you can tell me if it comes out of your plumbing in the same shape you took it in. This is a story about the summer of 2021, when everyone decided the plague had ended even though people were still dying, the year after Americans had grown so nostalgic for something bad and familiar to them while locked inside that hot dog sales leapt by more than 100 percent. This is a story about looking for a perfect hot dog and never finding it (spoilers ahead!), and you should know this trip doesn't end well for anyone. Did I mention there were two of us at the beginning? Well, there aren't now.

I traveled thousands of miles with a cat and a dog and a man, telling teenagers across this "great" "nation" that I'll have whatever their regular is. I experienced the full spectrum of what it means to spend seventy-five dollars on a hotel. I fielded questions about "the nitrates," questions about "the ketchup thing," questions about whether someone's aunt's ex-husband still works at this stall in North Carolina, which he doesn't because he died. I have had the arguments about whether it's a sandwich (sure), whether it's a taco (sure), whether there's any truth whatsoever to that study that says each hot dog you eat takes thirty-six minutes off your life (I don't buy it, and believe it is secretly funded by Big Lettuce).

I have had my ear talked off by business owners in it for the love of the game, by children of business owners who are in it out of obligation, by an actual child who runs a hot dog stand and makes them with steak, by an exhausted teenager preparing the tiniest hot dog I've ever seen and talking with the guy at the grill. I've seen all the signs: the neon signs; the distressed wooden signs; the all-lowercase, chic-font signs that tell you a quirky girl just got her trust fund and you'll never *believe* what business she's trying; the irrationally angry sign saying you'll have to fucking wait a little longer because it would appear that the *workers* don't feel like coming to *work* anymore.

I have become a hot dog snob, met a hot dog snob and wanted to walk into traffic, become a hot dog purist and fell asleep a snob again, all in the space of the state of New Mexico. I've woken up beside them, woken up from dreams of them, waved away sex after eating them, and been reminded of the sex I wasn't having while looking at them. I've seen people of all genders with natural C-cups whip their tits out to watch a group of men nearly kill themselves eating them on the Fourth of July. I have seen an old biker and a young biker about to either fuck or have a lovely family outing share one with their lips dangerously close to each other. I have seen the machines, the goop, the paste, been certain that this would be the video, the person, the texture, the bowel movement to transition me to Brooklyn podcaster veganism, and never been correct.

Hot dogs are the kind of American that you know there is something deeply wrong with but still find endearing. They're presented to people with no money as a filling and affordable alternative to health, all while people with too much money have found a way to charge fifteen fucking dollars for them. They're high culture, they're low culture, they're sports food and they're hangover food and they're *deeply* American for reasons that few people can explain but everyone has been told their entire lives.

The hot dog, my hot dog, is the delicious and inevitable product of centuries of violence, poverty, ambition, whispers in human ears and knives in the throats, shoulders, and legs of cows, pigs, chickens, and, if you're superstitious, maybe even the species they're named for. Today she rolls around at the front of the 7-Eleven, is vacuumed into the gullets of champion eaters, sits beside a flag you are told you love from the time you start to form memories. She is not American at all, and the most American girl you could meet—all marketing, no substance.

Our Protagonist

A troubled girl who is cagey about her origins.

I followed the hot dog across the country over the course of several months in 2021, a period of time hereafter referred to as Hot Dog Summer. Starting in the Southwest, we wore no more than five shirts apiece all season, squirreling around the South and up the East Coast, pausing before hovering north and back down the Pacific Coast Highway. There was a lot of ground to cover, but that's Miss Hot Dog's way—she herself is an immigrant.

A hot dog is a whole lot of something shoved inside of something else, but you cannot, *cannot* confuse her with her father the sausage. A sausage is any meat shoved into casing with as many spices as you like, is tougher and less surgically precise in its production, does not require a large vat of pink goo to be smoked through for hours before being declared food. The hot dog is born of the sausage tradition, but insists on her own nastiness.

Here is her secret—the American hot dog is not American at all. Hot dogs are part of a massive family of meaty scraps in meaty casing from all around the world, but she holds her familial recipe in Germany, Poland, and Greece. Their sausage and meat sauce traditions immigrated to the United States over a century ago, only to become possessed by the lunatic frenzy of American individualism. The hot dog was willed into existence in name during the late nineteenth century on college campuses, in vaudeville performances, and in editorial cartoons, but early traces of her existence predate goddamn Jesus Christ.

The "ancestral sausage" goes back twenty thousand years to the Paleolithic era. The Geico mascots of yore didn't have the machinery necessary to bring hot dogs to the masses, but they had the general idea: meat cooked in skins over open fires or in pits filled with hot water that, with all due respect, couldn't have been much dirtier than New York hot dogs cooking on the sidewalk as you read this. The primordial dog pops up again in the Middle East during the first millennium BCE, appearing in Assyrian texts, then again when Homer's *The Odyssey* turned blood sausages into a metaphor for you tell me what.

"As when a man near a great glowing fire turns to and fro a sausage, full of fat and blood, anxious to have it quickly roast," Homer wrote. What do you think?

We find Little Miss Hot Dog again in Italy on one of her many journeys made possible due to the oppressors' impulse to violently colonize and force their culture on others. I was raised to believe that commonalities between Greek and Roman mythologies could be chalked up to Italian insecurity and copycattery, but it's yet another imperial tale. Even so, the Romans beat the Greeks to the sausage punch—the southern Italian province Luciana produced a sausage of the same name between the seventh and eighth centuries BCE.

Once colonized by the Greeks, the Romans violently forged west, bringing sausage with them to the banks of the Rhine, where the ancestral hot dog makes her first critical contact with Germans. Germany didn't need the assist—there are German sausage recipes from as early as 228 CE, and hot dog historian Bruce Kraig has speculated that the two cultures likely developed their own sausage traditions without knowledge of the other. The exclusively pork sausage increased in popularity throughout the medieval era over the pork-and-beef-mixture alternative, becoming a staple throughout Europe and some parts of Asia for its ability to be preserved for long periods and its easy incorporation into working-class religious feasts. The dish continued to make appearances in pre-plumbing pop culture—in England, the fourteenth-century utopian poem "The Land of Cockaygne" features people filling themselves to the brim on walls of bright red sausages.

Germany continued to independently develop the sausage over the next few centuries, with the Thuringer, filled with pork, beef, and veal shoulder from the German Thuringia region, debuting in the early 1400s. Finally, between the fifteenth and seventeenth centuries, the hot dog's parents were born: the maternal frankfurter and the paternal wiener.

Let's not upset the family—frankfurters and wieners are not the same. German-style frankfurters are most commonly made with beef today, but began as smoked pork sausages prior to the beef-exclusive label from the Gef-Volsings company in the late nineteenth century. Wieners are of Austrian descent—precooked pork, beef, and veal mixtures most popularly canned as Vienna sausages in North America today. (In a confusing turn that will be far from the last in hot dog lore, the Chicago-famous Vienna Beef company serves all-beef dogs.) To the average consumer, the frankfurter and wiener are the same, but think of them as cousins in matching clothes on Easter.

Most regions of Europe developed their own form of sausage, with thicker ground meats finding local character in the form of Polish kielbasa, French boudins, and more than forty kinds of bratwurst. It's these characters, along with frankfurters and wieners, that made their way across the Atlantic in the seventeenth and eighteenth centuries in order for the "all-American" hot dog to take shape.

The countries responsible for the majority of brutal North

American colonization and subjugation of Indigenous people from the 1500s onward are Britain, France, and Spain, none of whom have a significant footprint in sausage or hot dog culture. Still, it's important to note that it's unlikely the sausage ever would have gotten to North America without western Europeans first perpetrating this violence. German families were present in the US as early as the 1600s, and sausage became a new tradition on stolen Indigenous land by the 1700s. The first cookbook to be published in the Thirteen Colonies, Eliza Smith's *The Compleat Housewife,* included a painstaking recipe for home pork sausage preparation that involved mincing meat, mixing with leaf lard, preparing pig guts, stuffing extensively, smoking, and finally frying or grilling the entire situation. The book was written for the "gentlewoman" of the higher classes, but the meal that was simply meat stuffed into other meat wouldn't achieve its status as a street-side staple until the Industrial era, thirty years after the publication of Smith's book.

Once again, violence for the hot dog to make her way into your hand. Prior to the American Civil War in the 1860s, sausage was handmade in local butcheries—more accessible to the general public than centuries past, but not yet automated for the masses. Meat markets around this time were still dominated by finely ground pork, but lack of regulation and the general mystery of butchery fueled (often rightly placed) superstitions around what was *really* in these sausage things. Butcher and writer Thomas Farrington De Voe vocalized these industry-wide concerns in an 1867 appraisal of New York meat markets in *The Market Assistant,* warning that "there is danger, also, in the kind and quality of the flesh which some use, it being almost impossible to tell, from outward appearance, of what animal or in what condition the flesh was."

This suspicion was compounded by the frequent presence of a bafflingly named "common pudding," said to consist of pork skin, head meat, and pig's liver stuffed into beef casing and cooked—a charcuterie of the supposedly inedible.

By the time the Industrial Revolution fully gripped the US, a new class of underpaid, overexerted workers was surviving paycheck to paycheck in the extremely dangerous meatpacking factories of the 1800s and early 1900s. This was where the most important legal intervention in the modern Miss Hot Dog's young life took place—by writer Upton Sinclair, somewhat unintentionally. Sinclair's 1906 novel-exposé, *The Jungle,* is a stunning work that remains one of the most effective recruiting tools to the socialist cause (about which I am enthusiastic—no, don't put the book down) but is primarily remembered for its influence on legislation regarding American meatpacking plants.

The Jungle had a massive influence on American culture, but only one element of its protagonist's complicated story had legal impact. Sinclair's fictional Lithuanian immigrant, Jurgis Rudkus, attempts to secure the American dream for himself from within the working class, only to be met with predatory landlords, illness transmitted through unsanitary factory conditions, corrupt politicians buying votes, male bosses abusing and coercing female colleagues into sex in order to retain employment, police corruption, failed unions, jailing the poor instead of rehabilitative solutions, alcoholism, depression, drug addiction, grueling work hours, and neglected children. The ending is stunningly optimistic, with Jurgis losing everything before learning about the concept of socialism—a concept, it's emphasized, that could theoretically land a nuclear bomb on the majority of obstacles he experienced in his American journey.

(An aside: I feel the need to include this rejection of *The Jungle* from Macmillan, the publisher behind the imprint that brought you the very book you're reading. It says:

"I advise without hesitation and unreservedly against the publication of this book, which is gloom and horror unrelieved. One feels that what is at the bottom of his fierceness is not nearly so much desire to help the poor as hatred of the rich."

Ha! Bitch.)

Sinclair's intention was to expose "an inferno of exploitation" stemming from his personal experience growing up as the child of poor immigrants in the late 1800s, then spending seven weeks undercover working at meatpacking plants in Chicago to accurately reflect the experiences of his protagonist. The American political machine had contempt for the labor issues expressed in the book, but its success couldn't be ignored, and so they hedged their bets by tackling an important but not establishment-shaking cause—hot dog rights.

"I aimed at the public's heart, and by accident I hit it in the stomach," he joked of *The Jungle*'s popular reception in *Cosmopolitan* in October 1906.

President Theodore Roosevelt absolutely hated Sinclair's work and loyalty to socialism, calling him a "crackpot," "hysterical, unbalanced, and untruthful," but did agree that some, *some* of the ammunition behind "the efforts of arrogant and selfish greed on the part of the capitalist" needed to be addressed. Reader, Roosevelt did not choose *actual* capitalism to address, nor the instances of police brutality or lack of healthcare access that so defined Jurgis's struggle—he chose meatpacking plant conditions. This somewhat flippant decision directly led to three critical moves by the government in the year following *The Jungle*'s publication: the founding of the Food and Drug Administration and the passing of the Federal Meat Inspection Act in June 1906, as well as the Pure Food and Drug Act, focusing on consumer protections and labeling, in January 1907.

The Federal Meat Inspection Act's history in particular has significant bearing on the journey of the hot dog. Roosevelt remained suspicious of the leftist leanings of Sinclair and other reporters whose work claimed severe safety and health risks in plants, and sent out his own goons (sorry, a labor commissioner and a dedicated civil servant) Charles P. Neill and James Bronson Reynolds to the same Chicago plants Sinclair had studied to confirm his findings. The boys returned similar reports—the working conditions *and* product were cutting corners in the interest of cost and time efficiency, resulting in an unsanitary environment for humans and animals alike. The Federal Meat Inspection Act was set into motion just four months after *The Jungle*'s publication. It demanded that livestock be inspected before slaughter, then again postmortem, in addition to implementing sanitation standards for slaughterhouses and meat processing plants with ongoing inspections from the US Department of Agriculture.

Roosevelt did not express interest in any of Sinclair's other concerns.

In the 1890s, the era Sinclair's 1906 novel examines, the meatpacking industry had reached a level of automation that made the modern hot dog possible, provided that menial immigrant labor was readily available and exploitable alongside emerging technology. The first steam-powered sausage chopper was invented in 1868, which led to various innovations in automation by the end of the century—American startups industrialized everything from transporting livestock to slaughter to rendering to meat grinding to shipping, all using low-paid labor to get the job done. Prior to the Federal Meat Inspection Act, meatpacking titan and innovator (exploiter) of vertical integration Gustavus Swift bragged that his meat used every part of the pig "but the squeal."

Miss Hot Dog and the meatpacking industry being featured during the Industrial Revolution as the Big Fixable Problem is fascinating. Without a doubt the horrific factory conditions and labor practices were a cause for national concern—hell, losing your appendages to the job was so common it became an inside joke among employees. If you lost one finger you were a great sausage maker, two meant magna cum laude, and three was summa cum laude. Still, unsanitary and unsafe conditions for all parties but the executives persisted throughout American factory culture at large—a then behemoth spanning from textiles to automobiles to stoves to shoes to furniture to fucking *chemicals*. It's an industry that still has a heavy footprint in the US but has largely relocated to China with little improvement in working conditions. The circumstances under which the Industrial Revolution hot dog was produced were an easy target to quiet the complaints of those who had read *The Jungle* because yes, placing regulations on the meatpacking industry had a positive effect and no, it did not help the working class in the way Sinclair was hoping. Hot dogs were getting more and more popular with Americans working paycheck to paycheck, and the Federal Meat Inspection Act laid excellent tarmac for the hot dog to land as a meal staple of the Great Depression.

There is a series of lies on how and who brought the hot dog to the starving masses for the first time. Like many modern folk tales, their origins range from old books to marketing campaigns to internet speculation, with no definitive story nor particular interest in knowing the absolute truth. Here are the ones I've seen most often, our Big Four, in ascending order of how compelling I find them:

The British Concession King: In April 1901, it was a rainy day at the New York Giants baseball game, and vendors weren't prepared for the inclement weather. Game concessions were simple—peanuts, cigars, soda, and ice cream—but nothing to keep the fans warm. This was an issue for magnate Harry M. Stevens, a British immigrant who began his concession company in 1887. It was acquired by conglomerate Aramark in 1994. No one wanted ice cream in the rain, so Stevens pivoted, instructing his son Frank to buy up all the German sausages in the neighborhood—"those long dachshund sausages—what do they call 'em, frankfurters" (oh, come on)—and rolls to place them in. "And get some mustard."

The Working-Class German: Ignatz Frischmann was a pioneering baker in the mid-1800s who put Coney Island street food on the map—it was his small bakery that "started the manufacture of a certain oblong roll that the frankfurter men needed for their business," according to his obituary, making the creation of the hot dog a collaboration among the German food community at large.

The Glove-Bearer: The St. Louis World's Fair in 1904 had twenty million attendees with more than one hundred places to eat, one of which was Bavarian sausage guy Anton Feuchtwanger's stall. In order to serve his sausages hot, he lent Michael Jackson-esque single white gloves to wear to avoid burns, but immediately started losing money when people wouldn't return them, possibly to start pop music careers. He consulted a baker at a nearby stall for a solution, and received it in the form of a soft roll slathered in mustard.

The Working-Class German, Part II: In either 1867 or 1874, a German immigrant named Charles Feltman started selling traditional German pies on the Coney Island boardwalk and asked a local wheelwright to design a new wagon with a burner unit inside where water could be heated. He experimented with cooking sausages with this setup and put them in sliced buns, something that became a hit among the new tourist population when trains connected Brooklyn to the rest of New York City.

Lies, one and all. Stevens clung to the false myth that he was a hot dog god in order to keep the marketing for his concession empire strong, there's no evidence the creepy white-glove story ever happened, and Charles Feltman never operated a hot dog stand at all. The commonalities of these lies are what to keep your eye on. Every one of these false origin stories has a hero—an industrious man who pulled himself up by his bootstraps and made something amazing, gaining notoriety and wealth in the process. It's the classic American individualist narrative, the same one that the tech billionaires of today are still trying to shove down our throats like a common pudding. Stevens's story as a steel mill worker who built a catering empire isn't all that different from Bill Gates's story about beginning Microsoft in a garage—they transform themselves not just into someone to root for, but someone who *could* be *you,* if you work hard enough. It's the false promise that brought *The Jungle*'s Jurgis Rudkus to the United States to seek his fortune, only to be met with the reality of American capitalism.

The hot dog is a player in this lie, a tool of American exceptionalism who obscures her own decentralized origin story to reinforce the bootstrap narrative while being sold to the Jurgises of the world, poor immigrants who could not afford something more nutritious. It's in these moments that she's at her most American, wholly adapted from the German sausage to be not just a demonstration of a false dream, but a symbol of it.

The truth is this: the hot dog was a dish that slowly became popular due to nameless German street vendors, and was turned into an icon by some of the most privileged people on Earth—shitbird frat boys at Yale University. Here's a poem that appeared in an October 1895 issue of the *Yale Record,* describing the lunch wagons on campus as "dog wagons":

> Tis dogs' delight to bark and bite,
> Thus does the adage run.
> But I delight to bite the dog
> When placed inside a bun.

Oh, shut up, don't you have a co-ed to be sexually assaulting? I'm kidding—not because Yale frat boys aren't sexual predators, but because Yale didn't let women in until 1969. Anyway!

The phrase "hot dog" began as frat slang for someone they didn't like, an old-timey insult that made their mothers blush. German sausages had already been called "red hots" among consumers, and the terms eventually mingled and merged when word of the elegant, stained glass–paneled "Yale Kennel Club lunch wagon" became locally famous for its paintings of dachshunds on the windows.

The term spread in a way that would have been impossible in the hot dog's earliest days—through mass media ranging from newspapers and editorial cartoons to vaudeville acts. (See: an *extremely* weird vaudevillian German-dialect character named Carl Pretzel, an offensive send-up that Chicago journalist Charles Harris toured around, insisting that there was actual dog meat in hot dogs.) The stiff-collared Yale shorthand trickled down to the middle class, and eventually to the underclass who mechanically produced, sold, and consumed them for the industrialists claiming the whole thing was their idea. Of course, the popular rumor that man's best friend's meat could be mixed into the product prior to the Federal Meat Inspection Act didn't hurt in getting the name to stick.

Most hot dog titans of today opened shop at the turn of the century and increased in popularity during the Great Depression. Hebrew National was started by Russian Jew Theodore Krainin in 1905 and became popular in the New York Jewish community when incomes plummeted during the Depression; Polish Jewish immigrant Nathan Handwerker founded Nathan's Famous on Coney Island in 1916; Bavarian Oscar Mayer began his company in 1883 but really finessed the company's iconic image in the 1930s with the Wienermobile. Nathan's products were being shared by the Sinclair-hating Teddy Roosevelt with the king and queen of England by the late 1930s; hell, the Austrian immigrant team that founded Vienna Beef in 1893 advertised that their Chicago-style hot dogs had a whole "salad on top" during the Depression to emphasize that it could be viewed as two meals by its poor consumers. The turn-of-the-century technological shift made information on the hot dog's production readily available through the developing mass media machine, but was often leapfrogged by the stronger American tradition—the sometimes irrational nationalistic branding that wanted you to *feel* harder than you tasted. Each company has their industrial hero, and each company relies on the labor and consumption of the underclass's very American belief that *that* could be *them*.

How is she *made*? Oh, come on, don't spoil the fun all at once.

The Five Hot Dogs You Can Purchase Easily in Heaven

Acknowledging the greats before going on a quest.

There are a few heavily franchised icons in the field I feel it is my duty to acknowledge, give flowers to, then leave in the night before we begin our journey to the independently owned hot dog joints of America—the few, the proud, the remaining fast food hot dogs. Presented in order of how much I would die for them:

COSTCO

If you see no purpose in finishing this book because Costco has the best value for the best hot dog in the United States, I understand. There is *nothing* like a Costco hot dog, not only because it is delicious but because it is, at the time of this writing, impervious to the evils of American capitalism . . . at least in the inflation sense. The Costco hot dog deal—$1.50 for a Kirkland Signature all-beef hot dog and a 20-ounce soda with refill—has remained in place since its debut in 1984, even as other once-reliable food deals like the dollar slice of pizza fell by the wayside at the same establishment.

If you've ever had it, congratulations on knowing someone who knows someone who has a Costco membership like I do, and double congratulations on having had the best hot dog for the best value in the game. The hot dog itself has a good snap and weighs a quarter pound, and like all good hot dogs, its vendor could truly give a shit what condiments you slather on it—for this consumer, the standard ketchup, mustard, and relish on a steamed bun with the Kirkland dog hanging a half inch over on each side is just right. To care more, for what hot-dog-slinging employees are paid, is sheer insecure projection.

There are two popular theories to explain Costco's non-response to inflation in their food court deals—one based in boring pragmatism and vertical integration, the other covered in CEO flop sweat and publicist-approved lies. The first goes as follows: Hebrew National was the bulk buyer's provider at the time of the deal's creation after a cart outside a San Diego Costco location made a killing, but the motivation behind the price consistency shows a rare, intense business ethos. It works in favor of only the customer who comes for the dogs exclusively—Costco admits that they lose money on the offer, which is more intended to get customers in the door than anything else. The business holds its ground on the pricing as a way to remind customers that they *are*, in fact, being promised a good deal when they come to the store, even if the items they actually need aren't on sale or within their price range.

Costco is a business marketed to working-class people, families, and businesses that buy in bulk and need to feel like they're a part of something larger than themselves in order to justify the cost of a $60 annual membership. In fact, the hot dog and soda have gotten *bigger* over the years to reassure customers that the brand is strong—the dog's size increased by 10 percent when Costco switched its distributor from Hebrew National to their in-house brand Kirkland in 2009, and the soda size was upped to twenty ounces from twelve. The same goes for their irrationally priced $4.99 rotisserie chicken, a product so popular that the company vertically integrated their chicken production in 2019 by opening Lincoln Premium Poultry in Nebraska. It's good news for the average consumer, and bleak news for those who know anything about factory farming.

If that's all a little opaque to you, you can always subscribe to the second theory, in which the cofounder of Costco threatens to kill his own CEO over hot dog prices. You're an adult, and so I feel comfortable reminding you that nothing that costs $1.50 and tastes delicious was made ethically and the Costco hot dog deal is far from an exception. According to 2021 data from the Bureau of Labor Statistics's CPI Inflation Calculator, this deal *should* cost closer to $3.65 in 2020s money in order to yield a profit. Around 150 million of these little fuckers are sold every year for about 60 percent less than they should be, and the company would like you to believe that the *only way* they could remain so would be if this frequently circulated clickbait anecdote were true:

Interior, Costco Industries.

Costco President and CEO W. Craig Jelinek, a man worth more than $100 million, confronts the business's cofounder Jim Sinegal about the losses incurred by the hot dog deal, according to an interview from 2018.

"I came to [Jim] once and I said, 'Jim, we can't sell this hot dog for a buck fifty. We are losing our rear ends,'" he said. Sinegal, a billionaire, replied: "'If you raise the effing hot dog, I will kill you. Figure it out.'"

Look, who among us isn't tempted to traffic in a fun little story about an eccentric billionaire defending the hot dog deal of the people? The story tends to go viral every few years in the way that Western culture is in a constant state of re-realizing that Keanu Reeves is a Pretty Awesome Guy, Actually, and it certainly hasn't deterred me from grabbing one any time I roll up to buy what anyone would agree is an absurd amount of tortilla chips for one person. What is never acknowledged in these pieces are the working conditions that exist in order for this folksy story to be sustainable at all.

During the pandemic lockdown of 2020, an executive order from failed casino owner President Donald Trump kept meat plants open so that Americans could continue to comfortably gorge themselves on cheap meat while the employees working to process it were put at an even higher risk for disease and injury than usual, a decision that led to hundreds of deaths and whose legal repercussions are still being sorted out. The Costco-owned plants that supplied meat for their private Kirkland label were no exception, and acted particularly carelessly toward worker safety in the interest of efficiency for profits and—as most would lie to your face—*patriotism.*

In May 2020, the Costco poultry producer, Lincoln Premium Poultry, was shut down due to what was then believed to be supplies contaminated by the coronavirus, the same day that one of twenty-eight employees diagnosed with the disease died. After the executive order mandating production remain at full blast—with little known about transmission and virtually nothing in the way of protection other than quarantine, masking, and social distancing—the underpaid, majority-immigrant staff were increasingly pressured to continue coming to work in spite of the extreme health risks.

An anonymous Latin immigrant worker who worked at Lincoln Premium Poultry spoke to *BuzzFeed News* in spring 2020 about the labor-health paradox presented to workers who couldn't afford to call in sick.

"Everyone is asking one another, 'Do you think you'll keep coming to work?' No one wants to fall behind on their bills. There are lots of people working because of that," she said. "Logically, the more time we spend at work, the more likely we are to get sick. A lot of people in the plant are saying, if the coronavirus kills us, who are the ones who are going to die of hunger?"

The fact is, if you're looking for unethically sourced tube-meat, there's no better deal that you should feel like an absolute asshole for taking Costco up on. But the mortal cost is extremely real, and that is the story of the hot dog that I learn over and over and over.

HOME DEPOT

The Hot Dog Summer of 2021 was not kind to the second-best reliably quick-and-delicious street dog available across the country, and it was completely decimated in some regions. I cannot overstate the number of friends, strangers, and strangers who believe they are my friends who have told me that the Home Depot hot dog is the best-kept secret in the country. There's something beautiful to me about the vulnerability of this interaction—if hundreds of people are telling me something I've known for years and are calling it a rare secret, it means Home Depot is doing something right to make their customers feel like members of a sex cabal instead of a hot dog customer who just bought a gallon of paint for their daughter's room.

If you don't already know of the Home Depot hot dog, it may be too late for you. If you look them up, the first result will be *why are home depot hot dogs so good,* closely followed by *what happened to home depot hot dogs.* They aren't everywhere—mainly found in the Midwest and the Southwest, so other unfortunates across the country are forced to go to taco trucks or even worse, a Burger King nearby. It's an "if you know, you know" situation.

Like many bizarre hot dog traditions, the Home Depot Dog is a concept that began and developed a cult following around Chicago. Writer Dennis Lee described growing up in the area assuming every Home Depot offered what are commonly referred to as Depot Dogs or Fixin' Franks, found at small hot dog stands that sold a loaded Chicago dog from Makowski's Real Sausage, as well as Italian beef and Chicago-style tamales. Fixin' Franks remain a staple in the already overloaded Chicago hot dog scene, but Michigan didn't make it through 2021 as lucky—their Depot Dog stands, Doggone It, were shut down by the company for good in the middle of July.

The backlash was immediate and severe—local vendors who had partnered with their nearest store for more than twenty years were left in the cold in the middle of the pandemic with nothing but a tacit "wishing vendors the best" message from a Home Depot spokesperson. More than nine thousand online protest posts erupted in the wake of the decision, escalating all the way to State Representative Darrin Camilleri using his platform to beg Home Depot to bring the dogs back—possibly the most people-centered move made by the government in decades.

"We're devastated—especially because there was no explanation," he said, mentioning that his aunt worked at one of the hot dog stands before its sudden closure. "That stand made my aunt so happy, and we know it made customers happy too. I hope Home Depot reconsiders this decision."

A similar upset took place in Colorado during Hot Dog Summer, with a number of local Home Depot stands being done away with and others left on thin ice. There are still places where Depot Dogs are available, but it's not that they're consistent in preparation or style; it's that they're sold by local people and make you feel like you know a secret that everyone actually knows already. It's a dish that makes you say, sure, I guess I *will* replace the lightbulb that's been flashing in my bathroom and making me dissociate from reality during my skin routine. There's something *in* it for me.

HOT DOG ON A STICK

Hot Dog on a Stick is far from the best corn dog in the world, but it's the one that brings the *aesthetic,* and that's 80 percent of the battle when you're sparring with the likes of Chipotle and Panda Express in the dim lighting of a food court. A local business that sprang up right down the street from where I live now, Hot Dog on a Stick has been a tradition since its opening on Muscle Beach on the Santa Monica Pier back in 1946. To this day, the seventyish mall locations across the country use founder Dave Barham's family cornbread recipe and an all-beef Nathan's Famous Hot Dog from Coney Island, clear across the country (with turkey and veggie variants).

The corn dog itself is decent, still the only menu item outside of deep-fried cheese, fries, and funnel cake sticks for dessert, so the trip through the line is more for a better look at the visual assault of the Hot Dog on a Stick uniform—bright horizontal stripes pulsing into your corneas while they deep-fry dogs to order. I can guarantee that you are less likely to get volcanic diarrhea with this third-place Muscle Beach original than the orange chicken at Panda Express, and I would know something about the state of volcanic food court diarrhea at this moment in history.

AUNTIE ANNE'S

Were I a Hot Topic teenager skulking the filthy halls of the Westgate Mall in Brockton, Massachusetts, maybe I would feel differently. I *tried* to be a successful mall goth in my day to no avail, met only with what was considered a valid complaint by my peers at the time—it's not that we don't *like* Jamie; it's that her back brace precludes her from playing hacky sack outside and if one cannot *play* hacky sack *outside,* then there's no use in initiating her into a group she could not possibly survive within.

And yet, you simply must hand it to the country's most popular pretzel dog and her mini-pretzel-dog spawn. While I could take or leave the product itself—seven dollars for a pretzel-wrapped hot dog that vaguely smells like preservative chemicals simply doesn't sit well with my spirit—the story of Auntie Anne's is an authentic hero's journey. Far from the fake-out hot dog origin stories, she keeps me coming back to the disgruntled teenagers peddling her product. Since opening in 1988, the franchise has exploded into 1,200 locations in malls, airports, and transit stations across the country, selling a charcuterie of pretzels, hot dogs (Nathan's all-beef wrapped in their proprietary, bready exterior), and lemonade at a slight overcharge.

Anne Beiler started the business after growing up in the Pennsylvania Amish community, helping to care for thirty nieces, nephews, and children of her own after dropping out of middle school and marrying at nineteen. She was your average Amish protagonist and had no intention of changing that, until the fatal loss of her young daughter in a 1975 tractor accident led her to seek guidance from her pastor. The pastor raped Beiler, then coerced and shamed her into a six-year abusive sexual relationship before she decided to sound the alarm in her community—something that was not widely accepted for any assault survivor to do at this time, much less an Amish one.

In spite of the stigma surrounding the subject, speaking publicly about this abuse had a *massive* effect on the area. It turned out that the same pastor had sexually abused Beiler's own sisters and most women she'd grown up with, then shamed them all into silence.

Beiler's husband was outraged at the news, and the couple became determined to open a counseling center where women could seek PTSD and trauma guidance after the pastor's credentials were stripped and he was removed from the community. Ever the Christian, Beiler still blamed herself for the "marital crisis" caused by the sexual abuse she experienced. Her husband pivoted from his career as a mechanic (can the Amish do that? anyway) to train as a marriage and family counselor so he could get the business off the ground—she describes this period in the early 1980s in a 2014 interview with *Fortune* magazine.

"He wanted to offer counseling services for free to our community, and we needed income. So I told him, 'You've stayed with me despite all that I've done. So do what you want to do, and I'll go to work.'"

Please tell Auntie Anne she didn't "do" anything wrong! The

fact remained that the Beilers didn't have the startup money to serve the community to the extent they wanted. Anne suggested they save up by starting a food stand—she'd never made pretzels before, but threw herself into the practice and expanded to eight Auntie Anne's locations within a year. She remains firmly connected to her Christian roots, and is currently on the board of directors at the Museum of the Bible in Washington, DC. She is, for lack of better descriptors, a Christian hot dog girlboss.

So yes, Auntie Anne is a legend among legends—but the hot dogs taste like chemicals and that's not my fucking fault.*

*And this goes double for her weird politics.

WIENERSCHNITZEL

What are you, five years old?

We Are in the Southwest

So what's in there anyway?

Any time I'm away from home for a while, I leave a Mike's Hard Lemonade in the vegetable crisper beside something expired for when I get back. There are plenty of ways to measure time—the moon, hot dog bowel movements, people you love who die—but this one is my very favorite. Before I leave on a tour, trip, or embarrassingly long sex commute to the Valley, I feel the Mike's Hard (okay, Hard*er,* 8 percent) in my hand and try to remember how it and I feel, then do the same exercise once I'm back. If it lays in my palm the same on both ends of the trip, something has gone terribly wrong. I'm late to jump in the passenger seat, I've fucked up the rental car reservation, I hold the Strawberry Harder tallboy against my cheek in the third week of June to return for in September. Don't worry, Mike's Harder is honey in a pharaoh's tomb; it won't go bad in my absence.

We pull out of our driveway to eat the motherfucking hot dogs. It's been an abrupt planning process, one that involves a LaserJet-printed map of the United States and a number of little foil star stickers snaking from our duplex in Los Angeles, through the desert, into the South, and shakily up the East Coast's torso to the hot, wet mouth of New England, where my family will engage in light psychological torture for the remainder of the summer.

One thing you should know is that I don't have a driver's license. The why, here, is elusive even to me, something I've vaguely managed to connect to my cousin's husband dying in a tragic motorcycle accident when I was twelve. My hot dog plan starts as a variation on a toxic theme I've been repeating since college—long, sweaty trips across the country, skipping from Greyhound to Greyhound until I get too tired or someone throws up on me, then stop for the night and repeat until reaching my destination. It's a system that's gotten me from Boston to Tennessee to go to a music festival where a bunch of aggressive teenagers from Albany hijacked my two-man tent to finger one another. It's a system that's gotten me from Los Angeles to Portland, where I met a man who still, to the day of this writing, sends the word *Hey* to my "other messages" folder every six months. It's a bad system, but it's the one I know.

My boyfriend, who offered to drive, doesn't like mustard. I don't know how I thought the trip would end *well*; he doesn't like mustard and I *knew* that, knew the mouths of hot dog vendors would tilt smugly upward or angrily down at the sound of "No mustard, please." I knew this reaction would send blood rocketing from my ass to my face, knew I would overcompensate and say, "I *will* have mustard," knew the look that would appear on his mustard-averse face when I said that, knew it might hurt him. It's critical, and I cannot stress this enough, to only go on a hot dog road trip in a relationship with two people who are mentally stable and both like mustard.

But he offered to drive, because he is kind and because we like to spend time together, especially with the dog and the cat. I pretend to like the podcasts he listens to, and he refuses to listen to my music or audiobooks because he says that those things make his head hurt. Fine, books are boring, bitch, but I'm actually writing one right now. Do you know why we're taking this trip? Still, he's driving and I'm paying, so we pull out and leave, dropping off the plant I got him last Christmas that he never watered with a friend. We never inquired after it again.

It is a hot dog mission, yes, but there's something else going on here as well, something more private and nebulous. My dad has lung cancer, and it falls to me to look after him while he has a portion of his lung removed, in the way it falls to an eldest to do certain things. Our first few days on the road are marked by waiting for his test results, surgery dates, associated costs, but these real, looming things are Not Discussed as my dad continues to apologize for falling for those ads where the camel was dressed as a gambler pimp driving a red convertible. But who doesn't want to be a camel having sex in a convertible? It doesn't seem fair to lose a vital organ to engaging with that fantasy, and now it's *my* problem.

He will be okay, but we don't know that now—there are still several months of masked hospital visits, crunching numbers with insurance agencies to see how long he can stay in recovery, scrubbing the walls of the house we grew up in with vinegar to get the stench of Winstons out so he's not tempted by the ghost. A poor, unsuspecting guy will offer me a cigarette after sex a few months later (What year is it? Am I awake?) and I will say, "I can't, cigarettes are killing my family." He will nod for a second and then say, "Oh . . . kay!"

The first night, we arrive at a low-rent hotel in Tucson, Arizona, after getting stuck at a McDonald's drive-through behind a Camry full of teenagers who had a free fry hookup. The man at the hotel desk is behind a thick wall of plastic wearing two masks, a system that makes our single-mask approach look reckless. He upgrades our room for wearing masks at all—without prompting, he shares that he is the caretaker of an elderly parent and works a second job across town, yelling through the plastic shield and two layers of mask fabric that most people "around here" are morally opposed to.

I fall asleep scrolling through emails, a series of rejections to my requests for touring hot dog factories dotting the country, claiming it's not permitted "due to present circumstances." The present circumstances this summer shift depending where you are and what day you happen to decamp. Turning back is not an option—one week because of the death rates spiking from COVID summer weddings, the next because tropical storms are taking out power grids, the next because fires are threatening the lives of Miley Cyrus's horses. We are pushing east in an overpriced rental car, landing up the coast where I will spend the summer and my boyfriend will, as he keeps telling me, figure it out when we get there. Consider my mind at ease.

There's a *Keeping Up with the Kardashians* marathon that runs for the entire summer, an unavoidable hotel cable staple. This first night, I fall asleep somewhere between Khloe croaking through her COVID symptoms in front of a ring light, saying, "God bless us all," and Kim struggling to take care of her children when her coterie of nannies fall ill. We are, of course, supposed to feel bad for *her*.

It's 107 degrees when we arrive at Hot Dog Ruiz Los Chipilones in Tucson and encounter the Sonoran hot dog, our first excellent dog of the summer.

The Sonoran hot dog, best consumed in Arizona, has a strong presence throughout the Southwest and is one of the best around. It's the only in the country to sport a banana boat bun, not slit from end to end but only at the top, so the slightly shorter hot dog can rest on the bottom and handily support its toppings. I start telling my boyfriend it's just like the experimental medical procedure my mom got done so I could be born, but he's already heard that one and it's no longer charming. The dog is grilled to a slight char, strangled in a strip of grilled bacon, and topped with diced tomato, onion (crude and fried), winnie (I cannot for the life of me figure out *what* this is), mayonnaise, mustard and—wait for it—*beans*. The sheer risk factor of beans on a hot dog is thrilling, and the fact that there is only one place in town that has the (stay with me) *bun infrastructure* to pull it off is even more so.

The dogs themselves were innovated by Noe Maciel and his brothers at the corner of South Sixth Avenue and East Twenty-Second Street, where they prepare the buns Sinaloan-style, named for the Mexican state south of Sonora. It's unreal—the butter-brushed-on-bun grilled breading gave me the first true dopamine hit of Hot Dog Summer. The Chipilon dog, a variant of the Sonoran, was so successful that the business expanded to include a taco joint and, inexplicably, a full-service car wash by the late 2010s.

On this day, we've just come off a disappointing first hot dog elsewhere in Tucson (wet bun, cardinal sin) and find an employee in a boiling hot food truck. A second, larger white trailer that serves as the dining area is full of locals who know better than to eat the bread slop at any other Sonoran hot dog joint. Mexican Coke bottles sit on ice, baseball bats from the Dodgers and the Diamondbacks are crossed at the entrance, and local news about people dying of the newest version of the plague blares as customers pull much-needed napkins from the pencil boxes they're kept in.

It's the second dog of the day, and I break my only rule right away. Never, ever, under any circumstances, eat the entire hot dog just because you think you will look like an asshole if you don't. I detest food waste, but at a four-hot-dogs-a-day clip in one car with another person for ten hours in 107-degree weather, you cannot do the righteous thing. Hot Dog Summer results in an absurd amount of waste.

The Jamie Loftus Hot Dog System is thus:

Take two bites, about thirty seconds apart. Consider the flavor, get a mouthful *with* bun and topping.

After the second bite, pass the dog off to the other person, who will do the same thing from the opposite end. In the industry, this is called nonsexual *Lady and the Tramp*ing.

Do not, unless you won't be eating for at least another three to four hours, finish the hot dog out of a sense of obligation. This *will* lead to a summer of unholy meetings with rest stop toilets.

Take the remainder of the hot dog to go and swear you're going to eat it later even if they don't ask.

Know you are lying. Don't eat it later.

I am, not proudly, among the most useless dumb white Americans, the hideous breed who took a dead language at a public high school under the guise of being "gifted." Ten years later, I am completely unable to communicate in Spanish, the language that much of the Southwest speaks, and am duly ashamed for believing that studying the ancient Romans would ever serve any practical purpose. The employee is gracious, charges only $3.50 for a quality Sonoran dog that would demand two and a half times that elsewhere, and wishes us well before we head out.

My boyfriend parks somewhere he can get weed, has an anxiety attack because he doesn't have weed, then spends the next three hundred miles annoyed that anxiety prevented him from going to get more weed in the first place.

Where we *needed* weed was in Albuquerque.

I am a woman of simple pleasures, which is my little way of telling you that when I see a billboard that says SEE THE THING! 15 MILES, I will loudly mention The Thing in Fifteen Miles at every subsequent billboard *until* we see The Thing fifteen miles later. The roadside advertisement is intentionally vague, but boils down to a rehash of the dinosaurs-versus-aliens conflict I could never get very invested in as a kid. Still, we want to make the detour worth it, and I loiter near the five-dollar-admission stand. Unwilling to pay, I hang out near a souvenir T-shirt rack to see if the employee selling tickets has loose lips about The Thing we drove fifteen miles to see.

"So what's in there anyway?" asks a man in an ostensibly handmade, unclear-if-it's-ironic DEMOCRATS 4 TRUMP T-shirt while he waits for his children to pee in the public restrooms that, if we're being honest, are the main reason people visit the attraction in the first place.

The employee smiles cryptically with a completely unmasked face in a summer when that was, uh, not medically okay. "Well," he says, "you gotta pay five dollars."

The tourist dad shrugs and turns his back, and the employee falls to pieces. I love unfounded insecurity in the wild. "Okay, okay," the employee says, folding like a piece of fucking origami, "it's like, this big RV that's parked down the hallway." Children start pouring out of the family restroom, one wearing a shirt that says LITTLE DEMOCRAT and the other, LITTLE REPUBLICAN.

"You parked a damn RV down the hallway?"

The employee doesn't seem able to stop himself from defending The Thing in Fifteen Miles. Everything is riding on this, for some reason. It is so stressful seeing a man in a DEMOCRATS 4 TRUMP T-shirt have the upper hand. "It's not just an RV," the employee says with a lilt of desperation that confirms it is, in fact, just an RV. "The Thing came to Arizona to help us form an alliance with them aliens." The politically maniacal family disappears, and I buy a shirt.

In New Mexico we're pulled over because our rental car's Oregon license plates are a "dead giveaway" for drug hustling in the West, a bored state trooper tells us. We had no luck getting weed and my Adderall stash is buried deep in my luggage, so the statie fuck lets us go after realizing it would jeopardize my boyfriend's trucking license to write us a ticket for driving eight miles over the speed limit. He lets us go because we're white; he lets us go because he doesn't want the hassle, his information comes from another state trooper, and he's not the type to fact-check.

It's in this spirit, sweaty and anxious, exhausted from making the cocker spaniel pose for a picture next to the fiftieth road-side alien sculpture we drove past, fresh off an argument about whether the dog we gave water to at a gas station was very sick or a coyote (I will not tell you what side I was on but I was right), that we arrive at The Motel.

Let's see how long it takes you to figure out what's going on at this place.

Once again there's a panel of protective glass between us and the receptionist, which is normal for the time in which we're traveling. We're staying a little outside the center of town in Albuquerque, but we're both well-seasoned shitbag motel guests and have spent the last few years mastering the art of the sleep-on-top-of-the-sheets, shower-and-get-the-fuck-out model that defines the deeply ingrained travel habits of any lower-middle-class kid who wants to see something more than four hours away from where they were born. The woman we speak to is older and in high spirits, appearing from the back office after several minutes.

"Oh my God, you're just in time," she says. Neither of us are sure what this means, but we're willing to ride on the energy. She checks us in, looking over her shoulder occasionally while slamming her fingers against the old keyboard, and asks us where we're from. She's from New Mexico, she says while blinking and moving her mouth circuitously. Born and raised, she continues without moving her eyes from the screen, but she *did* spend some time in Los Angeles in her twenties before returning here for reasons she mutters about incoherently. It's the plastic shield,

I tell myself as a man in an Adidas tracksuit enters with two exhausted-looking women who get in line for the bathroom in the otherwise empty lobby. Is there even anyone in there?

"And when I got back from LA we— Sorry, this Wi-Fi has been so bad ever since the hotel got struck by lightning."

I'm the de facto pleasant conversation haver of the trip, and zone in on the quirky detail. "This place was struck by lightning? When?"

Our hostess does not miss a beat, pummeling the keyboard with her life. "Today."

The corners of my boyfriend's mouth turn down as the guy in the tracksuit starts to get impatient, muttering to himself a few feet away about where the fuck Jay is.

"I've been struck by lightning *four* times, you know," she continues, picking up a crusty keycard and running it through the proprietary scanner repeatedly.

How are you doing? I still have no idea what's happening in the moment.

"That's so wild," I say. "I didn't know there was that much lightning in New Mexico."

"Oh yeah." She nods sagely, then takes a moment to shoot a glance over to the guy who's increasingly annoyed about where the fuck Jay is. "I got struck by lightning last week at the gas station."

She seems to have finished securing our motel room and starts to extend the key card beneath the plastic, but yanks it out of my grasp when the guy in the tracksuit decides he's done waiting for Jay.

"Where the fuck is Jay? That [abysmal language you can guess or not] needs to get the fuck out here, he owes me money."

Maybe I'm just the absolute pinnacle of feminism, but I'd assumed that our receptionist was the manager and it turns out I'm wrong. The bumps coming from the back office aren't a rogue air conditioning unit or, if recent claims are to be believed, lightning. The manager is Jay, and Jay owes the guy in the tracksuit money if he's going to get what I'm realizing is a Walmart bag of significance in this guy's hand. The receptionist is invested, and we are not getting into our motel room until this issue is resolved.

She looks back at the locked office, presumably full of Jay, but not the money Jay owes. "Jay's not in there," she says as another bump comes from the room. "He's at his poker game and—"

"Bullshit," the man in the tracksuit says, slamming down the plastic bag full of—and I don't mean to pigeonhole the area, but—absolutely meth. My boyfriend tries to see if he can reach the keycards from beneath the plastic as the receptionist busies herself swatting away the other two women who—okay, I'm with it now, I was extremely sheltered—are 100 percent high on meth. They try to push past the floppy plastic shield and toward the door where Jay is or is not.

The receptionist is able to fend them off with a small tap on the plastic, and the women shrink back to the lobby chairs, which look even more tired than they do. Albuquerque is, during this particular summer, experiencing a surge of drug-related homicides, more than thirty during the summer we visited, many of them at hotels and motels like, well, this one. There are plenty of contributing factors, most of which tie into the opioid crisis, violent incarceration as a more expensive and less effective substitute for rehabilitation, and the disproportionately high rate of violence toward and imprisonment of people of color found guilty of drug crimes in spite of similar usage and sales rates to their white drug-dealing counterparts. (For your reference, all parties in this particular lobby are white.) But in the summer of 2021, the reporting around the issue is inherently unreliable, often featuring exhausted local reporters taking soundbites from retired cops and presenting them as unbiased news.

Nicholas Huffmyer, a former Bernalillo County sheriff's deputy, told local outlet KRQE within weeks of our being there: "The lie that people are told is that drug crimes are nonviolent. It isn't violent for you to just sit and smoke weed, but do you have any idea how that got here?"

Huffmyer and the Albuquerque press remain stunningly incurious about solutions that aren't rooted in returning the violence right back, leaving the city to scoop up Golden Globes for the *Breaking Bad* expanded universe as the situation worsens. It's not my place, as a hot dog historian, to declare cops who fearmonger to lazy press outlets to be shit-sucking losers, but I'm going to anyway.

It's because of this institutional apathy, and my desire to stay somewhere that costs less than eighty dollars, that we are staying at a spot that, I find out later, local reviewers have cheerfully dubbed the Meth Haunted House.

Again, the key card is millimeters from my hand, but as the man in the tracksuit begins to shout "JAY!" at the top of his lungs in a syncopated rhythm, the phone rings and the receptionist drops the key to retrieve it.

"Casey! Casey, hello, I— Shut the *fuck up*," she hisses at the man in the tracksuit, jaw rolling again. "Oh my God, Casey, I thought you were one of my case managers. I'll call you back in a minute." She hangs up and, just before the man in the tracksuit resumes his birdcall for Jay, looks at me with some confusion: "Wait, you two were young a minute ago," she says.

Not wrong.

The receptionist coaxes the man in the tracksuit to give her the bag from Walmart and says Jay will be back any minute. Tracksuit has a soft spot for her and pushes it beneath the plastic divider, asking if she's still in pain. The receptionist nods, and it's possibly the first true thing she's said since we arrived. She pulls the plastic bag beneath the desk and gives us a key card to the room just around the corner, advising we turn in for the night before dark and not leave once we're inside.

With one last roll of her jaw, she tells me, "You've come at a good time. We just stopped letting locals in."

A short history of the rest of our evening: Yes, the receptionist followed us to the room and stood there while we brought our bags in for what she said was our "protection." Yes, there were cigarette holes in the sheets and a dark brown stain beneath the sink. Yes, we spent upward of forty-five minutes trying to make the best of it. Yes, we turned on the news and saw one of the more desperate local news stories I've ever seen, a one-two punch informing us that Albuquerque was experiencing "detective burnout" with a systemic lack of interest in helping victims of drug-related crimes, and that the South we were heading into first thing in the morning was about to be engulfed in a multiple-day monsoon. Yes, we left that night, and yes, we called ourselves pussies for putting a night at a Fucking Marriott on a credit card. And, please stop asking me, yes, there was an unsolved murder from April of that year that took place in the same motel and yes, an Albuquerque detective was too depressed to do the legwork.

"Who's gonna solve these crimes?" a local detective asks the camera with a sigh, not even needing to say that "solving" involved taking people from places like the fleabag motel where we stayed to jail without support, without efficient rehabilitation, without any high-level examination of how Albuquerque became so riddled with fentanyl to begin with or which communities these "solved" crimes would disproportionately affect. Who's gonna?

The next morning I swim in an overpriced Marriott pool and apologize to my boyfriend for the corner-cutting that landed us at the Meth Haunted House. There's still a storm coming, and we have hot dogs to eat before zigzagging across the South.

Clowndog Hot Dog Parlor in Albuquerque is as close as we get to experiencing the student life side of the city, a themed restaurant bar with a boiling-hot patio for retirees by day and blacked-out college kids by night. Opened in the fall of 2020, a time when around thirty thousand COVID cases were tracked in New Mexico a week and would peak at more than 120,000 a week within two months, Clowndog was the brainchild of restaurateur Rich Bartel. He optimized the business early on to be carryout-only and later opened an expansive bar featuring the kind of menu only found at such an aggressively quirky institution, a list of hot dogs that are all better in theory than in execution.

But you have to hand it to them—any of these would zap a hangover like, let's say, a bolt of lightning hitting a Meth Haunted House. Surrounded by framed photos of novelty clowns at a sticky, primary-colored table that fits the vibe of the cheerful but exhausted bartender, I make direct eye contact with the two-foot-tall painted hot dog in a bun announcing AMAZING! STEP RIGHT UP! and take in the institution's best and grimiest offerings:

> The make-your-own option, offering an array of hot dogs (turkey, beef, veggie, and brat) with what the website advertises as "a veritable FREAKSHOW of toppings, heretofore never even CONSIDERED appropriate for decent, moral Hot Dogs," everything from chopped peanuts to popcorn to a whole-ass fried egg. "AND WE WILL NOT JUDGE WHATEVER COMBINATION YOU DARE TO CHOOSE!"

> Hot Dog Jalapeño Poppers, your standard popper with little chunks of hot dog unceremoniously shoved inside

> The Three-Ring Circus, an all-beef dog topped with onion rings (okay), sliced jalapeños (okay), cheddar (incredible), and Spaghetti-Os (now hold on)

And the Frito Dog, a chili dog slathered in cheddar,
sour cream, onion, and everyone's fourth-favorite chip

For the less adventurous, Clowndog offers Chicago and Soronan-style hot dogs, but I came to get diarrhea at ten in the morning at all costs so I spring for the Three-Ring Circus, a concoction that holds up remarkably well on bread and proves that hot dogs are, indeed, sandwiches. With regrets, the title exceeds the dog itself. I have a steel trap of a digestive system, one that used to endure wet dog food onstage several times a week during my body horror comedy "I Will Do Anything for Attention and Love to Call the Suicide Hotline, I Crack Them Up" era, but this combination of vegetable and pasta rings is an incredible concept that I cannot abide by in the human world. It's all style, no substance. It is the comedian-that-wears-a-cool-jacket of hot dogs.

I successfully implement the Jamie Loftus Hot Dog System before taking in the establishment's impressive collection of clown detritus and head from the sticky high-concept hot dog laboratory to a stand with the best sweet chili these cracked lips have ever wrapped around. Welcome to the Dog House on Route 66.

The Dog House Drive In proudly declares itself "unfussy," a very clever way of telling you that there is no indoor seating. I've been to three or four different places that think naming their business the Dog House is an original idea—it is not—but this one commits to the imagery with a full, sincere, and unfussy heart. A wiener dog in an oversized hot dog bun smiles in neon profile as we pull up to a spot and wait for someone to come take our order—*they* have been coming to *you* for more than seventy years. Not knowing how the park-and-order system works, I get out of the car and look for a counter to order my slop.

NOW HIRING! a banner declares, displayed prominently across the barred front windows that used to say BEST HOT DOG IN

NEW MEXICO. The brightly colored walls of the room where people once ate footlongs and corn dogs are dusty and well over a year out of use. Below it, a sandwich board echoes a sentiment we'll see over and over this summer:

THANK YOU, it yelps in thick Sharpie, "FOR YOUR PATIENCE. DUE TO AN <u>EMPLOYEE SHORTAGE</u>, ORDERS MAY TAKE * LONGER * THAN USUAL!!

I return to our Subaru and relay the message in the cadence it was delivered in.

"Okay, but what about the cherry shake?" my boyfriend asks.

At this point I start googling the intricacies of the labor issues that haunt this summer. Waves of underpaid employees who survived more comfortably under unemployment during the COVID lockdown understandably have no desire to return to the hot Albuquerque sun to serve the Dog House specialty, a dish called a chile dog, to tourists dressed as Heisenberg. Before we can decide on one shake or two, an employee who *did* return to the fold is at our window and we get their classic with the cherry shake.

It turns out that a chile dog goes down so much smoother because it's *not* a chili dog, as most would expect it to be with just one vowel's difference. The hot dog world is full of small but significant linguistic contradictions like this—one needs to be able to distinguish a *chili* dog from a *chile* dog, know the precise differences between a *red* hot and a *white* hot, understand that Coney Islands are actually best eaten in Detroit, and Texas hots are nowhere to be found in the state they're named for. Any mistake made, no matter how understandable, will be met with a pitying chortle from the proprietor and whatever the regional parlance for "That's just how it is" as the answer.

Footlongs at the Dog House are prepared in a way I already recognize as The Best: Split down the middle, grilled, with a decent, hoagie-like bun and toppings plopped accordingly. Their chile recipe is unique to the area, not the undeniable diarrhea consistency that becomes fashionable as we head farther east. Instead it's smooth, sweet, and light, with onions, cheese, and mustard mixed in—slimy but pleasantly so, which I assume is a word that exists in another language but not this one. Jimmie Hartley, the Dog House's owner of more than fifty years who encourages the *Better Call Saul* crowd to keep a-comin', refuses to disclose the recipe in an attitude befitting a true Hot Dog Asshole.

Chili, to the proper New Mexican hot dog stand owner, is a perverse shart of Tex-Mex garbage and is to be avoided. *Chile,* on the other hand, includes local red chiles mixed into its smoother texture, and online chefs have speculated it also includes beef broth, oregano, bacon drippings, and cumin powder. The secret stays with Hartley, along with his reasons for not offering a wage high enough for his employees to return and serve the frothy tourist Jesse Pinkmans.

My boyfriend eyes the remainder of the saccharine cherry shake before putting it in a cup holder where it will separate into fifty mystery chemicals over the next twenty minutes. I want to chug the rest but in the first wise decision of the trip, toss it in the crusty trash bin on the drive out of the drive in.

It's somewhere between Albuquerque and Texas that I first encounter, and I'm so sorry to have to say this, the Gender Pickles (my naming convention, not theirs). For the rest of the day I try to get a refund from the Meth Haunted House, which is more a way to pass the time than a tangible goal, and we're stopping, stopping, stopping at gas stations.

I love a gas station. I love the smell, the feeling of surveillance, the long waits at the coolers that hold the hideous blend of energy drinks that you need to get to the next gas station, the sometimes watchful, sometimes threatening eyes that follow you down the hallway to the neon LADIES ONLY sign. I grew up hanging out at gas stations, spending long nights in the parking lot with my friends in different parents' Ford Focuses drinking seventy-nine-cent slushies because dumbasses of our caliber were not "invited" to "parties" or "having" "sex." I went exclusively to gas stations for meals throughout college when less, uh, petrified food wasn't in my tax bracket, and I am a known entity at every 7–Eleven I've ever lived within walking distance of.

Not coincidentally, hot dogs thrive in the gas station, usually on bone-cold perpetual motion machines where they shrivel like football leather over a period of days but still manage to soak up the White Claw you paid for in quarters earlier that night when shit hits the fan. In my late *Riverdale* years (this is my way of telling you I'm twenty-eight at the time of writing), I have become something of a connoisseur of the food at any given gas station. The sushi at 7–Eleven was briefly my party trick of choice—I eat it, I like it, I don't even throw up! The chicken sandwich at Cumberland Farms in New England is a delicacy, the cookie dough at Love's Travel Stop *hits,* and I would have unprotected sex with anything from a Wawa.

But it was not until a gas station in Texas, minutes after snaking past a car accident so brutal it reminded me why I never got my driver's license, that I saw the Gender Pickles. I was already a staunch evangelist of the Car Pickle—those two-dollar pouches you can seal and reseal that are friendly to anorexics on a budget like myself, a few calories in exchange for the driver insisting you crack a fucking window. These lesser gas station pickles, however, do not appear with a face, or story, or family dynamic, a given that the Van Holten company of Milwaukee has been subverting since 1898.

Allow me to introduce you to the Gender Pickles family— one that, once seen, continues to expand throughout eastern America. (This tracks, as it is canonically where the Perverts and Sickos tend to thrive. I digress.)

THE GENDER PICKLE FAMILY:

 **Big Papa:** This is a pickle that is all man, which you can tell because he is the lead character (always male), he is wearing sneakers (girl pickles would never), and he is otherwise completely naked. He's the blueprint, the "hearty dill pickle," the Fred Flintstone of the sour cucumber universe. Beside him, without fail, is *his wife*.

 **Hot Mama:** I don't know how surprised you'll be to hear that the gender pickles are sexist and, if others are to be believed, leaning pretty heavily on Latin stereotypes. Hot Mama is the Wilma of the equation, branded "hot and spicy" in a bright red package (see previous sentence), wearing a string of pearls (a pickle in pearls, I want to feel her pickle arms around my human torso at the door on Christmas morning), in a black side-swept wig with bright red streaks that remind me of my young, divorced jazz dance teacher from high school, the first woman I had dreams about kissing, except for that other one. I love Hot Mama.

 **Sour Sis:** I regret to inform you that this pickle is a barely legal teenager in a crop top and a miniskirt, and if you don't regret knowing this, please do not contact me. Sour Sis, the Van Holtens eagerly inform us, is "Tart and Tangy" and sports the same red lipstick as Hot Mama, black leggings, and little yellow shoes. She gazes adoringly at her own tart and tangy reflection in a pocket mirror, and she's right to. I send a picture to my friend, who replies that it "feels like Van Holten has some shitty opinions about Latinas," and the second she says it I know she's right.

Sour Sis is wearing the most clothes of any of the pickles but is the most erotic by a long shot—she has an hourglass shape that pickles aren't, well, known for and wears a blond wig with a stem launching out of the center like a unicorn's horn. She is a complicated image, designed by a frothing marketing man in the middle of nowhere before I was born, but looks like the sort of character that could be reclaimed, written about in poetry books and past-their-prime think piece sites, an image of a woman looking at herself all dolled up and liking what she sees, the semiotics of "tart and tangy," I have spent so much time in the lobotomy aisle of the internet and all I have to show for it is some of the worst sex of my life. The best sex of my life was with a prop comedian who *hated* me. I can't write this in the book. If you're reading this, it means it's the final draft, and someone has done me a gigantic disservice.

There's one last gender pickle.

 **Garlic Joe:** Who Garlic Joe is depends on where your threshold for chaos lies. He is the undisputed Chad of the Van Holten pickle expanded universe (VHPEU), a "zesty garlic pickle" who wears a crop top that says G.Y.M. (what this is an abbreviation for is unclear), fingerless gloves, workout sneakers, and dumbbells with onions on either end. He has chest hair—*chest hair*—biceps, and an absolutely pantsless Donald Duck situation beneath the chest, dickless unless Garlic Joe is *the* dick and this is just how you would style a dick that went to the gym. Which, fuck, means the balls are the sneakers, and I guess you could go from there.

Joe (Garlic) doesn't hold the same clear, nuclear tie to the family that Mama, Papa, and Sis do—a world of possibility opens. Is he hooking up with Hot Mama on the side while Big Papa is at work? Is he the jock to Sour Sis's Becky? Is he Hot Mama and Big Papa's son? Is he, my favorite permutation, Big Papa's trainer who becomes the secret, but evident, love of his life? Do Garlic Joe and Big Papa decide no, life is too short, Hot Mama deserves to know? Do they take her to the Olive Garden and tell her that it's been going on for years and she doesn't deserve to spend the rest of her life living a lie, it's already been so long, plus Garlic Joe has stage one pancreatic cancer, it's not fatal but it's certainly a wake-up call, no of course we'll get the check?

PROUDLY SUPPORTS BOYS AND GIRLS CLUB, it reads on the bottom of the package. What the fuck does that mean? Why is only Garlic Joe supporting boys and girls? Of the family, he is the pickle I'd want around a child the least. Okay, well.

There are other pickles. Hot, Kosher, Dill, Sour. Naked, genderless, completely free. They are the same pickles as the gender pickles, with the same flavors. It is your choice, as a gas station consumer, whether you want to be a pervert Or Not.

The Val Holtens are, to this day, very much trying to make the pickle family *happen,* though to a degree of success that seems to be limited to about a thousand Instagram followers and a handful of items in their online store, all of which I've purchased. My boyfriend takes pictures of the gender pickles, close up—my phone is dead, but he says he'll send me everything once we're back home.

There is a piece of my brain that reminds me to write it down myself. One thing that really puts a plug in the ass of love as a concept is that you really can only depend on yourself. This is something that people who are in love never want to hear, shoving this same plug into their ass so far that they—and I hate to say this because I'm pretty sure it will live on a shelf next to cookbooks—begin spewing their own shit from their mouths.

At the next gas station I take my own pictures because, reader, you just never know.

Here Is How You Make
a Hot Dog

*A note to my vegetarians and vegans and those who do
not engage with the meat-dog—you are right.*

There is a video on the internet called "How It's Made - Hot
Dogs" that has eighty-nine million views at the time I'm writing
this. I can't overstate how much I love "How It's Made - Hot
Dogs," a five-minute clip so informative, horrific, and completely
lacking in self-awareness that I'd estimate I've watched it once a
month since it was first uploaded in 2012. It does what it claims
to—shows you how a hot dog is made in the least disturbing
way possible—and it desperately wants you to believe that this is
a normal and good thing to be happening. A note to those who
don't want to hear the ins and outs of the modern slaughterhouse
and meat-processing factory: this may be the chapter you skip. If
you're on the fence, I encourage you to stick around if you can.
Some train wrecks are worth witnessing: who else will tell your
friends?

"How It's Made - Hot Dogs" consists mainly of footage from
a meat-processing factory in the late 2000s, tracking the journey
of a hot dog from raw meat "trimmings" all the way to a vacuum-
sealed package. It is cheerfully narrated by a Canadian host and
has a goofy organ soundtrack zipping in the background. What

accompanies this peppy narrative is some of the most horrifying footage you could ever want to see. Footage so visceral that you can smell it. Footage that makes you wonder why you can't see a dick on television but you *can* see how hot dog meat is pulverized while a man's lilting voice reassures you that this is *delicious*. It is a clip designed to be watched alone with your face one centimeter from your phone in the dead of night, to be watched with your college roommate when the conversation stalls, to be shown to your crush when you need to seem interesting.

What they present is the company line on how your average hot dog is made, one that is verified by the extremely corporate, somehow real National Hot Dog and Sausage Council and still manages to look stupendously unappetizing. In five minutes or less, the viewer is assaulted with knowledge I will faithfully reproduce here.

"A century and a half later," the voice says over a shot of three hot dogs scissoring one another on a white porcelain plate in front of a municipal building for some reason, "hot dogs are still the number one treat on the street."

A sinister fade begins as organ music plays—we see hundreds of pale brown hot dogs being shot out of a piece of machinery like T-shirts at a sports game, wet and slippery, precooked but aesthetically raw, slipping and sliding all over one another as hundreds, *hundreds* of them pile on top of the others and await human consumption. The organ music tinkles as we see three gigantic vats of liquified meat, the "slurry" that makes up your average hot dog—"pork, beef, and chicken," he says cheerfully, before bringing us back to the beginning of the sinister process. Empty your bowels and take a deep breath, for this is the journey of the modern hot dog.

We see the meat trimmings enter the factory and slap down a gigantic metal slide into a tenderizer. "Trimmings" are a gentle term for the wide variety of meat considered not good enough to be a part of a better-conceived dish—essentially garbage being repurposed as a mass-appeal food, though our Canuck judiciously describes it as "pieces of meat left over from cutting steaks or porkchops." A gigantic pile of randomized, pale raw meat said to include fatty tissue, sinewed muscle, head meat, and some liver is pushed into a tenderizer with a metal rake and pulses pornographically, bouncing as it smooths out in the same pulsed motions of a married couple doing doggy style on a Tuesday night. These are the cuts that are left on the slaughterhouse floor, only to find a third life in the soon-to-be thick goop I will spend an entire summer punishing my body with.

The trimmings are cut and ground, going through a series of pressurized metal plates and grinders that shoot out a flesh-colored meat slurry in thin spaghetti strands into another metal bucket. "How It's Made - Hot Dogs" elects to show an extended shot of pinkish ground meat as a drum solo plays for the longest ten seconds of my life and yours, before crossfading to something even more horrific—a hundred pounds of liquified processed chicken meat being heaped on top of it, followed by food starch and salt to bind the meats into a uniform pudding of food deemed edible *enough*. It's interesting that the program readily admits to using a basic starch as a binder, as the uptight Council only uses the carefully chosen phrase "curing ingredients," along with whatever proprietary spices the company uses.

"These flavorings vary depending on where the hot dog is to be sold," the narrator drones on as a dandruff snowstorm of said flavorings cascade onto the diarrhea-looking heap, "because people in different regions have different tastes." This is a not-so-subtle nod to how particularly vile hot dog brands and generally unhealthy processed foods tend to be pumped into predominantly poor and Black neighborhoods in the US that have little in the way of affordable, healthy alternatives, a deliberate decision that has been impacting the health of these communities for decades. "How It's Made - Hot Dogs" has no interest in the social impact of their subject.

They're too busy switching the music to a royalty-free farting techno as the meat reaches its next form—a sloppy, creamy batter—as shots of water and a golden shower of corn syrup piss onto the hot dog soup, turned over and over into a thick slime by the next industrial blender. How are you feeling? The narrator tells us that this added sugar and moisture serves to make the hot dogs juicier as syrup squirts onto the soaking wet batter, before being pushed through *another* metal tube to force out air and shart a mountain of shiny, thick emulsion into the next vat.

It's at the cellulose tubing phase that we get to see the employees of the hot dog factory at work, all blue smocks and hairnets and big red earmuffs to drown out the sound of hot doggery. Their job is the one that Industrial Revolution–era factory employees would regularly lose their fingers to, as emulsion is forced into the shiny, precisely measured casing and shot out of a machine in a long, linked row. The children holding hands across the world have nothing on these fuckers, and every few seconds the employees guide hundreds of dogs through their gloved fingers and into the next industrial-sized bucket, hovering just a little too close to a piece of machinery that could hack off an appendage and is loud as a machine gun. Once in links, we see for the first time something that resembles the eventual hot dog.

The football field's worth of links are sucked into a spiderlike robot that hangs the long meat chains onto racks in rows of six and sends them into what the narrator describes as a "liquid smoke shower" but more closely resembles a yeast infection exploding into a cloud of liquid with no warning. The hot dog chains are dripping with hot, yellowy something as they're hustled through the next oven, where the ejaculate mixture is baked in and finally rids the dogs of their sickly pale hue in favor of a darker brown.

The hot dogs descend into the sixth circle of factory hell, cooled in a shower of cold, salty water and sucked back up into the Giger tarantula onto a conveyor belt toward another work-place liability, *the peeling machine*. This will slice off the cellulose casing the employees dutifully shoved hot dog pus into earlier in the process and liberate them from the case as a rubbery solid. It's a miraculous Jell-O-like transformation happening hundreds of thousands of times every day, but some miracles aren't good miracles.

"Inside the peeler machine, a tiny knife slits each casing along the top," the voice continues over footage of an employee in a white smock tensely smiling at the camera while his hand lingers near the lethal tiny knife machine. What kind of direction are the people at *How It's Made* giving these poor employees? "Then, steamy air blows the casing *right off the dogs.*"

A sick bassline drops as we see this demonstrated by a machine called the Townsend 2600 (currently $15,000 used), shooting out peeled hot dogs at the rate of seven hundred a minute, then examined by the sex god of the meat plant, The Inspector. They look just like any other employee but stand straighter with purpose as they run their fingers across hundreds of hot dogs at a stunning pace, an octopus feeling their way around in the dark and plucking out undesirables that are too long or thick or misshapen to make it into the hands of the foamy-mouthed consumer. It's here where some hot dogs meet their true end, the death where not only have you died in physical form, but the last person in the world who remembered you has died too. These dogs are tossed off the conveyor belt and onto a metal counter, solidifying their status as the least desired meat product in the world as their surviving almost-identical comrades are prepared for packaging.

In any given shift at a hot dog factory, two and a half million dogs go from being head meat to a vacuum-sealed Jell-O meat mold ready to enter a refrigerated truck and then your home.

And that's the *nice* version of this process.

People love to ask me what's in a hot dog, as if I have an

answer that will make them feel better. Dead animals is the answer. But the hot dog's reputation is for *extremely* dead animals—ones killed in unsanitary conditions with no mercy, with only the worst working conditions and least appetizing sections of the animal shredded and deuce-dropped into a cellulose casing somewhere in New Jersey. These rumors have followed the meatpacking industry for as long as it's existed, and with good reason—Bruce Kraig, author of *Hot Dog: A History,* details suspected ingredients including wild dogs, cats, rats, and sometimes human meat as potential risk factors going back to the nineteenth century. The anxiety is a well-placed one, regardless of how many times the Council—I imagine them sitting in flowing robes at a long table made of fossilized hot dogs—tries to put your mind at ease.

Yes, the meat used for hot dogs are scraps, barely edible, but what's more important is how the animals whose head meat is fashioned into factory-certified shapes are treated at the facility that comes just before—the slaughterhouse.

Again—the choice not to eat meat is the correct one. Vegans, you are right. Humans eat a shitload of it, though, and so it matters that when animals are killed, they are given lives worth living and death with dignity, something you know, if you are reading this book, does not often happen. This was the general philosophy of Indigenous Americans whose land was stolen by future industrialists—bison were hunted in the wild with the cooperation of entire tribes like the Cree, who tricked herds into running themselves off hills and dying all at once, nearly painless. A well-executed hunt could yield more than ten thousand pounds of meat without affecting the quality of life of the bison at all, a practice that was halted when European colonists not only nearly wiped out the buffalo and bison populations, but committed genocide on the Indigenous people of America for hundreds of years. They built their own, harsher slaughterhouses where humane hunting once took place.

To humankind's credit, industrialization was at least in part a response to a rapidly increasing population—the species swelled from 1 billion to 6.5 billion people between 1800 and 2000, leaving a lot more mouths to feed that were, statistically, mostly underclass. Even so, factory farming (or, large-scale industrial slaughter) hasn't haunted the *entire* history of the hot dog—her early years found her produced mainly by local butchers who tended to practice more humanely. Its rise in popularity came alongside new technology and the ability to vaccinate animals in close proximity against diseases, which began in England in 1947.

The concept was developed not with a mind toward nutrition, but "was seen as a way of providing food security" without the expense of importing meats, according to the United Nations–endorsed Agriculture Act. Never keeping her eyes on her own paper, the US had already been in the habit of mass raising and slaughtering chickens going back to the 1920s and got in on the barely regulated industrial farming game in the 1960s. Between 1980 and 2010, conglomerates swallowed smaller operations into the dark, poorly ventilated, disease-ridden, and highly efficient factory model as hog farm numbers plummeted while the price of meat in grocery stores fell by around half. This affected not just the quality of product and the treatment of the animals, but the benefit to American farmers—in this same time period, a farmer's take-home pay fell by half, as well.

Humans have always bent toward the destruction of species they deem fit for consumption—going back thousands of years, the very existence of humans means that local mammal populations will be all but wiped out. Still, what happens to the animals in the hot dogs I eat during the summer of 2021 is particularly cruel—creatures that exist in the millions and are bred to multiply, but not to strengthen or preserve their species. The chickens, pigs, and cows in our hot dogs are bred to be helpless by design, not just to cut costs (which it certainly does), but because the suffering is the point—providing a life means money and time and labor and a creature that has something to lose. By suppressing the natural bonding instincts of a calf, removing her from the social aspects of the herd's maternal bonding, and providing her with only the bare minimum to survive before being inseminated with bull sperm, the logic is that she will never know what she's missing. But she does—there are thousands of years of ancestral knowledge telling her this is not how things were supposed to go, that this process cheats natural selection by denying nature the opportunity to select at all.

All right, last warning—this is the truth of the contemporary meatpacking industry. I think you can handle it; you're an adult or interested in adultlike themes (boring, murderous) but the powers that be have advised I give you one last escape hatch into the hot dog ignorance abyss. I am about to describe to you exactly how livestock turns into hot dogs, and my opinion is if you've got the stomach to eat it then you should know who suffers for you to do so. No judgment—I've eaten hundreds of these things, we're strangers and we'll stay that way. If you want to imagine holding my clammy phantom hand, here it is.

Here is what happens to one of the nearly eighty million pigs being raised for slaughter in factory farms this year, the one whose head meat landed in the last industrial meat tube you bought off the street. The only federal laws that exist to protect them at present are from 1873 and 1958—respectively, the Twenty-Eight Hour Law, which requires that animals not be confined for longer than that length of time during interstate travel, and the Humane Methods of Slaughter Act, which requires "the proper treatment and humane handling of all food animals except chickens." The hot dog process is completely legal in most states.

A slaughterhouse pig's life begins in a gestation crate, an enclosure with nothing but slats in the floor to drain piss and shit.

This is also where a mother gives birth, but is often unable to nurse without assistance, having spent her entire life between inseminations in a series of small crates. The mother would have just spent around four months pregnant in the gestation area, then moved to another tightly enclosed farrowing crate to nurse her newborn piglets behind bars, unable to bond normally. She will be inseminated over and over until her body gives out, at which point she will be sent to be slaughtered by stun gun and throat slitting.

Her babies will often have their tails clipped without anesthesia to prevent biting, and males are frequently castrated and have their teeth removed so that they will not bite cage bars. Runts are slaughtered. All slaughterhouse pigs live in crowded pens and are vaccinated to remain healthy enough to be deemed food, but this doesn't prevent all injury or disease by a long shot. After six months, they're loaded onto trucks, prodded onto the killing floor, and most will be successfully stunned before their throats are slit—reports say that those that aren't successfully stunned are killed while conscious. After slaughter, pigs are dunked into tanks of water, with cases as late as the 1990s resulting in pigs being boiled alive or drowned after their throats were slit. Meat is then harvested for bacon, pork, and ham, and whatever is left over goes into the vibrating vat as the *How It's Made* bassline slaps.

Of course, pigs aren't the only animals slaughtered—chickens in particular face a stunning amount of abuse as they're not covered under the Humane Methods of Slaughter Act. A short-list of torture methods that end as pale brown hot dog goop include *forced molting,* a practice that is continued in the US but illegal in the EU that induces simultaneous molting in a flock by withholding food and water for as long as two weeks to reset a chicken's reproductive tract. Cattle has long been a source of concern for disease spread due to lack of oversight and caution regarding the care of animals being bred for beef and veal—most famously, mad cow disease (bovine spongiform encephalopathy if you're nasty) made headlines in the early 2000s as a neurodegenerative disease brought on by malnutrition on a slaughter farm. This was better regulated beginning in the late 2000s, but not before it had spread to humans.

Look, I'm not posing naked on a PETA billboard (I would but I have weird boobs and no one asked), but you don't need to be a soldier for the cause to realize that the reality of factory farms is an integrated scheme to exploit everyone involved but those at the top—the animals are treated without mercy by underpaid employees, who in turn make an unhealthy product to be marketed to the poor, who consume and shorten their own lifespans by enjoying it. Maybe she is American after all.

A largely ignored subject, even in the world of animal rights activism, is the dignity and labor rights of the employees at slaughterhouses and plants, all of whom are undercompensated and most of whom are immigrants. The information is there—a watershed 2001 report from Jo Warrick at *The Washington Post* detailed the reality of the turn-of-the-twenty-first-century slaughterhouse laborer, accounting the work of "second legger" Ramon Moreno, whose cheeky job description entailed the brutal work of chopping more than three hundred legs per hour off of steer carcasses. He reported that many came to him still alive.

"They blink. They make noises," Moreno told Warrick. "They die piece by piece."

This is technically an admission to breaking a law requiring that cattle be stunned before execution by the Humane Slaughter Act, but Moreno was acting at the behest of the slaughterhouse he worked at. Further sources, including inspectors and overseers, said the law was not well enforced at the time of publication—some slaughterhouses racked up more than twenty violations that were never pursued by the government. These issues were further complicated by significant privatization of meat inspection and ghoulish "ag-gag" laws emerging in the 1990s that made it a crime for anyone, though primarily targeting activists and employees, to document anything on the grounds of a meat plant in order to prove abuse or other legal violations.

In the early 2000s, the meatpacking industry held the highest rate of job-related illnesses and injuries at around 27 percent, with workers describing the need to wear chest pads and hockey masks to avoid being injured from improperly killed or distressed livestock.

Warrick spoke with a Florida beef plant technician in 2001 about the worker's reality at the slaughterhouse—speak up, lose your livelihood. When hidden camera footage was released of Tyson Foods (then IBP, Inc.), slaughterhouse employees—then making nine dollars an hour to kill more than two hundred cattle in a single shift—could be seen stunning cows that later woke up and were killed while still conscious. Pressure was put on workers to sign statements saying they had never seen live cattle on the slaughter line.

The company's reaction was a predictable one, scapegoating individual migrant workers and bullying others into doing the same in order to retain their employment. Similar reports have been made of many American meat-processing plants, notably a report from the *Los Angeles Times* in 2015 revealing that the USDA had declined to punish Farmer John Hot Dogs in Vernon, California, for repeatedly failing to stun pigs being prepared for slaughter.

By the 2020 COVID-19 lockdown, worker and animal protection issues had barely improved, setting the meatpacking industry up for a metric fuckton of trouble. Once again, Tyson Foods, purveyor of Ball Park hot dogs, and their more than one hundred thousand employees were at the center of the controversy, with the country's largest food provider allegedly obscuring positive COVID-19 tests from local officials and bullying workers into remaining on the job.

The corporate patterns were similar to those from the early 2000s—*ProPublica* reporting from 2020 revealed that Tyson employed private companies to handle the issue of disease spread among employees, leaving public officials in the dark about accurate numbers or precautions being taken to prevent spread. In North Carolina, the company had to be threatened with "injunctive relief or prosecution" in 2020 before the health department learned that 599 workers had tested positive—a fifth of their workforce—and two employees had died. Meatpacking executives had planned for how to handle a pandemic when it came to managing animals to be slaughtered. What they had not done was consider the low-income workforce who did the slaughtering, leaving employees extremely vulnerable in the interest of upholding the American supply chain.

At the end of April 2020, President Trump's executive order stated that "critical infrastructure food companies continue their operations to the fullest extent possible."

With a few years' distance from the wave of labor atrocities at Tyson Foods, reporting from the spring of 2022 revealed more intentional collusion between meat executives and the Trump administration than originally thought. A new *ProPublica* report from Michael Grabell in 2022 revealed *direct collusion* between Tyson Foods, Smithfield Foods, and the American government to push the executive order that needlessly cost hundreds of vulnerable lives.

Here's a strong case for bringing back the guillotine: the CEOs of Tyson and Smithfield chatted over email in April 2020 about how to avoid their production and profits suffering. Types Tyson CEO Noel White: "Anything we can do to help?"

Smithfield CEO Ken Sullivan is typing . . . he wishes there was. His bestie replies, per Grabell: "Would Sullivan like to discuss the possibility of getting President Donald Trump to sign an executive order to keep meatpacking plants open?"

Reader, the executive order that cost lives in their factories was *their* idea, one that tested exceptionally well with the Trump administration. The executive order eventually bore strong similarities to a suggested draft that Julie Anna Potts of the North American Meat Institute, a trade organization representing more than half a million meatpacking employees, sent in April 2020. The loophole she suggested invoking was a clever one—a law implemented during the Korean War called the Defense Production Act allowed the president to order an entire industry to remain on the line regardless of labor conditions.

Trump's agriculture secretary arranged a call between White, Sullivan, and then vice president Mike Pence—Pence, cuck of the planet (pejorative) would say in a White House press conference *later that day* that meatpacking workers should "show up and do your job." The same CEOs were in regular contact with Trump chief of staff Mark Meadows up until the executive order announcement on April 28, 2020.

But the exact strings being pulled to endanger the lives of Tyson Foods employees internally was not public knowledge in the spring of 2020. At that time, the damage of demanding plants remain open no matter what was significant, immediate, and under-discussed—the Tyson plant in Waterloo, Iowa, tested 58 percent positive. Fifty-eight percent. Just before major lockdowns, the same Tyson CEO who privately pushed for an executive order contacted the governor of Nebraska to inform him that "social distancing is a nicety that makes sense only for people with laptops." The company's largest plant, located in that same state, had only one nurse employed when the workplace had nearly eight hundred positive COVID cases, nearly a year before a vaccine would become accessible.

The CDC floundered about the plight of these "essential workers," initially saying that employees testing positive should quarantine for two weeks, then changing their tune to say that asymptomatic positive testers could return to work immediately. For an industry where the average employee makes under $30,000 a year at a time when COVID stimulus checks were issued in America at unlivable amounts, it's not hard to understand why disease continued to spread within plants. What the fuck are you supposed to do?

Likely thinking their emails with one another would never surface, executives and the government hummed a familiar tune: blame individual workers.

This level of labor abuse can seem unprecedented, but particularly in places like the aforementioned Tyson pork factory in Waterloo, Iowa, a town previously idolized for its strong meat-packing labor unions. In a brilliant report from Bernice Yeung and Michael Grabell, Waterloo's unique history as the former proud "Factory Town of Iowa" is laid bare—in the early 1900s, Black workers from Mississippi on strike from exploitative railroad jobs were drawn to the area as a way of joining the middle class. Even then, the recruiting language was deeply racist—ads from the 1910s said that the Black American had "proven himself a capable workman" and was superior to "cheap foreign help."

At the time, a steady meatpacking job at what was then the Rath Packing Company made a middle-class life possible, building up a stable, union-powered community that made Waterloo an ideal place for civil rights and labor victories throughout the mid-twentieth century. The "Smokey Row" area of town became known for its dense population of workers coming to Rath from the South, where racial violence, Jim Crow laws, and floods terrorized Black communities. In Waterloo, the inclusive United Packinghouse Workers of America unionized meatpacking employees and gave workers influence over their conditions that are unheard of now—when conditions worsened, wages dipped, or Black workers were treated as inferior at the Rath plant, the entire line walked out and their needs were generally met. Strikes . . . work.

It didn't last—during the 1960s, the arrival of industrial machinery in meat plants reduced the perceived importance of the individual worker, and the 1980s-era Reaganomics spiral and farm crisis permanently disabled what had been a vital and growing Black middle class. Rath laid off thousands, and by 1985 was shuttered.

A company called Iowa Beef Processors, the same company that would later pressure employees to say they'd never seen live cattle on the line, filled the void where Rath once was, lowering wages and standardizing packing factories with employees standing shoulder to shoulder for what amounts to twelve dollars an hour in 2022. Many employees used to the comparative dignity of Rath walked, leaving IBP to recruit from marginalized communities with fewer options—namely, unhoused people brought in from shelters and non-English-speaking immigrants looking for work in the South. This new system of fractured communication and exploitation established, Tyson acquired the factory in 2001 and furthered recruitment efforts to refugee immigrants new to the US from Africa, Asia, and the Pacific Islands, with new employees from Myanmar and the Congo in particular starting jobs in the Waterloo plant. It was this environment, with a vulnerable population that had largely missed the town's union salad days, that COVID hit.

"This is a culture issue," an official on a conference call for Tyson said in the spring of 2020, blaming a Kentucky plant's COVID outbreak on thirty Burmese refugees holding an Easter gathering. The disease's spread at the plant predated the scapegoated celebration by more than a week. Communications among employees, the plants, and local health departments were further complicated by language barriers, as both entities were understaffed in communicating with the groups they were intended to serve. Workers still experiencing symptoms were told to remain on the production line without social distancing, per the *ProPublica* report, unless they had fevers. In Iowa, a plant manager created a winner-take-all betting pool for higher-ups to guess how many low-ranking employees would test positive for COVID—at the end of 2020, some of these Iowa employees would receive between a $300 and $700 holiday bonus for surviving (sorry, bravely keeping the American food supply chain afloat, completely out of patriotism).

Workers continued to show up. A 2020 *ProPublica* report called "The Battle for Waterloo" details the story of a Haitian immigrant named Félicie Joseph whose primary concern while deathly ill was whether Tyson would fire her if she asked to extend her quarantine—she died before she was due back at work. A white Tyson laundry worker, Jim Orvis, was taken off life support by his brother over Zoom this same month, followed by his upstairs neighbor Arthur Scott, who worked at the Tyson pet food plant nearby. In these early days of the pandemic, a local community health clinic reported that 99 percent of COVID-infected patients were Tyson employees or lived with someone who worked for them.

In a CNN broadcast in April 2020, Tyson president and CEO Dean Banks said, "From everything we've seen, the spread of the disease in the community is affecting us in the plant."

The message was clear: if you died on the job in an environment where you are already marginalized with massive communication barriers and intentionally weakened union power, for a company knowingly pushing the government to keep you at work in circumstances that they should know could kill you? That was *your* fault. It would be incredibly far-fetched to suggest the companies misunderstood the potential dangers of COVID-19—why else would Tyson have implemented far more comprehensive protocols in their Chinese factories in February of the same year?

As of this writing, Sullivan of Smithfield is retired and White of Tyson remains an executive vice president, whatever the fuck that means. By their definition, the ghoulish campaign to keep their factories open during the plague was successful—the meatpacking industry profit margin has grown 300 percent since the beginning of the pandemic as late 2021 numbers indicated that 59,000 Tyson Foods employees contracted COVID-19 and 269 died. Numbers reported previously were nearly three times fewer—probably because symptoms were reported as absences, and in five cases at Foster Farms chicken plant in California, COVID fatalities were reported as "resolved cases" and "resolutions." In the larger sense, research indicated that by July 2020, a few months after Trump's executive order, 6 to 8 percent of national cases were a result of community spread from meatpacking plants—upward of eighteen thousand casualties total.

How we feeling about that guillotine?

This is the story of the meatpacking industry—there is some outdated, theoretical governmental oversight, but it's not enforced to a degree that actually protects animals or humans. The USDA has some authority, local health departments have some authority, the CDC can recommend this or that, but no one has the ability to override a president who desperately wants meat to remain available in grocery stores at any human cost, or profiteering CEOs from goading him.

It may not surprise you to hear that during the summer of 2021, I was not able to find one meat-processing plant or hot dog factory willing to let me inside, with virtually all of them claiming that denial was due to an abundance of COVID safety precautions. Similar COVID outbreaks continued at large plants including Farmer John Hot Dogs, then still the primary contractor for the iconic Dodger Dogs well into 2022.

The comments made by a meatpacking employee to *The Washington Post* in 2001 apply just as much to the cost of human and animal life in the American meat supply chain more than twenty years later.

"I complained to everyone—I said, 'Lookit, they're skinning live cows in there,'" he said. "Always it was the same answer: 'We know it's true. But there's nothing we can do about it.'"

But sure, employees just don't want to work this summer. Why could that be?

We Are in the South

You can't leave. Where would we go?

We get into Oklahoma City late after snaking past miles of dried-out VW bugs without wheels on the side of the road. It could have been an art installation but I think it was what art installations are supposed to be *about*. I don't understand that sort of thing, but I have friends who really think they do. I've gotten us a room at the Days Inn next to the Hustler store, which is interesting, but I've accidentally gotten us a room that allows smoking, which is not.

There is an unspoken rule of road trips, and it's that you can't fuck up two nights in a row. One night is a story for when you get to your destination, two means Jamie is a cheapskate and a bad girlfriend who is not sure enough she will finish the book she is being paid to write to spend the entire advance on the research stage. Does that make sense? If you're reading this, I was being irrational.

The smoke alarm hangs from the ceiling almost as a joke as we bring in fast food I've never tried from Whataburger—I mean, we're here, he's sick of hot dogs, and the *Keeping Up with the Kardashians* marathon that started the night before we left has finished and begun again on a loop. I let myself be transported for a millisecond: it's 2007, Obama is running for president, everyone is calling each other sluts, I am sitting at home in my back brace and refusing to go to a birthday party because I'm tired of questions about my torso. In the present, we almost go to the Hustler store as a joke but don't. They're shooting amateur porn next door and the men with the cameras smoke cigarettes and ask each other which superhero movies the others have seen. One guy says between cigarettes, "Sorry, and I hate to say this, *Wonder Woman* just *wasn't* that *good*, and it's not even the woman thing!"

I worry about our cocker spaniel inhaling this much cigarette smoke, but there's nothing we can do. We go to sleep. I get my period on the sheets and we need to leave first thing in the morning; my head is pounding and the knockoff Thomas Kinkade I stared at until the sun came up is sticking to my eyelids like a phone protector. We have four hot dogs to eat today.

Coney Island Hot Weiners [sic, their spelling is not our business] opened in Oklahoma City in 1924 in the wake of one of the region's most gruesome historical moments. An hour and a half away in Tulsa was a hotbed of violent white American racism in the few years leading up to the shop's opening. The Socialist Party had been destroyed by the early 1920s and the Ku Klux Klan existed above the law when areas like Tulsa's predominantly Black Greenwood District was attacked in 1921, and twenty-six Black Oklahomans were killed in what's now known as the Tulsa Race Massacre. Those who threatened the KKK's idea of "100 percent Americanism" were threats to the state, and economic struggle continued in Oklahoma up to the freefall of the 1929 stock market crash. What remained by the time Coney Island Hot Weiners served its first dog in 1924 was poverty, severe racial unrest, and an impending depression—the last of which is a kingmaker for hot dog joints.

A century later, it's still a fraught time in Oklahoma City. Arrests were made there and in Tulsa during the George Floyd protests in the spring of 2020, a pickup truck with a horse trailer plowed through a Black Lives Matter protest, and unemployment peaked at 13 percent. By the time we drive through a year later, the unemployment spike has settled but the industrial park across from Coney Island Hot Weiners's painted sign—advertising Greek-style spaghetti, beer, and the best chili in town—is completely deserted. Its storefront features one of my favorite cursed images in the world: an anthropomorphized, throbbing red hot dog with Mickey Mouse appendages in the middle of an awkwardly staged dance, lurking in the corner of the window with too-real eyes. It's a tiny building beside the midsize office structures that flank it, completely empty on a Saturday morning.

Here's the thing—a hot dog joint *never* closes. I have been to a trillion hot dog joints, their names overlapping, their stories all meshed together, dozens of dancing hot dogs grinning menacingly from their buns. *None* of them have closed. Places burn down, relocate, switch hands from one Greek guy to another, but never truly close.

Coney Island Hot Weiners's interior is like walking into a station wagon blown out to five times the size. Wooden panels and linoleum line every surface, a clean-dirty scent hangs in the air, and two old men catch up loudly in front of a chess board as a television older than I am blares the local news fretting over No One Wanting to Work. The woman at the counter eyes me suspiciously enough that I don't touch my phone the entire time I'm inside, afraid of having it swatted from my hand.

"I ain't going anywhere," she reassures the local news, asking me what I want. I get the signature—Our Famous Coney, $1.20 for a dog with chili, mustard, and onions prepared right in front of you with a toasted bun. It's good, really fucking good, and I feel her eyes on me as I try to figure out the last time the banners for the "New Coney Island Record" were switched out. A whole wall is dedicated to University of Oklahoma football statistics written in large Comic Sans.

"You can't leave, honey," one of the old men at the chessboard hollers over the linoleum back at the owner. "Where would we go?" She grins at the boiler, not him.

Tulsa is desperately trying to be self-aware this summer and it's about 40 percent of the way there. The Coney Dog–saturated city is offering artists small grants to move there, the parks are sprawling and squeaky clean, the plaques acknowledging the Tulsa Race Massacre look suspiciously new. There's a Scorsese movie shooting here this summer, literally everyone I encounter tells me; maybe you'll see DiCaprio, did you see *The Aviator,* it was his best (this was my mom on the phone and she's wrong, but who cares).

My friend is living here now, back to his hometown after a spectacular cross-state breakup that left him without an apartment in Los Angeles or a girlfriend. He *needs* to talk about it in a way that used to make me want to kiss him on the mouth when I met him five years ago. What is that? I forget what book it was that I got at the mall and left on his doorstep for his birthday in 2017, or why I am unable to express romantic interest without doing something a twelve-year-old would. He's the best, I love my friend, and the three of us catch up on the stoop of the Coney I-Lander hot dog restaurant while my eyes keep drifting to a Halliburton truck with a *Punisher* decal.

Coney I-Lander has been open for ninety-five years and the employees appear to have been working without a break for about as long. My boyfriend gives our cocker spaniel water from a cleaned-out Slurpee cup outside while teenagers give me and my friend free soda when we tip, one of us going for a regular Coney (two bucks) and the other a cheese Coney ($2.25). Too much shredded cheese—Mexican bag cheese from the grocery store, I'd bet my life on it—wet bread, mustard, and onions, tired teenagers I hope were paid enough to have it be worth their while to return to work in the first place. Should I tell them that no one is going back? Maybe they haven't heard.

CHUCK LOVED TWO THINGS MORE THAN ANYTHING, the walls announce about a person I'm assuming is or was the owner, PEOPLE AND CONEYS. A line of families wilting in the June heat winds through the restaurant and onto the sidewalk, where my boyfriend listens to my friend describe his last performance before lockdown, the one where he woke up in the hospital the next morning and remembers nothing. He has the footage but is afraid to watch it. I bet it's good.

The hot dog, on the other hand, is not great, and my friend asks if we want to stay longer. Did I know he's in the Scorsese movie? Did I know his dad is a twin? He *needs* to tell me this and I need to know it. I ask a question about twins over forty because I forget twins age past twenty-five; people tend to lose interest after that. It sounds like they fucking hate each other.

My boyfriend tells me he will kill himself if I try to get him to eat another hot dog today and then we get a call from our landlord, a chipper woman who gave us the place because her husband used to do comedy before realizing that the sensible thing to do was move back to the Midwest. They want to sell the duplex and we're fucked if they sell it. We panic, are polite, ask each other where we'll go if the place where we lived together was suddenly turned over to some television executives who think it would be "more comfortable" to take meetings in a "proper home" and then use it to cheat on their wives. (I have certainly never witnessed something like this, who would do something like that?)

On our way out of town I tell him that if we can't keep our apartment, I'll just apply for an artist's grant in Tulsa. At the gas station, an old man whispers "White power" to my boyfriend, confirming that his most recent facial hair attempt scans as fascist. After that, we don't need to say the grant plan is off to know it's off as we speed past an impossibly large wooden sign declaring THE TEN COMMANDMENTS.

Our third night on the road, sometime around the World's Largest Cedar Bucket and the Damn Yankees official restaurant, is spent in the first state where there's no hot dog of note: Arkansas. In a display of stunning incompetence, I have booked a hotel room in Little Rock for a month from the day we're staying there and bravely continue to plow through my book advance by paying for a hotel room twice for no reason. The good news is that it's not covered in cigarettes and no one tries to kill us. We walk to a nearby takeout place where I get frog legs and he gets some gnarly hot wings, and unlike the Okies, the unmasked Arkansas employees are *thrilled* to hear about the book I'm working on. Have I ever heard of a Chicago hot dog? There's not an Arkansas hot dog. You could put catfish on a hot dog though—anything you want, they say, and they're right.

That night we go to a hotel bar and I ask him to pretend to pick me up, which we get about 30 percent through before one of us, I don't remember who, gets more interested in the fact that there are regulars here. While we're eavesdropping on a pair of women gossiping about the teen beauty pageant contestants descending on the lobby ("they must know their angles because I'm just not seeing it") and an aunt with a terminal illness ("it's all right though," she says before ordering another pickleback), our cocker spaniel is eating frog legs in the other room from the box my boyfriend thought was placed out of reach but was not. When we get back and discover this, I call the emergency vet while he cries in the corner. The dog looks at me with confused eyes: the frog legs were good, what are we so upset about? A deep-fried Southern voice tells me the dog's size and the consistency of frog bones mean he will be fine by morning.

"Oh, he's over twenty pounds, honey?" she says. "He's gonna digest just fine." And he does. We leave early and make a beeline past Crazy Rob's Fireworks near the Oasis Church to make it to Atlanta by dinner.

I had every intention of getting hot dogs in New Orleans and sending Bud's Broiler my regards, but the problem with the South is that every damn place is closed on Sunday except for church. So okay, I can't drink a White Claw on the road, but I *also* can't get a goddamn hot dog, which hadn't even occurred to me. The gas stations in Mississippi appear between swamps, and old ladies gossip at the tables inside. God, every gas station should have gossip tables inside. It's all so charming to me until I think about what their personal politics are, and then I remember shit, yeah, the nostalgic gaslighting of the American road trip is strong. I couldn't do it on my own without getting murdered, and there are at least three instances in our first few days where I'm protected by being white, by being tall, by knowing how to smile until someone leaves me alone instead of asking for it. *Asking for it.* Still, gossip tables at the gas station—an idea worth considering.

I'm almost as tall as 4 Way Lunch in Cartersville, Georgia, a bright red building with its name interrupted by a huge Coca-Cola logo that every business in the state must feel bullied into hosting. It opened ninety years ago when a man named Fred brought a sack of meat and buns to a street corner and started making sandwiches, and evolved into the low-ceilinged lunch counter we pull into around ten in the morning, a long red table with plenty of elbow room. It changed hands from Fred's family in the early 2000s, but at the 4 Way Lunch, the food being wet is the *point,* and asking a question means opening yourself to a friendly firing squad of locals. They have the high ground, as they should, surrounded by news clippings and advertisements that are hieroglyphics to the average outsider. One stray comment could leave you on the wrong side of the gravy vat, and yes, there's a gravy vat—a vat full of liquid meaty *something* is a near staple of any respectable independent establishment. It's special here; you're cheating yourself by not pulling in.

THIS ISN'T BURGER KING. YOU DON'T GET IT YOUR WAY, a small sign reads. YOU GET IT OUR WAY, OR YOU DON'T GET THE DAMN THING. At first sight I am tempted to declare them the comedians of the hot dog world, but it turns out it's a pretty common sign—I come across the same one at Olneyville New York System in Providence, an equally charming and grouchy establishment.

There are three women running the place, two on the counter who I know are not married but I hope they're secretly in love with each other like in *Fried Green Tomatoes*. The men sitting at the counter all seem to be laborers who have been there a thousand times before, and they treat us with polite interest when I laugh to myself about the difference between a Happy Meal (one egg on a brown gravy biscuit) and an Unhappy Meal (one egg on a white gravy biscuit). We're here for a hot dog "ALL THE WAY," which is listed on the menu as the standard southern chili, mustard, and onions, but arrives ass-deep in a kiddie pool's worth of refried beans.

"Are we the first people to get hot dogs today?" I ask one of the women at the counter. There's a framed faded newspaper clipping of the two that declares them the best cooks in the South.

"Not even close," she says, serving me the wateriest coffee I've ever had (but keep in mind, the coffee isn't the point). "Chili burgers already went out this morning, people get around early."

She loses interest in me the moment the hot dog hits the water and turns her attention back to the two elderly regulars to our left. One of them calls her a tomboy in a pointed way that turns the room back into 1996 for a fleeting moment, but she rolls with it—yes, she grew up on a farm, likes doing farm work, has strong arms, so what? Her dad taught her how to milk a cow, regular milk and sweet milk, but the one thing she would not and will not do is go into the chicken coop. Those little fuckers are scary.

"Daddy would say, 'You're not afraid of the horses but you're afraid of the damn chickens?'" She laughs, flipping my hot dog into a bun from a standard grocery store eight-pack, as the 4 Way's signature is what lies inside. She tosses the rest of the bag on the counter next to one of the little blue bowls filled with a sherbet-colored spread of sour sugar substitutes, the kind my great-aunt got kicked out of Old Country Buffet for stealing. She works quickly, lining the bowl with beans before drone striking the dog and bun with them, spiking a scoop of chili and mustard that gets hot the moment it hits the plate, a fistful of onions and a *second* scoop of refried beans for good measure. It looks like the second day of my period but it tastes okay, which I can't tell you is true in the reverse but if you can find a guy named Dave who I knew in 2016, he could tell you.

I'm not hungry, but it's the sort of place where you can hear the insult the moment the door closes behind you if you didn't clean your plate, so I eat a billion beans and a beautifully boiled hot dog while the second proprietor wipes down the grill in a yellow T-shirt that has a dog wearing sunglasses on it. I entered the building unconvinced that a hot dog could be a breakfast dish in the way her sausage father was so famous for, and left gladly corrected—breakfast has more to do with how you feel than what you're eating, and the people and dogs of the 4 Way make me feel awake, full, and not to be fucked with. Another couple comes in, and as they begin ping-ponging with the server about where they know each other from, I put down twelve dollars that miraculously covers two breakfasts, two coffees, and a 30 percent tip. God, I hope they're in love.

TRAFFICKERS ARE TARGETING KIDS ON THE INTERNET, banshee screams the billboard closest to our next hotel in Smyrna, Georgia. KNOW WHO YOU ARE CHATTING WITH! There is no website or advice on how to know, but you know . . . just know that that's happening.

The Varsity in Atlanta is one of the most popular hot dog joints in the entire country, and with that comes the same unreasonable level of expectation that hangs over the other hot dog states of New York, New Jersey, and Illinois.

"What'll ya have, what'll ya have?" is the phrase so closely associated with The Varsity that it's printed on the front door in bright red letters, a reference to the words that tens of local news junkets have shown employees chirping cheerfully from the counter in downtown Atlanta. It's a compelling story, and one the institution has had nearly a century to land the plane on. In 1928, founder Frank Gordy dropped out of the Georgia Institute of Technology to open their first location, then called The Yellow Jacket, with the idea that male students would drop by before college sports events to get a hot dog and—I'm speculating here—complain about women being able to vote. The franchise quickly became associated with its chili dogs, boxed "while-you-walk" onion rings, and sprawling parking lots, which could hold around six hundred cars at the peak of finger-me-in-a-parked-car culture in the 1950s and '60s. The Gordy family continues to run the franchise, which has waxed and waned in location numbers across the state.

In the summer of 2021, everyone is tired. The downtown Atlanta location, sporting the familiar Coca-Cola logo in its gigantic, Instagrammable V-shaped outdoor signage, is full of employees making between ten and fourteen dollars an hour in a city where more than sixteen an hour constitutes a living wage. They're not being paid enough to fake The Varsity's signature enthusiasm, and they know it. Whole areas of the city-block-wide dining area have been taped off—not because of the virus, but ostensibly because The Varsity can't afford to employ enough people to look after the nearly eight hundred guests the indoor area can hold, much less the six hundred cars that could cram outside.

"What'll ya have?" an older cashier asks us when we get to

the front of the line. Like every car-park location we've been to so far, management has been careful to remind people why the restaurant is still swarmed with customers but not with employees. THANK YOU FOR YOUR SUPPORT DURING THESE CHALLENGING TIMES! declares a banner with the signature Varsity football player tossing a ball toward the restaurant's logo.

I've been nervous about ordering here for days. The Varsity has capitalized on the diner lingo associated with the heyday of its operations in the 1950s, though short-order cooks in American diners were known to rename egg prep styles after biblical characters going back to the post–Civil War era. I want to be game for and supportive of diner lingo but ultimately feel that anyone with a generalized anxiety disorder, which is the entire population of the planet this particular summer, will find it more stressful than charming on both sides of the transaction. You want me to call a hamburger a "naked steak" in public to an employee not being paid a living wage? It's perverted and I'm not going to.

"Could I have a, uh, a Varsity Orange and a, uh, Naked—"

She's tired. "Are you getting a combo?"

Thank fucking Christ. "Yeah," I say, letting the sweat that's been threatening to release through my shitty T-shirt loose. "Chili dog combo, orange shake, Diet Coke. And a can of chili."

In the YouTube video I watched to prepare for the visit, an employee from ten years ago shouts, "Red dog, yellow dog, N.I.P.C., and strings!" For me, our kind and somewhat annoyed cashier slides the chili on the counter into my hands and passes a receipt to the kitchen. No one makes eye contact.

It's overpriced but who cares, my boyfriend is looking at the closed merch store and shuffles across the red-and-white tiles as we wait. As crater-hole depressed as it is at present, the trail of twentieth-century history inside the massive building is impressive—tiled mosaics of football players lead you to comforting and filthy bathroom stalls with still more mosaics inside.

Apple pies come in old-fashioned wax paper bags with the same graphic design that my grandparents associate with "the good old days" when they meant there were social safety nets and culturally acceptable racism. A series of framed pictures tell the story of not the restaurant, but what it is supposed to represent.

Erby Walker, one of The Varsity's most beloved and notorious figures, is *the* symbol of the spirit The Varsity is selling. Starting as a janitorial staff member at fifteen in 1952, Walker worked at The Varsity for more than fifty-five years before his death in 2008. One of the first Black employees who worked at the front counter following The Varsity's desegregation of the business in 1964, Walker assumed the role of unofficial spokesman for the white-owned business that, to this day, continues to promote to the executive level primarily from within the Gordy family. He was the ultimate counterman, known for keeping the line moving during rush hours without aggravating customers or coworkers—for anyone who has worked a service counter, a close-to-impossible feat. He served the likes of Muhammad Ali, carried the Olympic Torch on a relay during the 1996 Atlanta Olympics, and was told to stop eating Varsity hot dogs in 1990 after suffering a heart attack in his fifties. He was inducted into the Hospitality Hall of Fame in 2003 after a botched attempt at retirement left him eager to return to the counter. He's credited with coining the iconic "What'll ya have, what'll ya have?" and would keep going, telling customers "Have your money out and your food on your mind, and I'll getcha to the game on time!"

So much of what is associated with The Varsity is tied to one employee, who received publicity for shaping the restaurant's homey feel at the height of the Civil Rights Movement, but it's unclear what compensation, if any, he received outside of his counterman's pay. For a business that rakes in more than $11 million a year in sales and sells "What'll ya have?" merchandise—everything from hoodies to Christmas ornaments—the benefit of his legacy in the financial sense still very much appears to belong to the Gordy family.

We eat our chili dogs and something's changed about the meat slop again—the chili of the Deep South is *goop*, it's a darker, thinner, messier straight line of meat that you can buy canned to go alongside a strong mustard that pairs with it perfectly. Our second hot dog, a chili cheese slaw dog, is the first of its kind we've tried, and the style will tail us all the way to Washington, DC.

Varsity dogs are prepared with an efficient line system consisting of three tubs—the boiled hot dogs leave the first tub and are dressed with the Varsity chili from the second tub, then the cheese and mustard that mix with the chili better than anything we've had so far are slopped on the bun at the third tub. Vintage video shows the process as dynamic and loud, and today it's just as busy but tired and quiet by comparison.

One of the strangest holdovers from The Varsity's trappings of the American mid-twentieth century are its TV rooms, originally devised by the Gordys during the medium's earlier days in an effort to keep people in the restaurant when the public's interest shifted from car parks to indoor dining. In the political climate this summer, it feels aggressive—the ESPN Room on the restaurant's bottom floor is closed, along with the CNN Room, which blares a broadcast about "AN AMERICAN ASSAULT ON DEMOCRACY: Special Report on the January 6th Insurrection" to nobody. It stands to reason—the only figure that looms larger than Coca-Cola in Atlanta is Ted Turner, whose loathsome traits include being a billionaire and whose single good trait includes being Jane Fonda's ex who doesn't appear to have gotten over her. Upstairs, the Fox News Room is not just open, but dare I say bumping with exclusively older white couples while younger crowds cram themselves into the undesignated rooms that remain.

The television in the most easily accessed room plays a loud Fox News story yelled by the ugliest newscaster I've ever seen, comparing insurrectionists to *looters* (the subtext, I can hear it) and asking why arrest one if you didn't arrest the other (you did, what did it accomplish). Regardless, this room has one of my favorite hot dog parlor fixtures: The Wall Filled With Pictures of Celebrities. Like the hyper-partisan rooms, The Varsity's celebrity wall is equally adamant that *all* famous people matter—Barbara Bush beside Burt Reynolds beside Matthew McConaughey beside Bill Clinton beside comedian Nipsey Russell, a former Varsity carhop who went on to become a game show icon in the 1960s. There's also just . . . a picture of Elvis, asking you to believe the long line of managers who claim he loved the burgers there.

We've arrived right before the joint closes and grab two red paper hats from the counter, the Burger King crowns of Atlanta. My boyfriend's back has been hurting since this morning after the cat found a corner to stow away in last night's hotel that required circus-level contortions to extract him. I rub his back with oil and promise we can take a pause and stay an extra day. We can't afford it but we have to, so we do. It's across the street from a Chuck E. Cheese—a good omen for old James Loftus.

The pool at this place reeks but we're making out in it. They don't have the Kardashians channel here and it makes me sad. I feel bad for feeling sad; there's so much prestige television and I know I'm supposed to like it, but I want to see women arguing and forgiving each other in unrealistic situations.

The day my boyfriend spends at the hotel recovering, I walk around the industrial section of Smyrna, Georgia, a town on the fringes of Atlanta where locals can get their fill of big-box stores and sparsely attended local carnivals. I walk through a Barnes & Noble and feel a pang of embarrassment for someone I haven't been in more than a decade. I used to come to high-ceilinged bookstores like this and pretend to know who Murakami was in high school, then take secret pictures on a point-and-shoot camera while holding my cup of Starbucks because my dad was so convinced of the brand's sophistication that he regularly proclaimed it "fuckin' French."

A mother puts four manga books on a credit card while her kid browses the magazine rack a healthy distance away.

"I don't get these," she tells the cashier, "but I don't have to." She looks over at the twelve-year-old. I cry about it later, in the nice way I hope will crystalize my ability to do the same one day.

He's feeling better by sundown and we go on a date night, pizza for the pizza book that will ruin my life in five years.

We Are in the Southeast

R U HUNGRY?

Is this where they started coming when Florida got full? Charlotte, North Carolina, has an aesthetic beauty that immediately gives away that it's being heavily gentrified—sprawling streets that scream, "We'll *definitely* get to that affordable housing initiative that's been kicking around City Hall for the last decade." Still, the trees, the air: it's nice. I would love to go on a walk instead of eat a hot dog, but that is not the order of the day.

The order of the day is JJ's Red Hots, a joint that opened in 2012 and has since been blessed by King Guy Fieri himself. The theme of JJ's prior to Guy's arrival is unclear, but by the time I get there the restaurant is a haunted museum of "that time Guy Fieri came here"—a spray-painted metal lunch tray of Fieri's head hangs on the wall above an autographed photo. It's a place for the *boys,* and the low ceilings and cheap beers get the message out loud and clear. If you can hear over the sound of Fieri's hair, the building rings with the *thunk*s of Sahlen's hot dogs hitting the grill in the signature, delicious char-broiled style. I don't even care that the sweet cashier doesn't know what the *Cathy* comics plastered across my crewneck sweatshirt are because he's selling two-dollar PBRs and says he'll have someone personally come up to the outdoor deck we're sitting on to bring our cocker spaniel some water.

I order JJ's "No. 1" Red Hot—the char-grilled dog, hot relish, diced onions, Weber's mustard, and a long dill pickle spear that would make Chicagoans cream but honestly is A Bit Much. The second, which I'll only get a few bites into out of sheer Dog Exhaustion, is part of JJ's Dog of the Week program. On the day we're there, it's a heavy goddamn thing called the Summer in the City—kraut, onions, and deli mustard covering a barely visible hot dog. Now that we've hit North Carolina, in-house is the name of the game, from homemade sausages to pickles to— and they *love* this shit—tangy slaw.

Look, there's simply nothing better than a char-grilled hot dog. Anyone raised on boiled dogs will attest that their first grilled meat tube is life-changing—there's *flavors* in there, there's the char on the edge that's the same as the one coating a campfire marshmallow. After the boiled, wetter dogs across the South, it's a welcome relief.

"Do you want to just wait a few minutes to pay?" the cashier asks me with a smile. "You can get the special if I check you out after three o'clock." Heaven. I let our cocker spaniel finish the Summer in the City.

This is what we at Jamie Industries call a five-dog day. Our next stop is Jay Bee's Hot Dogs in Statesville, North Carolina— or, if their website is to be believed, JaybeesHotDogs dot Biz and their world-famous footlongs. Hot dog stands have a lot in common with mediocre comedians in that their websites always say they're famous when they aren't, and claim they are bringing something New and Interesting to the table when their mouthfeel is nothing special.

There's a gorgeously abrasive personality to this drive-through, whose line we spend the better part of a half hour waiting in, the sort of line that would give you an aneurysm if it were just a Wendy's. JaybeesHotDogs dot Biz does not give a shit that you're waiting, something they remind you of at every turn of the wheel or scroll of your meat-stinking finger.

"If you are looking for fast food, you've come to the wrong spot," the website yells at you in a mid-2000s serif. "We pride ourselves in making your food to order . . . and it takes a little more time." I poke my boyfriend's arm and show him the website, and he points to the faded yellow sign reading WE DO NOT PRE-COOK OUR ORDERS. PLEASE EXPECT A LITTLE WAIT. THANK YOU.

With this kind of wait, you would hope things would be above average, so I take my time choosing between the World Famous Footlong (no citation), John's Double-Dog Dare, and the few specialty dogs on the menu before ordering a footlong "John's Way," with mustard, onions, chili, and slaw with a Diet Coke.

The Jay Bee's chili is the reason to wait through the multiple spankings that come before the reward of the footlong, the restaurant's specialty since husband-wife duo John and Sherry Baker began the restaurant out of his father's convenience store in 1980. The chili and slaw are slopped onto a boiled dog and un-grilled bun, delicious on top in particular. I appreciate the weird intensity of the place—people are still not allowed to dine indoors here, so we sit at a picnic table beside a dumpster that warns that GREASE THEFT IS ILLEGAL.

Winston-Salem is our final stop of the day, after driving for the better part of an hour behind a pickup truck with a *Punisher* decal we are doomed to see plastered across the ass of a minimum of forty vehicles a day, past a church with signage reading ALWAYS BE READY beside a different sign insisting Donald Trump actually won the election that he had lost nearly a year before. It's not my region but it is my class—we drive past stores full of cheap, stiff prom dresses arranged in rainbow formation, and pull into Kermit's Hot Dog House drive-in. There's an unspoken rule I've taken care to learn ahead of time as we pull into a spot that's been there since 1966, complete with teenagers bringing food to your Subaru like they got shot out of a T-shirt gun. The method: turn on your parking lights once you're in the carhop spot, switch the lights off once your food is delivered, and switch them on again if you need seconds. Honk? You're an asshole.

For all the modern, Fieri-led pomp and friendliness we found at JJ's earlier in the afternoon, the dramatically poorer neighborhood Kermit's has been a staple of for more than fifty years isn't looking for attention, at least not in the same way a business founded during the age of social media is. The carhop mainstay has no online presence whatsoever but is full to the brim when we arrive in the early evening, overrun with older regulars and an entire team of high school volleyball girls, their long legs hanging over the roofs of Hyundai Sonatas and Ford Focuses while they grip a shake in one hand and a teammate's hand urgently in the other. Olivia Rodrigo's "good 4 u" blasts from a teenager's borrowed four-seater because yes, it's *that* summer.

I walk inside, where the menu is yellowed with the exception of a few numbers rearranged to update the still exceedingly reasonable prices. The folks at Kermit's offer three styles of hot dog, but the real draw here is the distinctly Southern pimento cheese, a blend whose ingredients become obvious the second you know what they are—cream cheese, shredded cheddar, and mayonnaise with sweet pimento peppers and a few spices tossed in, depending on whose recipe is canon to you. The hot dog itself is grilled this beautiful pink, and not as overwhelmed beneath the weight of its own slaw and pimento as the last one.

We sit in the car together with the cat and the dog and the fourth hot dog of the day while I look for a hotel where we can stay the night. Now safely out of the South, Kermit's proudly displays its Pepsi endorsement beside photos of chili dogs and (delicious) fries. We will lament not getting banana pudding, the only reasonable post–hot dog dessert, along with other mysterious menus item labeled THE BIG K: $7.35 or BEEF WEENIE: $5.70. In this moment, we are so full of processed meat that we are quiet, playing a podcast about a roller coaster neither of us have been on or plan to, but I remember us driving to the last hot dog of the day in Roanoke, Virginia, as if we were starving and very much in love.

Texas Tavern in Roanoke, Virginia, has the second-best hot dog for your dollar in the country, and you can argue with the wall if that bothers you. The brick building, painted white and looking for help, had the most striking architecture I saw on our trip by a long shot, all red trimming and prices painted in three different fonts. $1.60 HAMBURGERS AND CONEY ISLAND HOT DOGS, one sign read. OPEN ALL NITE in bright white letters stuck onto the takeout window, $2.00 MEXICAN CHILE AND $1.40 COLD BUTTERMILK printed just below. It's the only place I've been to that is truly open all nite, closing early on Christmas Eve, entirely on Christmas Day, and open every other moment.

There are two employees on hand at the Tavern when we walk in around sunset on the five-dog day, the standard double act for any independently owned fast-food counter across this great nation—a guy in his late forties who has worked there for decades, and a teenager who has worked there for seven minutes. The elder employee, Chris Dobe, has worked at TT's, as it's known locally, from time immemorial as the head cook, grilling hot dogs right beside the takeout window to ensure that the smell of cooked-through beef wafts onto the sidewalk to trick the closest kid with two dollars out of their allowance. This window-wafting technique is a trend that snakes up the East Coast, mainly because of the need for a permanent structure to survive the seasons—the South and Southwest skew toward pop-up locations and trucks because they can afford to work in the open air year-round, but TT's is far enough north that there's a time of year to close the doors and turn on the heat.

"Hey, I, yeah!" the teenager, a tall redhead who looks to Chris for guidance, greets us. Chris is in the process of grilling at least fifteen dogs in spite of the empty dining room—COVID has redirected a lot of their business to pickup—but he's easy to talk to and says that we're not the first "hotdoggers" to come through with questions. I resent the implication that I am a hotdogger like the others, but realize what a ridiculous correction it would be as I take out $3.20 to get us in on the signature TT's chile dog. Sometimes you need to be knocked off your P. F. Chang's horse and be told the God's honest truth: you are *exactly* like the other hotdoggers. And yes, I can confirm it's the best chili I've ever had.

For all the marketing that some of the bigger hot dog joints do to emphasize the culture around their place, Texas Tavern barely needs to try. It's (and I mean this with love) a weird place with a weird history. Opening in a more densely populated area than most of Appalachia the year after the Depression ended, TT's shares an origin story with the vast majority of thriving American hot dog joints, with its longevity connected to a blend of nostalgia and the ability to feed poor people cheaply and quickly, and keep them full. What it does *not* share with its peers is being founded by a circus employee.

Isaac N. Bullington worked as the advance man—the guy who finds the place to have the circus—for the Ringling Brothers for years before opening the Texas Tavern in Roanoke. He brought with him not just an eye for location, but a chile recipe he'd come across (read: stolen) while traveling through San Antonio, Texas. He was encouraged by the success of early fast food chains like White Castle and started in the parking lot of a furniture store, eventually migrating to the building on Church Street where it stands today. Even now, it features the same grill, white walls cluttered with menus and accolades, and ten-stool counter. The third generation of Bullingtons runs the place now, the current top dog a younger guy named Nick, who plays along with the Roanoke media and has participated in stunts that make him look like a local tyrant. The man himself is the current leader of the unofficial organization that has been a part of Texas Tavern since it began, the Roanoke Millionaires Club.

Roanoke is a politically purple area, going for Hillary Clinton by five points in 2016 and shifting significantly to Joe Biden by twenty-five points in 2020. In the final stretch of the 2016 Trump campaign, Michael Pence, the pee pee man, Mother Lover, and future Vice President himself (per the "alleged" "myth" that he called his wife Mother), stopped by TT's to declare their food "one of the best cups of chili I've ever had in my life." He was then heckled by a passerby on the way to a town hall, and the only comment provided by a TT's employee was, "I kind of wasn't thinking as much as I was observing."

It is a beautiful and weird place, where ketchup is called Sissy Sauce and asking for a "bowl with" will yield a jug of thick chili with onions. Chris gives us our dogs and promises they will be the best of our day. And they are.

I find a Howard Johnson hotel at the top of a mountain in Lexington, Virginia, that is painted orange. There are some beetles but they're mostly dead, and the concierge casually posits that a case of COVID from early last year permanently affected his short-term memory. Our cocker spaniel takes a hot shit during golden hour, the kind of night you want to peel the skin off and rest on your face. Everything in the room is orange, the comforter and the walls and the curtains, and I'm glowing with the feeling you get when you're halfway heckled by a teenage boy from the balcony above yours, who stops when you look him directly in the eyes. I hate my body so much at this point, I do a million sit-ups and walk all the way around the abandoned Howard Johnson sign that lies flat behind the hotel, sprouting with flowers and worms. It feels like a metaphor for something I didn't go to enough school to understand. Mostly, the room cost sixty-four dollars and everything else is a coincidence.

This is one of the last good nights, and I remember it differently than it was. In my memory my stomach is not buckling under the weight of five very different hot dogs, buns, and mayonnaise blends, is not gag-reflexing against the well-intentioned but ill-advised peanut butter shake we drank a third of back in Statesville, although I can get there if I focus enough. Why bother though? You replace the good memory with something better, so you can miss it more once it's over. It's a hell of a trick. I can almost miss it now.

"I'm sorry this is so hard," I say from the other bed. Some nights I say there were only two-bed rooms available and I'm telling the truth, but tonight I'm lying. I want to be by myself.

"It's hard," he says, and returns to his work.

It's two hundred miles to Washington, DC.

Ben's Chili Bowl in the U Street Corridor is famous for many reasons, primarily its status as a Black-owned American institution, still owned and frequented by cofounder Virginia Ali. She and her husband, the eponymous Ben, opened the business with a $5,000 loan in 1958, a time when the odds were not only stacked against Black business owners but business owners at large—one in two businesses failed in the Virginia area the year Ben's Chili Bowl opened. Virginia's husband passed away in 2009, less than a year after Barack Obama made Ben's Chili Bowl his first outing as president. Ben was a Muslim Indo-Trinidadian immigrant whose plans to become a doctor in the US were thwarted by a fall down an elevator shaft, leading to his eventual graduation from Howard University and beginning a business with his new wife. In a move that strikes me as near suicidal, they opened the business seven weeks after getting married and less than a year after meeting.

Ben's is the home of the half-smoke, the DC and Virginia area's signature hot dog prep that's thought to have been innovated in 1930 by Raymond Briggs, owner of the DC Briggs and Co.'s meatpacking operation. Broken down, the traditional half-smoke is half-pork, half-beef, often split down the middle for grillability and dramatic effect, and generally smoked before being grilled. It's known for being a little bigger and a little coarser than your average flaccid dog, more closely resembling a sausage but still considered Hot Dog Canon. They can be found at carts across the region, but only two brick-and-mortars are known for them—the Weenie Beenie in Arlington, Virginia, and Ben's Chili Bowl in DC.

The red, white, and yellow storefront is one of the most beautiful we see on the trip, as if the Texas Tavern back in Roanoke were a little bigger and with a completely different, busier history. Once the home of DC's first silent movie theater, Ben's was a key stop on what was known in the 1950s and '60s as Black Broadway, the go-to stop for Miles Davis and Duke Ellington and Ella Fitzgerald after performing at U Street jazz clubs. The whole thing is American enough to give you a thick chili nosebleed, but Ben and Virginia's influence on their area and country is still expanding.

"I've got this idea," a BCB regular told Virginia Ali in 1963, "I just don't know how to execute it." The regular, as Ali tells it, was Martin Luther King Jr., and the plan was the March on Washington, prepared over a few thick, garlicky chili dogs. Ben's Chili Bowl donated food to the organizing event, just as they had in 1960 to the Poor People's Campaign.

Five years after Virginia circled up with Dr. King, the riots that followed his assassination devastated U Street as grieving protesters locked horns with DC police, just as they would again in 2020, the summer before our shitty rental car circled the now heavily gentrified block to get a six-dollar chili dog.

Ben's Chili Bowl didn't close during the 1968 riots—in fact, loyal customer and Student Nonviolent Coordinating Committee leader Stokely Carmichael specifically requested they stay open to help feed activists. After obtaining a permit to stay open following the federally imposed curfew, Ben and Virginia fed both activists and cops, hanging a sign that said SOUL BROTHER in the window to signal to protesters that they were a Black-owned business.

Virginia watched the protests that ran down U Street in 2020, her sons Kamal and Nizam now in charge of the day-to-day at Ben's, and remains conflicted. Her concern is how it affects the Black businesses that came up on U Street and other districts across the country in the long term.

"The neighborhood that we were in provided everything we needed," she told *The Dispatch* in the fallout of summer 2020. "We found the architect, the contractor, the plumber, the electrician, and the cabinet maker within a few blocks. They were African American owned businesses."

This opinion chafed with protest organizers then and still does now, but Virginia's anxieties in context aren't illogical—the aftereffects of the riots in the 1960s were incorrectly blamed for the twenty-odd-year economic downturn on U Street. At least, according to Virginia—the 1970s and '80s in DC gave way to the crack cocaine epidemic, an issue the government largely blamed on low-income Black residents who dealt or consumed the drug while failing to examine the systems that made its flourishing possible.

Nooooo, Jamie, don't start discussing the government's role in the crack epidemic in your book! Sorry, I have to for a minute. Virginia Ali presents the events of the 1970s and '80s to *The Dispatch* as follows:

"Businesses did not reopen," she said. "The middle class began to move away. And then after that, heroin moved in, and then crack cocaine moved in, and we became a ghetto. And that lasted, as I said, twenty years."

It's true that U Street, an area with many Black-owned businesses, was hit particularly hard in this era and that the damage sustained during the riots of 1968 did put many out of business. Theories have been floated for decades about crack cocaine's sudden influx into poor, majority-Black neighborhoods following the rise of cocaine proper as the vanity drug du jour in the 1970s, primarily used in popular media by upper-class white people. The CIA has been repeatedly accused of flooding crack cocaine into Black neighborhoods during the Iran-Contra affair in an attempt to fund Nicaragua's Contras versus the Sandinista government. The CIA denies this—of course they do, I can deny drinking a Mike's Hard Lemonade at 2:00 p.m. but you can still smell it on my breath—while National Security Archive senior analyst Peter Kornbluh testified in 1996 that the US government was largely to blame. Crack hit the streets of DC in 1986, relatively late in the year-span that Virginia attributes to the drug's initial prominence.

Kamal Ali, Virginia's son who works the register the day we visit, speaks of the second-generation era at Ben's Chili Bowl to the press with similar concerns. The business reduced its menu and staff when Ben and Virginia deemed the neighborhood too run-down to operate as normal, cutting out pies and cakes (claiming these attracted addicts), leaving only one employee on-site at any given time, and allowing DC police to conduct surveillance from a window upstairs.

"There was always a family presence and the locals protected us," Kamal said in 2005 of the era of the 1980s and '90s.

In typical American fashion, low-income and Black dealers and users bore the incarceration and negative cultural stigma associated with crack cocaine, while institutions like the CIA were permitted to deny any or all culpability. By their own admission, DC police were arresting as many as nine hundred people in a single weekend—a number that would escalate further by 1989, the year that George H. W. Bush declared crack cocaine an "epidemic."

"It's as innocent-looking as candy," he said in a direct address to the nation, holding a little white baggie that he claimed had been found across the street from the White House. "But it's turning our cities into battle zones." The drugs and the story the president told his people were, it turns out, props—the majority of crack was sold in a few city blocks nowhere near where the speech was given.

That's not to say that the fallout of crack cocaine in DC during this era was anything short of devastating, or that the Alis were wrong to worry about the safety of their employees and customers. The way this crisis was framed in the media ultimately didn't serve the community that crack cocaine was most severely affecting—instead, it was used as a way to further "prove" that poor Black Americans, Black women in particular, were negligent drug addicts not worthy of respect or anything more than further incarceration. But who the fuck put the drug there to begin with?

What emerges in Virginia's framing of local history is a common but pernicious obfuscation—*because* the businesses impacted were, in some cases, negatively affected by the 1968 riots, *then* the area became particularly vulnerable to drugs like heroin and crack cocaine, *therefore* the riots in 2020 should come with the same anxiety. It's not quite that simple, but Virginia's outspokenness during 2020 maintained Ben's Chili Bowl's status as a place for all to gather, rather than a radical hot dog haven. Yes, police were welcome to get their half-smoke hot dog during the George Floyd protests, but an institution like Ben's has earned its place in the American Hot Dog Pantheon. And institutions tend to support other institutions.

The company line is that Ben's Chili Bowl survived every

wave of challenges on U Street through good product and a shrewd eye for their community of interest. This is undoubtedly true, but their sixty-five-year endurance also required navigating and sometimes appeasing the forces that oppressed their community—after the crack cocaine panic subsided, the business stayed afloat as the DC Metro train line swept through the U Street neighborhood in the 1990s, decimating several more Black-owned businesses. Ben's solution? They fed the construction companies displacing the competition.

We can't park, or he can't park in this narrow spot and I can't drive, and it's my job to keep the animals calm. We enter Ben's through the back, where additional seating and a mural of iconic Black Americans, from untouchable icons like Prince to an awkwardly timed rendering of Dave Chappelle, months after he was dragged across the internet for transphobia and months before he was dragged across the internet again for, you won't believe this, more transphobia. Not the establishment's fault, and the mural is beautiful—we walk around to the front, where the early lunchers are already perched just outside the door, into the very 2021 outdoor patio tents that extend into the street. Five white lobbyists ignore their hot dogs in favor of their phones while Harriet Tubman looks on. Across the street, a major bank proudly proclaims that it's June, Pride Month, and they don't hate gay people anymore.

Ben's keeps the legacy-hot-dog-joint aesthetic going strong, so there are pictures of celebrity visitors everywhere: Anthony Bourdain, Kevin Hart, Serena Williams, Pope Francis, and a former DC police chief, all in plastic frames across from the main counter and into the high-ceilinged back dining room, where the silent movies used to play. In the most PR-conscious city in the country, Ben's Chili Bowl is an expected stop from any public figure who expects to be taken seriously.

Their street-facing hot dog aroma can assault the senses of an unsuspecting resident trying to make healthier choices these days—"I swear," they'll say, "the *hot dog* attacked *me*." An Ali son is at the register as a handful of other employees have the flow of the early-lunch rush down to a science: two flipping half-smokes, some on the register, others still wiping down surfaces to keep up with COVID standards and grabbing Ben's absurdly good dessert menu. There are more grills lining the back of the counter, but these are reserved for their chili burgers and fry baskets. The dogs themselves—available in beef, turkey, kosher beef, veggie, or the half-smoke signature that observant Muslim Ben Ali could never try—are fucking gorgeous. They are thick, split on request and laid on the grill in rows of sixteen for around fifteen minutes at 315 degrees, showing you where every penny of the admittedly tourist-facing prices are going. I'm not one for a steamed bun, but I make an effort for Ben's. The smell is overwhelming, enough to keep you in the line that wraps around the corner.

As we stand in line waiting to order the chili half-smoke, Virginia enters from the back room in a lavender jacket, flanked by two employees. The whole line recognizes the eighty-seven-year-old, and I suddenly wish I were wearing something nicer—what? But this is the reaction one has when suddenly confronted with Hot Dog Royalty. You couldn't have put your contacts in this morning, Jamie? Virginia fucking Ali is getting behind the counter to "check up on some things" while you order your chili half-smoke! She knows every employee by name, and I order the banana pudding that has her face on it.

While we wait in a crowd of people—some I can tell are regulars from the way their bodies navigate the building, others tourists like us—I decide to try to flush something out of my body before we slam two chili dogs. I do a lap around the back room, still closed to diners in the summer of 2021 for safety reasons. It's here where you can see the side of Ben's Chili Bowl that isn't haunted by photo opportunities and sticky framed pictures of Jimmy Fallon (where does he find the fucking time, his picture is everywhere, surely one of these is photoshopped). It's here where you can see Ben and Virginia Ali grow older or younger together depending on what direction you walk. Here is Virginia with a longtime cook; here is Ben smiling with regulars who are just people, his friends and neighbors; you can watch their family grow up and two Ali sons open their own restaurant called Ben's Next Door in 2009.

Ben and Virginia loved each other, that much is clear. You can't tell by looking at their picture whether it is the kind of love that feels soft every morning or the kind of love that feels like a strong agreement, like love I know and have seen and understand. Whichever way it skews, it's there; she is still here every day at the restaurant where her name has to find its way onto banana pudding to get top billing over her husband. I take a piss and try my half-smoke.

People are so eager to say that something commonly considered to be good is bad, actually, and Ben's Chili Bowl is no exception. In 2016, the *Washington Post* food critic, famous bad-toupee-wearer Tom Sietsema, called the chili half-smoke "awful," giving it one star. The truth, as far as I'm concerned, lies somewhere between politicians claiming the food is flawless (they are liars) and a food critic claiming the food is dreadful (you didn't hear it from me, but the toupee is controlling his thoughts).

The chili half-smoke isn't bad, not by a long shot. Does it snap perfectly? Not really. Is there such an absurd amount of chili on the dog that it should really have a bun that's grilled instead of steamed? Absolutely, but the chili itself has the nicest blend of pepper and mustard I've tasted, even when it runs over the bun. The half-pork, half-beef Junior Dog tastes incredible, and once I run back inside to get a fork from the counter, I'm in business, matching every bite of dog with a bite of banana pudding and sweet potato pie engineered by the legendary woman in the lavender jacket standing inside. I stop after a few bites, aware of the cardiac arrest that awaits me in Baltimore, and think there is no clearer evidence that once-frequent customer Bill Cosby was a man cut from devil's cloth than the fact that he could eat six of these in one sitting.

Ben's Chili Bowl has an incredible story and place in its community, surprisingly untouched by the big-bank-Pride-float gentrification that's swept U Street in the past thirty years, and in spite of the historically Black neighbors either leaving or being priced out. Two years after Martin Luther King Jr.'s assassination, the U Street Corridor was 90 percent Black, a figure that fell when the 1990s brought a surge in a mostly white queer population, then again when white millennial hipsters descended in the 2000s. But Ben's Chili Bowl looks, sounds, and tastes just as it did in 1958—except for that six-dollar price tag.

We pull out of the alleyway and snake along to Baltimore, where I accidentally get horny for a sign.

There is a Murphy's Law of hotdogging: if there are two hot dogs to eat within an hour of each other, they will both be covered in gut-ravaging chili that starts to leak out of your skin if you get too close to your own reflection in a gas station bathroom mirror. The days are passing and my relationship with my body is falling to shit—we listen to food podcasts in the car and I quietly clock how much they're enjoying the food—it's always men, they get so much of it and finish every bite. I can't *do* what the Doughboys *do* but I'm glad that they do it. Every sweet guy I talk to says, "It's not even a show about food, really, it's a show about a *friendship*," and it's like, okay, relax, I wasn't disagreeing with you, I like it.

"Do you know anyone in Baltimore?" my boyfriend asks me, and I lie for some reason and say no. I used to come to Baltimore with my mom to visit her cousin, who she didn't like, and my second cousin, who I *loved,* even when she made me eat dog food. I should call her, but I don't want to make everyone suffer the same food punishment I am subjecting myself to for content.

Attman's deli in Baltimore is a fucking trip, that I will tell you.

This is somehow the first Jewish-owned hot dog business we've been to in our migration from the Latin-owned Southwestern businesses into the poor white-owned Southern joints, then the gentrified Carolinas and legendary Black-owned Ben's in DC. It's also the first place we've been that has actually crested its centennial birthday—the vast majority of legacy hot dog stands were begun sometime around the Great Depression in the late 1920s and early 1930s. This one beat everyone else to the punch, opened in 1915 by Russian Jew Harry Attman, a stone's throw from the Lloyd Street Synagogue in East Baltimore.

By the summer of 2021, the historically Jewish neighborhood that Attman's has been built and rebuilt on for the last century is predominantly Black, which is reflected in the deli's current employees and customers—this is one of the most diverse lunch rushes I've seen on this trip or, honestly, maybe ever. The Attman family still owns the deli—now in their third generation of ownership—and claims on their website that they are the oldest Jewish deli in the country still operated by the original family. Where is Jewish deli *Succession*? That's a free idea.

Attman's was once a popular deli in an area so full of Jewish dining options that Baltimore mayor William Donald Schaefer felt comfortable referring to it as "Corned Beef Row" in the 1970s—a welcome change to how the area had been referred to before, "Jewtown" (sheesh). While the latter title had been used primarily by Polish locals, third-gen owner Marc Attman insists his grandfather was never bothered by it.

"We never used [the term] ourselves, but we heard it all the time," he told *JMore* in 2017. "No one got upset."

Someone must have, because Corned Beef Row was a welcome name adjustment to the community, a marketing tactic by the mayor to bring business and awareness back to the neighborhood after Attman's deli *and* a local dairy burned to the ground on the same block—we'll get there. Still, even that name didn't stick when long-held Jewish businesses began to fold, leaving Attman's, the synagogue, and a handful of other places as the last remnants of a once-legendary area. Now, it's just East Lombard Street.

Throughout the Depression, Attman's primarily made its living as a grocery store, then repurposed as a deli in the '40s—Harry and his son Seymour focused on hot dogs and sandwiches, eating kosher at home but not at the deli where they worked on the Sabbath. Harry died in the early 1960s. The history of the business is an interesting one, but not as much as the bedlam going on in this place when we rolled up, stomachs at near-full capacity on Virginia's banana pudding.

The line for Attman's is out the door, but not into a bustling neighborhood, instead winding into a ghost town with the neighboring school abandoned on a late June day and a few empty businesses nearby. I've got my eye on their signature—Attman's World Famous Jumbo Jewish Hot Dog, $5.50, in a thick roll with mustard, relish, onions, ketchup, and, wait for it, all wrapped in a slice of fried bologna.

Now hold on. You, Baltimore, want me, Jamie, to suck down runny District of Columbia chili and then, *then,* deep-throat a Maryland hot dog swaddled in deep-fried bologna? What of my ass, Baltimore? What of my holes?

Food critics will tell you that the Baltimore-specific recipe works because the hot dog and bologna grease cooperate to marinate the bun, but as with all things hot dog, it comes down to class and affordability. Attman's tends to take credit for the bologna innovation ("the bologna innovation," she wrote in her book, and was serious), but further investigation traces it to a

Ukrainian bologna entrepreneur ("Ukrainian bologna entrepreneur," she typed with a straight face) in West Baltimore during the Great Depression. The recipe made his product relevant, the cost of the hot dog low, and the sandwich extra-filling on days when the average poor Baltimore resident likely did not have the budget for three full meals. Attman's and a few other delis ripped the idea off, and it remains one of the business's biggest sellers today, appearing alongside a menu with sandwiches like Sara's Dagger (turkey, pastrami, corned beef), the Italian Stallion (salami, ham, provolone) and my favorite, the Gay Liveration (corned beef, chopped liver, Swiss).

The thing about the line at Attman's is that it doesn't move very quickly, so I get to catch all manner of chaotic lunchtime conversation as employees and regulars jitter around the small white building, the smell of corned beef in kettles ripping through the air from the back room. I get a spot in line just by the door, eavesdropping on an older white woman in the middle of explaining to a bored teenager how *she* used to come to Attman's every day at lunch when *she* was a girl. They're both from here and take no interest in the close attention to the details of Baltimore history that Attman's includes in its decor. A photo of the fire that decimated the deli in 1967 is displayed prominently beside a photo from May 2020 in which masked Baltimore residents stand in line waiting for pickup during the coronavirus lockdown. Their branded mustards, featuring a cartoon of Harry Attman, line the shelves.

There's a conversation happening behind the counter. It's between two employees—one who appears to be a shift lead, and the other his twenty-one-year-old son. The elder employee is a man who grew up in South Baltimore and has worked at Attman's for "longer than I can remember," he says to me later. There's a woman in line who "doesn't have a mask on her" in a way that could mean anything—does she not believe in them, did she forget to bring one—but she's cut off from the corned beef if she doesn't wear it, so she accepts the mask the employee offers. She asks what will happen that July, when the mask mandate is set to be lifted, and the employee shakes his head.

"We're already at full capacity here," he says, "I'm not taking my fuckin' mask off. Are you crazy?" He looks over to his son, who chuckles under doubled masks. "I don't trust the mayor. I don't trust the people that come in here, shit."

He's not wrong—the Baltimore mask mandate was dropped a few days after our visit, only to be reversed a month later after positive COVID tests in the area increased by more than 300 percent in the space of four weeks. To quote one of the greats, "I don't trust the people that come in here, shit."

"So I'm vaccinated," the employee continues, observing the line with some amusement, "*but*—"

Standing in this line, I'm less than two months fully vaccinated against COIVD, having spent a weekend in early May sweating through my sheets while four seasons of a Netflix reality show played in the background. I got my shot in a hospital parking lot while "Man! I Feel Like a Woman!" played and I quietly tried to ignore my Little Kissing Urges after getting the jab from the most beautiful nurse I'd ever seen. Was she more beautiful because she was giving me something that would let me go to a Six Flags? We can't know.

"*But*," the Attman's employee continues, "you know there's those microchips in the shot to worry about." He seems to be sort of kidding, sort of not, staring in the middle distance as his coworker uses his Popeye forearms to grind meat at the front of the store, and the woman in the mask agrees harder than he's anticipating.

"Shit like that happens!" she says, looking over at a pair of boxing gloves hanging on the wall. "Tuskegee!"

This actually gets his attention—it's not every day at the deli that a customer references a profoundly unethical study from the 1930s in which six hundred poor Black residents of Tuskegee,

Alabama, were allowed to die of syphilis over the course of forty years when a cure was widely accessible. When she, a Black customer, says Tuskegee, she's saying that the Center for Disease Control and Prevention in America doesn't have the ethically spotless record that people this summer need to believe they have, that public health services are historically racist, and she's right. Her son wants to be a boxer, she says, she's feeding him corned beef to make him strong, that's why she's here.

The employee's son returns to the counter, tall and lanky and quiet in a way that's impossible to be after your twenty-second birthday.

"I'm glad I was born in 2000," he says to no one. "I don't understand what these kids are up to these days." He looks to his dad for an endorsement, and the older employee puts a hand on his son's shoulder.

"You got the vaccine though," he says, laughing. "Now they can recruit you to become a super-soldier whenever they want."

There's something very beautiful about a deli that dares to be horny. So many places we've been are too corporate to get you hard, too underfunded to frame something perverse, too online and fearful of cancellation to hang a cartoon of a naked Jewish woman in a cowboy hat asking R U HUNGRY? right beside a sign that reads THANKS TO OUR LOYAL CUSTOMERS! 100 YEARS IN BUSINESS!

Attman's Deli does not suffer from fear.

Look, I was alive and "absolutely" "going" "off" on the World Wide Web in the early 2010s. I know that women are not meant to be objectified, that every woman I've ever known has suffered from this deep-fried, centuries-old cultural delusion that women are property to be surveilled and controlled. A few months after I leave this deli, my reproductive rights will once again be in the toilet of history, a few months after *that,* they'll be legally gone when *Roe v. Wade* is overturned, it's a nightmare, I know, it's a worse nightmare for other people put in peril by these same laws. But *this* woman, a naked lady in the middle of an ancient deli, is staring me down as my boyfriend orders one bologna hot dog; oh my God, there's no way a bologna hot dog will be kind to my ass, but the ass that expels the bologna hot dog and the ass on the horny deli sign are very different.

R U HUNGRY? I'm not, but she's eye-fucking me and I don't want to be rude because she's naked and wearing a little hat. Does she know that her body has been marked up like she's a cow about to be slaughtered?

She knows. Her name is Ms. Schtick Fleisch, a joke in German that roughly translates to "Ms. Sitting Meat." Her shoulder is labeled "roast beef," her arm a "Jewish hot dog," her thigh a "Hungry Man's Special," her tits "Jewish corned beef." One of her shoulders is just labeled "sex," and in a sick joke designed specifically for me, her ass is labeled "Jewish hot pastrami." I'm trying to get myself into the world she lives in, Ms. Sitting Meat looking over her shoulder wanting to fuck me one last time before she gets cut into a million pieces and sold back to me as corned beef. I can't help but think it's funny—how hard was the man who drew this thinking about it? I want to take her seriously, her predicament is so dire, but she's still pulling her hair back for me, asking *me* if *I'm* hungry for *her* soon-to-be-severed torso. Sure, I've been her. Something terrible is about to happen to me, do I look okay from this angle? I am not safe, are you hungry?

I sneak over to the Kibbitz Room, a veritable shrine to bygone patriarchs Seymour and Harry Attman—yeah, there are the expected framed photos of their Restaurant Association medals, the newspaper clippings about the business, but there are also photos of a shirtless Seymour catching a gigantic fish off the coast of Florida in 1974 and a massive oil painting of Harry looming over the room. Unlike the other hot dog photo parlors I've spent time in, this isn't an ode to celebrities—it's a tribute to Baltimore itself and the Great Men who sustained a business for more than a century. It's admirable and worthy of a Kibbitz Room, but the masculine urge to show oneself shirtless with a fish to prove one's virility makes my skin crawl the smallest bit. Aren't you embarrassed? They're not. These are the kinds of men who hang butcher maps of women's bodies in their lobby to ask them if they're hungry. They're hungry, not ashamed.

Like most places on the East Coast, at Attman's the dogs are prepared in view of the customer, grilled by an employee beside the vat where the fried bologna bubbles. They have options—the Bulldog is topped with corned beef and Swiss; the Stray Dog comes with pastrami, Swiss, coleslaw, and mustard, but I want the special and they deliver. It's not the careful service with a smile like the others, it's a brusque "$6.50!" and return to the meat grinder. Don't protect my feelings, I'm just here for the nastiest dish on offer.

Am I in an emotional place to enjoy this hot dog? No, but I eat half of it anyway, and it immediately calcifies into a brick and sits at the bottom of my stomach for the next three days. The Attman's dog is delicious and has a decent snap to it, the bun is ungrilled and boring, but it's the bologna that really pulls you in. It doesn't belong or make sense there, but it's talking to you and saying, "I am here because you are going through a difficult time right now." It's not something that someone who is "doing well" would eat. But I eat it. R U HUNGRY? It turns out I was.

We Are in Fucking New Jersey

You don't wanna stay for the ahm-bee-ance?

I love Fucking New Jersey.

It could be because of its status as spiritual partner to Massachusetts, which residents of both states deny in spite of their mutual insistence on being loud and diabolical and allegedly Irish Italian. The very suggestion would send a lifelong resident of either location into a fugue state, frantically arguing that this could not *possibly* be true in a variation on the accent that starts to sound English if you listen long enough. These people are wrong and I am right. I love Fucking New Jersey.

Newark is a city so ugly that its official website has no choice but to identify it as "the largest city in New Jersey." Since stealing it from the Lenape tribe, European colonists and their descendants have spent four-odd centuries really making a shithole of the place, though I say that with love. There *are* things to love about Newark—it's one of the most diverse cities in the state, with the insidious gerrymandering record to prove it. "We love our diverse city," the officials say on-camera with their gray little teeth, moving around the political board game pieces necessary so that their diverse city residents cannot take them out of office with a messy little thing called their right to vote.

And still, Fucking New Jersey could be worse: it's one of only thirteen states that passed laws to prevent prison gerrymandering, a phenomenon that counts incarcerated Americans as residents in the district they're jailed in, not where they lived before being arrested. It's a filthy little trick for a state that incarcerates Black men at a higher rate than nearly anywhere else in the country. Prior to the law's passing, over-policing low-income neighborhoods served a dual purpose for the police state—not only would it separate families and use tax money for jails over rehabilitation or building up public housing and income, but it disempowered those same communities further by taking the incarcerated out of the census population count. Some states, adjacent Pennsylvania included, have fought to reverse the legal empowerment of this practice and succeeded in early 2020, when the (still incarcerated, majority Black male) population were finally considered members of the communities they had been removed from. This decision particularly affected Newark's Twenty-Ninth District, where the Northern State Prison housed more than nine thousand prisoners at the beginning of the decade, roughly 4 percent of its population. That, combined with rapid population growth without the infrastructure budget to match, makes for a strange, uniquely Jersey drive to our next destination—the home of an Italian hot dog in the North Ward served by an unreasonably horny person.

This is another five-dog day and no one is required to feel good about it, so I go in alone. Dickie Dee's, known primarily for its pizza and not its more obscure hot dog, is the first on the journey to aggressively reject the reality of ketchup, an issue that will spin me into a stupor in Chicago. There are three men who look my filthy body up and down on instinct when I enter the empty parlor, just past three red signs reading NO PANHANDLING. I've made the critical mistake of wearing a shirt from another state (three dancing tamales from New Mexico, is this okay to wear?), and they act accordingly—this woman isn't from New Jersey, so let's see what's possible.

"What can I get for you, sweethawt?" the *Sopranos* extra asks me, leaning over the counter. I don't know what to tell you, it's not my fault that the first person I meet is a cartoon character. I feel right at home, and by that I mean I'm deeply uncomfortable.

I order their signature—an Italian hot dog (father, son, house of Gucci), yet another starchily dressed double meal that comes with peppers, onions, and potatoes on thick, mercifully toasted Italian bread. In keeping with the showmanship of the East, the Newark institution opts to prepare the potatoes and peppers at the front counter and lightly deep-fry their dogs in a small pocket of hot oil beside the grill. Maybe it's the constellation of blackheads on my nose that take the younger employee in, but he cooks contentedly as something quite different goes on between the two older employees behind him.

It's my preference to be an anonymous diner in moments like this. Established by Dominick A. D'Innocenzio, *thee* Dickie Dee, the business has been run by three generations with the same spectacularly Italian American naming convention—at different points the joint has been run by D'Innocenzio's late wife and notorious wedding singer, Toni Dee, his sons Ricky Dee and Jacky Dee, and now a crop of Dee nieces, nephews, and grandchildren. The men on-site today don't wear nametags, and at one point a customer who's holding a mop but definitely isn't an employee enters the building. I don't ask.

The man with the mop comes to the counter while the younger guy rings me up slowly, shooting the shit, where am I from, you know I don't usually like glasses on a woman *but,* and I'm trying to keep my focus when the man with the mop matter-of-factly pulls out a black plastic bag and hands it to one of the older guys who makes the pizzas. It's not a tense interaction—the older man has something for him and knows what's in the bag, they talk about the Mets, why does he have a fucking mop? I desperately try to apply my acquired wisdom from the Meth Haunted House but I've arrived at my sensory maximum; there are too many men from New Jersey doing weird things at one time, and I need a minute.

Do I want to stay or take it to go? I look to the bathroom I desperately need to use, but it's not worth it. To go, I say, and take the forty-pound paper bag they hand to me, giving a polite smile to the hideous hungry-man mascot on his T-shirt.

"You don't wanna stay for the ahm-bee-ance?" he flirts, and I'm in eleventh grade again, knowing I should be grateful for Ryan Sullivan's attention but wanting to date the five-foot-five Juggalo who doesn't know I exist. I need to go, I tell him, there are three men outside waiting for me, and I'm technically telling the truth.

It's an impressively large dish that sags the bottom of a paper bag even with just the single dog I order—generally, the Italian hot dog means *many* dogs, usually two but as many as four, wedged into half a pizza roll. Mustard is launched into the bottom of the bun, a rarity for a dish that tends to have its weak-bunned infrastructure shot to hell by even the suggestion of moisture below the meat. The dog is fried to a light snap and topped off with about ten home-fried potatoes, left on the grill and edged into the frying oil for whatever amount of time a Dee deems appropriate, finished off with paprika, parsley, peppers, and—*according to Rob Dee himself*—ketchup, in spite of the website's insistence that there's "no ketchup allowed." It's too much bread for my taste, but the Italian hot dog truly is something special, and the Dees know how to get the slightly fried dog, which I'll soon learn is called a "ripper," just so to complement its toppings. Call me a delicate, feminine flower (and you should), but I could have done with a few less potatoes. I did appreciate the ketchup though. You know . . . the ketchup that's on the hot dog that keeps telling you there's no ketchup on it?

I'm sorry, in this lifetime I will not allow myself to get gaslit by another man from New Jersey. I was told there would be no ketchup by virtually all marketing from Dickie Dee's, an establishment whose mascot is a sicko in a hat brandishing all five hundred of his teeth to chomp down on an Italian hot dog. I second-guess myself in the moment, thinking maybe there's some other sugary tomato-adjacent paste in the most recognizable generic red bottle in the country, a signature sauce known only to the Dees. The world's worst detective work reveals that this is bullshit—there's a Travel Channel segment on the restaurant from the mid-2010s, shortly before Dickie Dee died, in which the same bottle is identified as ketchup.

It raises the question: Why do you perverts want me to hate ketchup so much? It's not something I'll be able to fully confront in this region, certainly not in the bologna-addled mental state that is me getting hit on by a man who is actively ignoring an exchange of either vegetables or drugs from a person who is holding a completely dry, upright mop for, I can't stress this enough, reasons unclear. They're fucking with us.

"It's good for your sex life," Dickie Dee said in the same Travel Channel segment, shortly before his death. Speak for yourself (RIP).

There's no bathroom at the first Jersey gas station on our route, which means we are about to get into an argument. "What is life but arguing between hot dogs?" I punch into my notes app while my pelvis threatens to explode. It makes me sad to read now because there are at least two other things in life— cumming and calling your mom on the phone—but we pull into a nice hotel where we're not staying so I can pee discreetly in a lobby I look too cheap to walk into. We're arguing but have one more hot dog before the day can end. I'm so tired, but things are about to change. Because.

I am about to have a hot dog that will change my life.

Twenty minutes from Newark is Rutt's Hut, a hot dog parlor hanging over Route 21 in Clifton, New Jersey. It is here, on my fifth dog of the day, that I will experience something as close to Christlike as is possible for meat shoved into a meat casing to be.

Here's the thing—it's by no means a hot take to consider the signature Ripper at Rutt's Hut one of the best in the country. In fact, it's been declared the best hot dog in the country by *The Daily Meal* four times in a row (whatever that means) and is something of an American institution, the kind of place you get unsolicited emails about for years after if you don't mention it in your hot dog book. With the proper movie scoring, the building could present as a warm family hangout, a close-knit but dangerous workplace, or a place to grab a bite after disposing of a body in the Passaic River, and there's no doubt it's been all three at different times.

We arrive on a Wednesday night at dusk, and the lights of the perpendicular sign can be seen from the highway. The dining room to the midsize building, outfitted with an absurdly large parking lot, is closed due to COVID—definitely the right call as the Delta variant (what variant are you being fucked over by, reader?) is raging through areas of the country we seem to slip out of just in time to keep testing negative—but the decision leaves the main corridor flooded with a group of people who all appear to be wearing the same leather outfit, and oh my God, it's biker night at Rutt's Hut.

I look down at my shitty, sweat-stained outfit and want to bolt. It's *biker night* at the greatest hot dog joint in the country, and I've come sauntering in here four hot dogs deep thinking I'll be treated with respect. The place is mobbed by at least a hundred vest-clad and hungry Jerseyans, snaking through the lobby and outside to see each other's bikes and touch each other with an intent that makes whatever is lurking beneath the surface of my skin twitch. I walk into the cold rush of crummy air conditioning from a window unit with wood paneling like my high school boyfriend's dad's station wagon. I start to listen as we begin what becomes a half-hour wait for a hot dog that makes me want a hot dog after eating four, sorry, pretty brutally dense hot dogs. Last night was classic car night, and I silently thank whatever force brought me into a room that reeks of leather and Old Spice instead of death.

"Came here since I was four years old, maybe," says a young man who clarifies that he's "actually twenty-four," thick with Jersey accent and talking to a somewhat shorter, much older man in a black leather jacket that has seen thousands of Jersey miles, you can just tell. I start by thinking they're friends and end by thinking they're going to be lovers by midnight. "My dad and uncle used to come here and get all fucked up on Coors while I sat with them. They used to stack the empties over there," he says, pointing to the sticky white counter the line wraps itself around. The older man replies softly and makes his new acquaintance laugh.

There's no shortage of cheap beer here to get unforgivably fucked up on in front of your young nephew, along with a menu that expands far beyond the Ripper hot dog that Rutt's is so famous for. The gigantic menu also leans heavy on seafood—no one expects a hot dog joint to have a shrimp creole casserole, calamari, and a tuna platter, but fuck you, guess who does— boiled ham, seasonal Jell-O, and my favorite in the world, fried clam strips. Their signature is the Ripper, $2.80 with cheese and $2.35 without, and there is a tried-and-true *system* one has to be prepared for when approaching the counter with cash as exact as you can muster.

Like The Varsity in Atlanta, Rutt's Hut has a specific if-you-know-you-know ordering style with a slightly disturbed we-don't-care-if-you-wear-a-mask-in-the-middle-of-the-pandemic edge. It's a lobotomized steak order, having everything to do with how much of a heart condition you want to develop from a single half-beef, half-pork Thumann's hot dog high-diving into 350-degree vegetable oil in their little bikinis. Let's meet the ladies, shall we?

The **in-and-outer** is a teenage girl taking a dip in the pool to impress her crush. She plunges into the oil and sinks to the very bottom, stays there for a moment to prove she can touch the tile floor, then swims back to the surface to peek her head over the water, hoping her bangs don't fall in her face and it looks the way it does in movies. It never does. The in-and-outer is a rare steak, pale and tender in a way that some people love and others think is too raw. Give her a few years, she'll sort herself out.

A **ripper** isn't as shy, a medium-fried hot dog that proves the most popular in the restaurant and at the public pool. She takes the same dive as the in-and-outer but floats for a few minutes at the top of the oil, checking to see if anyone is looking at her. They are, so she stays in the pool until her skin splits and begins to crinkle, creating a crunch on the outside, juicy animal entrails on the inside. She's got a suntan and is delicious and yes, fine, does make you feel like you could die of a heart attack at any moment, but who cares? A ripper is the girl next door, popular but not in a threatening way, oh did they use *my* picture in the brochure? I didn't notice, ha ha.

A **weller** is the girl next door's mother who is ready to get herself back out there after The Event but forgets how, staying on the surface of the pool a little too long and getting a little too fried in the sun waiting for the right person to show up. She's not the most popular choice with pool clientele, but the ones who love her do so fiercely; she is the well-done steak of hot dogs that implies experience with the same taste—you love her but you want her to relax a little, it's okay to be a little crunchy, all your skin being tender is overrated anyway.

And then there's the **cremator,** a succubus of a hot dog that haunted the local pool for centuries before there was a pool and will for centuries after. She has no hot dog flesh because she has no heart to speak of—she is so fried through that she will take your soul with her, an eight-inch meat chunk to chip your tooth on, unfuckable in theory but what does that even mean in this context, she's daring you to fuck her. The current proprietor describes her as "very well-done bacon" that you need a "select appetite" for, and the old owner of Rutt's made people who ordered her sign a waiver signing their lives away before handing her over. She will not force herself on you, but if you fuck her you will die and some try it just to know what it would feel like. Every lifeguard who's looked at her for too long turned to stone.

I'm not feeling lucky enough to look into the eyes of Hot Dog Medusa today as I approach the man at the counter, who is not impressed with our status as the only masked people in the building. I order two rippers, one with their famous mustard-based relish and one with ketchup, hand him my ten-dollar bill, and head down the counter before shit gets too wild. There are four line cooks flanked in the back, tossing hot dogs into oil while ready-to-go rippers wait closer to the counter. The young biker shows the older man the two knives he has with him while they wait, sipping on a Coors in an ancient ritual.

This particular summer marks ninety-three years of Rutt's Hut, opened in 1928 by another scrappy working-class couple, Royal "Abe" and Ann Fedorchak Rutt. They started in a one-room restaurant, the hut, and began to roast their own pigs in the 1940s for their less famous but equally good barbecue sandwiches. Abe's wife, Ann, dutifully made their famous secret relish at home, much like the pepper relish I'll try in a few months in Philadelphia from the Danze family at Johnny's Hots. A wife makes the relish, her husband gets the credit.

There are some stands whose histories are told by the owners—your Varsitys, your Ben's Chili Bowls—and others who don't mythologize themselves intentionally, leaving the story to be written by customers and employees who care about it. Rutt's Hut is the latter, displaying nothing but their awards and some tchotchkes in the red-and-white interior brimming with leather daddies, without the customary framed photos of its founders. It's possible that these live in the currently closed dining room, or the absence could be connected to the fact that Rutt's is one of the few Mount Rushmore American hot dog stands that aren't still owned by the founding family.

In 1974, Abe Rutt sold the forty-seven-year-old business after a severe decline in health, replacing the old days of pigs and Rheingold beer on tap in a shack. The lucky buyers were a group of enterprising Greek American businessmen who he made apprentice in the kitchen before becoming owners in order to ensure the continuity of quality. The second generation of the Greek Rutt's takeover has yielded more interesting results, including a neurotic one-time co-owner named Johnny Karagiorgis, who was featured as a villain on *Real Housewives of New Jersey* in the early 2010s, only to die in 2016 of a massive heart attack at age forty-five. Customers left flowers in his parking spot at Rutt's the day after he died.

The mythology of the founders lies with the customers who survive to tell it, chatting on obscure message boards in pursuit of someone who's interested. God bless the grandchildren who taught these people to connect to dial-up internet, because it gives us a look into the heavy-drinking, pig-roasting patriarch of the country's best hot dog stand.

"I met him at a party at my brother's house," said a user on a defunct message board in 2003 who claimed to have been a Rutt's customer for seventy-five years. "Roy was a heavy drinker which eventually killed him. His widow continued making the sauce in her basement, even after the place was sold."

Another user, a woman named Lorraine, who claims to be a niece of the Rutts, replied to interrogate the first user's story, down to the texture of the stand's chili sauce and the character of a famous employee from the 1940s who only went by "Sparky." She too was in the dark about the Rutt's relish recipe, one that currently sells about 120 pounds in a single week and is said to be a secret family recipe from Abe's grandmother back in Germany.

"Upon his dying bed," she wrote, "the Rutts begged him for the recipe, but he took it to his grave."

The Rutt's ripper is fucking magnificent. It's the only dog in the country that really delivers on the *snap* that's so often promised in a hot dog with natural casing, and the residual grease rests inside an ungrilled bun. The relish, one that (speculators guess but cannot confirm) features coleslaw, pepper, and onions mixed in with a signature mustard, is all that's necessary to compliment the snap and chew of the Thumann's hot dog, resulting in a hot mouth full of perfect tastes and textures. The heat of the dog is cooled by the tang of the relish is softened by the grocery store white bread, and the pork flavor mixes with the finely chopped coleslaw like a *Fantasia* short. The ahm-bee-ance is Jersey, abrasive and unwelcoming, and the product is Jersey, intense and perfect in a way that you don't want to hand it to them, but must.

We pull out at sunset, right as the older biker leans into the young biker's ear to tell a secret I can't hear.

It's our last night before getting to my dad's house in Massachusetts, a house I grew up in that no longer looks the way it used to. It was always sort of broken down ("this reminds me of Charlie Bucket's house!" said a sixth grader to me, oh shit oh fuck), but there's no time to get into generational trauma on this trip— we're here to make sure a man stops smoking cigarettes before they absolutely murder him, an emotionless, tactical drive. I get us a room with two beds for the second night in a row to see if my boyfriend says anything, which he does not; the cocker spaniel chooses my full-size bed to fall asleep in and that pings the little scoreboard in the back of my mind. I can kill the land-lord in my head (cool T-shirt), I can kill the capitalist in my head (poster I saw in a trust fund kid's living room), but I won't kill my little scoreboard of which pet likes who more.

I have a note here that says, "I TAKE A SHIT! But not the shit I needed," which sends the sensation of five interstate hot dogs rushing back into my body. The backseat of the rental car is the home of the dog and the cat and a graveyard of half-finished meat tubes, the remainder of Virginia's famous banana pudding from DC, and three-fourths of the Dickie Dee's pasta meatball hot dog that I could only get a few bites in before real-izing I was eating a pita pocket full of meat and not a hot dog proper. You're telling me people are still fighting over whether a hot dog is a sandwich when there are real and present paradoxes in my backseat?

We Are in the Northeast

Do you ever get sick of hot dogs? Of course.

Did I ever tell you I've never cum in my home state and I think it's connected to taxation? Of course not, we're strangers.

Blackie's in Cheshire, Connecticut, has delicious food and the most puritanical energy for what is allegedly a fun business to run. Has it burned down before? Of course, any halfway-decent hot dog place has. Does it have a sign that prominently states NO DANCING? Is the stand closed every Friday because Catholics aren't supposed to eat meat then? Is the clientele we find in the late morning exclusively old men who are lightly harassing the teenage girl behind the counter? Take your guesses.

This place is no fun, and that's how I know I'm almost home.

As always, I order the signature—an all-beef hot dog manufactured especially for Blackie's by Martin Rosol's Inc in nearby New Britain, cooked in oil long enough for a light snap with none of the decadent options those secular freaks in New Jersey offer. It's served on a toasted roll with the *strong* suggestion that customers show their respect by slathering on brown mustard and Blackie's signature hot pepper relish, the recipe of which is by far the least menacing Catholic secret in New England.

Like Rutt's, Blackie's started in 1928, just months shy of the stock market crash that led hot dogs to become the cheap eat of choice for the average poor American. Irish immigrant Mary Mahoney left her hometown in County Kerry, Ireland, to try for more in the US and ended up with Waterbury, Connecticut, native Art Blackman—who, by all accounts, could be described as "some guy." The two opened a gas station on the edge of town in 1925, which quickly became a local hangout in a place there wasn't much to do, and started selling hot dogs, slathered in the secret pepper relish recipe of Art's family, for additional revenue.

The whole thing gets triggeringly Irish Catholic from there— when Mary's three siblings joined the operation and started slinging hot dogs and talking shit in the cutting, red-faced way the Irish Catholic family I grew up in did, and the spot became a popular place for customers to eat and dance and generally be from Connecticut. Art died just before World War II began, leaving Mary to run the business with her sister Nel—the Irish broads did the damn thing, expanding the menu to include burgers, ice cream, and never fries, which they seemed to be proud of for some reason.

Something even *more* Irish Catholic happened in 1945— Blackie's burned down under mysterious circumstances. Two kids noticed that the kitchen had gone up in flames in the way that rooms full of flammable things tend to when employees are not paid enough to keep an eye on them. The cause, according to the newspaper clipping the joint has framed on the wall, was a "lighted cigarette which shouldered in an accumulation of waste papers in the kitchen of the restaurant"—this is just good Irish cooking praxis, as far as I'm concerned.

After scooping up some insurance money, Mary and her brother rebuilt an identical restaurant in a nearby location, adding two multi-floor octagonal structures on either side for additional seating. It's this dining room where the iconic NO DANCING sign is hung beside the customary black-and-white photos of the founders and their family, as well as locals who could eat more than ten hot dogs in ten minutes. Their names are Lewis, Dan,

Joe, and Tough, something the community could leverage into a boy band, or not.

The exterior of Blackie's still looks very much like a gas station, its two-floor dining area topped by a sign that looks suspiciously like an old Shell gasoline ad that's been painted black. The food counter looks identical to a bar but, you will not be surprised to hear, is not one—having a bar would be fun, and there is a tax on fun in New England. Instead, you can get something called birch beer on tap, a cousin to root beer made from birch bark and sap, and Utz potato chips in lieu of fries. For the first time in many states, the garage door entrance to the not-bar where you can't dance, drink, or have a Friday hot dog means that we're all technically outside, making it impossible to know which of the dads perched on the not-barstools are anti-maskers and which are not.

The hot dog itself is damn good, and not only because it holds the promise of being the only one I need to eat today. The snap of an all-beef hot dog is unique, and the hot mustard and signature relish make for the spiciest hot dog experience I've had since I was sweating through my clothes in Arizona. The presentation makes me laugh, because for all its flavor it still looks like drab Irish cooking—the pepper relish is delicious but somehow gray, the mustard is hot but somehow gray. We have to meet my dad by one o'clock, so there's not much time to shoot the shit with the employees, who have absolutely no interest in shooting the shit with us.

But I have to ask about the NO DANCING sign, and the teenager behind the counter forces a laugh. "That was to avoid some tax," she says, referring to a still-active Puritanical law called the Cabaret Tax, a 5-percent wrist slap imposed on any food or admission income to the government for establishments that furnished "dancing privileges."

We pull out of Blackie's, an hour and a half away from the city where I grew up.

"Do you ever get sick of hot dogs?" a local newscaster asks an older employee who has been working at Blackie's since he was a teenager.

"Of course," he replies, and returns to work. "I bring my own food in, you can't eat hot dogs every day." Oh, shit.

We are a few miles from my hometown, where our trip will take a pause as we really expose ourselves to the elements of a family after a year and a half of pandemic-induced isolation. I keep returning to my front camera, convinced I look different after the mix of punishing quantities of early-lockdown Franzia and compulsive Jane Fonda workouts that turned out to be pretty bad for my knees.

We get to the house, park, and let the animals out, and my parents are older. We take the rental back and my boyfriend is frustrated, my dad asks if I'm okay, I say sure, I am just happy to see you. He drives slower than he used to and seems less sure; his anxious words come faster and for longer periods of time because there's a chunk of his lung that will be horked (medical term) out in order to save his life this summer.

I don't eat a hot dog for an entire week and I miss them.

We Are in New York City

I would like to ask my question, Joseph.

Coney Island on the Fourth of July was always a nonnegotiable event. In a flagrant display of hot dog propaganda only bested by the persistent phallic force of the Oscar Mayer Wienermobile, the annual Nathan's Hot Dog Eating Contest is not only the most horrific television broadcast of the year, it's the one that most closely connects the image of the rubbery hot dog with the rubbery concept of American jingoism.

I arrive in New York City the way any self-respecting Bostonian does—on the Megabus at 2:00 p.m., sweaty and a little drunk from the can of pinot grigio I dumped into a rinsed-out Dunkin' coffee cup. The two rows in front of me are crowded with a flock of college girls loudly discussing *finally* being able to go to *fucking New York* after being locked in their parents' homes for the duration of the pandemic, in (if I may hazard a guess) hastily constructed Midwestern McMansions with asbestos issues. This is a moment I've witnessed a hundred times: the nineteen-year-old girls gasp when the skyline comes into view from the rancid bus.

We've got plenty of places to deep-throat hot dogs before tomorrow morning, when American hot dog eating champion

Joey Chestnut (Westfield, IN / Age: 39 / Weight: 230, according to his Major League Eating stats) competes for his fourteenth title at the Nathan's contest. It's a contest between Joseph and himself—beginning in 2012, he won by more than ten hot dogs swallowed from his nearest competitor, a chasm that widened to nearly thirty by the audience-free coronavirus edition of the competition held inside for some reason in 2020. In his fifteen years of competition, Joey has risen from being Some Guy from San Diego to a national symbol on par with the hot dog itself, someone worthy of trophies and sponsorships and titty-whipping-out-in-hundred-degree-heat. I'll have a crush on him in twenty-four hours, but you couldn't pay me to believe that now.

The only dignified way to begin a three-day New York hot dog binge is by spotting the nearest Sabrett umbrella. It's not hard—my Megabus armpit sweat hasn't dissolved into the city stink before I spot one, just steps from where we slither out the side of the bus. It's a signature blue-and-yellow signifier that borrows the similarly iconic look of Chicago's Vienna Beef stands. For a couple dollars almost anywhere in the city, a wanderer can find a natural casing garlicky all-beef dog with a snap on the street, as well as Sabrett's skinless frankfurters in Madison Square Garden. The Sabrett company was founded in 1948 by Latvian immigrant Samuel Ogus and business partner Fritz Frankel, and their hot dogs are traditionally served boiled in the signature built-in cart "dirty water" that other regions turn their nose up at, with the company's classic tomato-based onion sauce produced with the rest of their food in Jersey. I order one topped with mustard and kraut at the nearest stand.

"How long have you worked here?" I ask the man at the stand, who yells over the sound of traffic to complain about something mid kraut heave.

"Who knows," he says, and looks to his partner. They both laugh. "I try not to keep track."

There's been a snag in our accommodations—did I say

accommodations? I meant my friend's fiancé's aunt decided that a couple who have been eating nothing but hot dogs are too vague an acquaintance to trust in her nice Manhattan apartment. The solution is to stay with a sweet friend of a friend all the way out in Ridgewood, Queens, at the tip of a dead end, where we find our host playing *Tony Hawk* on an old PlayStation with his older brother. They are so kind and almost interested in why we're here, inviting us to their rooftop party at the brother's place nearby while I scan his shelves of rare comic books. The futon is stiff but surrounded by beautiful things. Where did all the crust punk boys from 2013 go? I scroll through my phone and check—they're engaged to graphic designers named Stephanie who "completely changed their view on what life could be."

My boyfriend isn't in the mood for another hot dog tonight, but I'm relentless and meet up with my friend Grace (she's really impressive, you'd love her) at Schaller's Stube, a German sausage stand that's serviced the same Yorkville neighborhood since 1937 by three generations of Schallers. I grab their eight-dollar "Classic"—in-house bratwurst, Dusseldorf mustard, and sauerkraut served on a thick, toasted Danish Balthazar bun. He is a big boy, a pale boy, not technically a hot dog boy, but *delicious.*

"I've been watching Joey since I was little," Grace admits, one of my few friends who was a hot dog sister-in-arms. I bonded with her over our college habit of buying up 7–Eleven hot dogs and leaving one in the bottom of a purse or a backpack in case of emergency. "Like, in middle school on the ESPN broadcasts, I wouldn't miss it. He's a legend."

This is what I'm turning over in my mind at six thirty the next morning as we make the long trek from Ridgewood to Coney Island to make it in time for press arrivals—a distinction I am thrilled to announce I scammed my way into. It's not that I need more access than the free admission pedestrians who wandered into (or crossed state lines to get to) Maimonides Park that morning, but it can't and doesn't hurt.

There's a couple frantically making out at DeKalb Avenue Station before one breaks away just in time to slip through the doors and onto the Q train. The girl who left turns to look at who she was kissing as the train pulls away, then looks at her lap for the next four stops smiling. I try to put myself where she is sitting, where I sat once, and feel bad for the person who gets on and sits next to her three stops later. He has no idea he is sitting next to the most in love person in the entire world.

Coney Island reeks, a place that's a shithole but it's *our* shithole, and I piss like a helicopter in a beachside bathroom that smells like eggs and Febreze. We walk past the century-old Cyclone roller coaster, past the overpriced theme park, and toward the reason crowds have been assembling here on "America's birthday!" (imagine me screaming that with a throat coated in mustard and beer) since the Nathan's contest formally began in 1972. Up until the plague hit, it was held at their flagship location, the looming yellow, green, and white building where Nathan's Famous Hot Dogs earned their name.

Getting from the family vacation postcard of Nathan's storefront to the jaws of Joey Chestnut takes a little myth-sifting. The restaurant itself is still on the corner of Stillwell and Surf Avenue, just as it was in 1916 when a Jewish immigrant from Poland named Nathan Handwerker and his wife, Ida, got a $300 loan to open their business. Handwerker's connection to the hot dog myth extends further back still—in the Coney Island edition of the hot dog origin myth, it was Handwerker slicing the bread into what are now standard-issue hot dog buns before striking out on his own. A tall red cartoon hot dog on the building's roof reminds you they've been open for more than a century, while the sign below features a disembodied white hand pointing to the line, advising you to FOLLOW THE CROWD.

That the company had a gigantic impact on New York's role in popularizing the hot dog is without doubt—the *rest* of its history involves a bit of free-form informational jazz. A promoter for Nathan's dates the contest back to their founding year, claiming that four immigrants held a hot dog eating contest at the pier on the Fourth of July to determine who was the most patriotic. That same promoter, Morty Matz, *also* once stated the contest's annual tradition began in 1941 as a protest of World War II, then corrected this to a different story that it had begun in 1971 as a protest of the Vietnam War. In 2010, Matz came clean with the very American truth—he was lying about the whole thing for publicity, and the real contest started as a marketing stunt in the early 1970s.

Of course, the Nathan's Famous legends interact directly with the Americana of Coney Island itself, a sight best seen, never smelled, and God help you if you touch it. The park was built on land taken from the Lenape tribe, and after aggressive colonizing, Coney Island was connected to the city by rail and developed as a resort by a series of wealthy railroad tycoons in the 1870s. One area would be renamed and constructed into a luxury hotel called Brighton Beach by developer William Engeman, and the eastern shore was developed by the wildly anti-Semitic Austin Corbin and named Manhattan Beach, which banned Jewish people from the resort in its early years. As transportation to the area continued to improve, amusement park elements began to crop up—by the 1880s, the pier was rife with carousels, sideshows, zoos, and brothels that became increasingly accessible to the lower classes. Early roller coasters followed; tunnels of love encouraged covert touching; a gigantic brothel shaped like an elephant was built and then burned down. When you weren't fucking in a gigantic wooden elephant, the hot dog in the Coney Island Charles Feltman myth (see a lie published in an earlier chapter of this book) became the park's signature identifier along with the Wonder Wheel. It's a place of weirdness and excess that's been burned down, pummeled by weather, and rebuilt countless times with the strange, violent and dark corners worthy of anywhere worth visiting—a corner the Nathan's Hot Dog Eating Contest slips into unnoticed.

Matz may have been the contest's first hype man, but the marketing executive who built it into the ESPN-broadcast event it is today is a showman in a straw hat with a history of racist actions and a dangerous amount of charisma named George Shea. He's one of two men responsible for the contest's steep increase in popularity beginning in the early 2000s—the other is Japanese eating champion Takeru Kobayashi, who made the competition a must-watch event with his skill and showmanship beginning in 2001. The contentious relationship between the two is laid out in stark terms in Nicole Lucas Haimes's 2019 ESPN *30 for 30* documentary episode "The Good, the Bad, the Hungry"—a seventy-six-minute journey into how Kobayashi popularized competitive hot dog eating in America, only to be forced out of the sport for not being the champion George Shea or many bigots in the crowd wanted. Who did they want? You guessed it! Some white guy from San Diego named Joseph Chestnut.

George Shea is still a massive presence in the sport, and is set to emcee the event for the thirty-first time in 2021 the day we're waiting for our coffee from a Ridgewood cat café to kick in. He was an employee of Morty Matz's beginning in 1988, where Shea says—and we should always take what Shea says with a grain of salt—that he first found his calling in 1990 after noticing that a hot dog eating competitor was cheating.

Shea went to his boss to report the indiscretion quietly, but Matz was a publicity man through and through—"Morty told me to go over and get a cop to arrest the guy, which I thought was crazy," he told *MEL Magazine* in 2021.

But Shea took the chaotic instinct to heart and went all out, conjuring PR stunts that far exceeded Matz's. There was the scholarly article he once attempted to submit to *The New En-*

gland *Journal of Medicine* called "The Belt of Fat Theory," a still-unverified theory that Shea made a stink about upon its rejection in 2000. He and his brother Richard founded the International Federation of Competitive Eating and Major League Eating in 1997 in order to legitimize the sport and take it on the road. With this came a steep escalation in the publicity around the Nathan's contest, with Shea's invention of a coveted "Mustard Belt" (an old belt of his covered in Pearl paint and rhinestones on the floor of his friend's apartment) quickly stoking rivalries in the eating community. This was around the time that Shea's role as emcee, one that involves him introducing aggressively normal-looking competitors as if they're WWE wrestlers, became a key component of the hype surrounding events. I mean, you're not gonna whip your tits out for someone without being riled up a little first. I would know.

"A lot of what I say *literally* isn't true in terms of words," Shea says in the *30 for 30* documentary, "but it's *emotionally* true."

Of the many ways to see through Shea's evangelical attitude toward the hot dog and into its hollow ad-man origins is how his own wife reacted to his work. Carlene Shea has written for soap operas and the WWE, according to a profile of her husband for *Time*, and was interviewed on camera about her opinion of his work as Nathan's emcee in a 2000s-era video featured in the 2021 hot dog eating documentary *Scarf Face*. Affectionately noting his penchant for being the center of attention, she commented, "He's a brilliant PR man and I think there's plenty of other things he could be promoting. I'm breaking his heart saying this but competitive eating to me is not really a sport . . . I don't see the athleticism in competitive eating."

Don't get me wrong—I find George Shea to be a singularly vile person, a spiritual embodiment of the clearly fake but aesthetically fascinating set of porcelain veneers in his mouth. He is a shameless promoter who seems willing to take advantage of the worst instincts of his audience to get a reaction, including but not limited to racism, sexism, body-shaming, and exploiting the personal lives of competitors. But. *But.*

He's fucking *effective.*

Here's how he once introduced legendary eater Crazy Legs Conti—I'd tell you his legal name, except he had it changed to Crazy Legs Conti so that *is* his legal name. Please stay with me. Shea bellows this on national television:

"He was buried alive under sixty cubic feet of popcorn, and he ate his way out to survival. And that's why we call him the David Blaine of the bowel, the Evel Knievel of the alimentary canal, the Houdini of cuisini, Crazy Legs Conti!"

There's a part of me that's glad Shea is content to merely ruin the lives of hot dog competitors and not aim his cyclops's eye on larger prey, but the negative impact his jingoistic marketing approach had on Takeru Kobayashi at the height of his career cannot be overstated. It's why Joey Chestnut is about to win the contest for the fourteenth time in 2021, and why as many as twenty-five thousand spectators have gathered to see him do it in person as millions more watch on ESPN.

Kobayashi was born in Japan in 1978 and was already well-known for competing in televised eating and chugging contests. Major League Eating in America very much followed Japan's lead in presenting eating as a potential sport—there had been a thriving scene going back to the 1990s before George Shea ever caught on. The broadcasts were as goofy as Nathan's, but there was an emphasis on the physical training it took to trick the body into eating absurd amounts of food—the vast majority of Japanese champions are built like Kobayashi, muscular and slim with deliberate training rituals.

"My dad said, 'you don't necessarily have to study, but whatever you decide to do, be the best at it,'" Kobayashi says in *The Good, the Bad, the Hungry.* He quickly rose through the ranks of Japan's *gurgitators* and became known for his big, sometimes emotional personality and passion for the sport. His signature was his six-pack—before and after coming to America, Kobayashi would pound his hard stomach after eating pounds upon pounds of food as the people who lost to him passed out from the meat sweats beside him.

By 2001, the Sheas had built enough clout around their operation to get the attention of Japanese eaters, bringing Kobayashi to Coney Island for the first time. The Americans didn't have a lot of faith in the spindly twenty-three-year-old with frosted tips, but he *destroyed*, virtually doubling the national record by downing fifty hot dogs in twelve minutes. The Sheas and Kobayashi mutually benefited from this victory—all of a sudden the eyes on the contest multiplied, and Kobayashi became a sensation in the US. Still, his otherness was emphasized from the beginning.

"There is nothing greater than the belt, the victory, and the trophy," Shea said to Kobayashi, handing him the oversized generic trophy in 2001. "And even though it wasn't an American who won, congratulations."

Most American competitors would agree that Kobayashi's victory combined with his raising the bar for performance legitimized American competitive eating in the 2000s. Shea took advantage of the tidal wave of reality TV of that era to get shows like *The Glutton Bowl* and *Gutbusters* on the air, bringing out Kobayashi and emerging domestic champions to eat cow brains and compete against live bears in the recesses of cable TV. In 2002, a Japanese schoolboy choked and died attempting to imitate competitive eating, slowing its growth in Kobayashi's home country and pushing him further still into American eating—at his second Nathan's contest, he was brought out on a raised litter like a Roman senator, fans throwing carnations as he passed.

It was around this time that Joey Chestnut and his brother saw Kobayashi on TV losing a hot dog contest to a grizzly bear, and Joseph decided that he was going to be . . . that bear. Under the tutelage of his mother in the San Jose area, he began as a local asparagus-eating champion at twenty-one, then placed

third in his first Nathan's contest behind Kobayashi and Sonya "Black Widow" Thomas (more on her in a moment). People
were excited about the kid from California presenting a viable
challenge to five-time champion Kobayashi, and the Sheas
threw their entire operation behind encouraging competition
between the two men—they at no point tried to establish a serious rivalry between Chestnut and any women competitors, and
were just five years out from separating women from the main
contest altogether.

"If you consider yourself a competitive eater, [Kobayashi]
wasn't an eater, he was a god," Chestnut said of his rival and
inspiration. For his part, Kobayashi recalls feeling proud that
his success had spawned real competitors.

That the Sheas wanted an American champion from the beginning was no secret, in spite of their debt to Kobayashi and
Japanese speed eating's outsized influence on their own success.
MLE videos insisted that "Joey Chestnut is our hope" and promoted him as an American hot dog eating savant, and the two
champions were pitted against each other at contests as much as
possible.

Rivalry aside, the cultural differences between Kobayashi and
Chestnut's attitudes toward food are fascinating—Kobayashi
was raised by a father who advised that eating to excess was
indulgent, while the Chestnut family believed that "food was
comfort, was your friend," according to his music teacher father
(whose name, I *need* you to know, is Merlin Chestnut). Rather
than acknowledging this contrast at face value, the Sheas
praised Chestnut's rearing as the correct one, even as Chestnut
continued to look to Kobayashi's undeniably more artful and
measured eating technique while developing his own effective
but less graceful approach to the sport.

Even now, over twenty years into the competitive eating's
American surge, there isn't a lot of infrastructure for training
for a Nathan's contest. Like in any fledgling industry, this has

its benefits—for the first ten years, competitors would develop techniques through trial and error and by observing each other. Kobayashi trained intensely with signature moves that included breaking two hot dogs in half at once while dunking buns in hot water to create one fluid eating motion; Thomas developed a system of intermittent fasting and workouts, limiting her number of competition dates to stay sharp; Chestnut, once again, motivated himself in training at first by watching videos of Kobayashi. His technique eventually grew into something more elaborate, with Chestnut keeping his jaw from locking up by chewing on a rubber ball and doing sit-ups while gulping gasps of air to expand his stomach.

On the Fourth of July in 2007, the tides turned—Joey Chestnut ate sixty-six hot dogs to Kobayashi's sixty-three, including an impressive moment when Kobayashi ate his own vomit to salvage his final hot dog. In a year when he'd lost his mother and considered backing away from the sport altogether, it wasn't enough, and Chestnut took the day, immediately revealing Major League Eating and the watching American public's low-simmering prejudices.

"Go home, Shanghai boy!" frat boys screamed at the six-time champion the moment he lost. "Go home, kamikaze!" They shook the American flag in approval at Joseph and began to chant "USA!," solidifying Chestnut's newfound status as more than an individual weird guy determined to beat the reigning champion, but instead a symbol of masculine white America.

Kobayashi describes being shocked at how the American public turned on him once Chestnut became a viable competitor, after he was originally thrilled to have found an opponent who could keep up.

"I didn't understand American culture," he said in 2019, "so it scared me."

No one was more ready for a white American champion than George Shea.

"The dark days of the last six years are behind us!" he declared, raising the new champion's fist in the air.

Joseph was thrilled—several years of intense training and devastating losses had yielded the victory he'd fought for, and he wasn't shy about bragging to the press. Footage shows George Shea coaching Chestnut on his answers in the wake of Kobayashi's loss, punching his optimistic statements of a job well done into malice and encouraging Kobayashi to antagonize Chestnut through a translator.

Between the language barrier and Chestnut's own shyness and desire to hold the public's attention, the Sheas and Major League Eating got exactly the answers they wanted. In one unedited talking head video from a contest where Chestnut defeated Kobayashi at eating turkey and cranberry sauce on TV, George Shea turned the bullshit up to 11.

"After that event, I went back to my room and I wept," Shea said straight-faced to camera. "I silently wept because something was lost . . . we had a hero, and he was no longer invulnerable. I wept." Assuming the clip he needs is done, Shea cracks a smile and repeats the lie with teeth. "I wept!" He and the camera crew start laughing—no one truly gave a shit, save Kobayashi and Chestnut themselves.

Following Chestnut's ascent, tensions between Kobayashi and Major League Eating escalated sharply. Chestnut's income had skyrocketed with his victory, and Kobayashi signed with a Japanese agency that informed him that Shea had roped him into an unreasonable contract that meant that he could only compete in America with the permission of MLE. This greatly affected his ability to capitalize on his popular image in America—when Chestnut won again in 2008, Shea would not budge on Kobayashi's contract.

"I have always used pro-American rhetoric," Shea said in 2019, "and the belt is a national prize, from the day the belt was made. You think I want Kobayashi to win six years in a row, necessarily? If he wins, he wins, but that's not great for the narrative." He continues, "You need to understand that there's an American hero, and you can be a hero in the same exact way, but you can't be an American hero. Because you weren't American."

After contract struggles, Kobayashi refused to participate in the 2010 competition. He instead attended the contest in protest of Shea's treatment of him, wearing a T-shirt reading FREE KOBI and leading the crowd in cheering "Let him eat!" as Chestnut competed onstage for another win. Kobayashi was in full possession of the showmanship that had made America love him— he's since stated that he was just there to support, but media of the time suggested he hopped onstage to make a statement and shake Joey Chestnut's hand in a show of public goodwill. The Sheas saw the ruckus, and called security—twenty years after George Shea's mentor first encouraged him to have a hot dog eater arrested at an event.

Kobayashi was thrown against the barricade beside the stage and arrested in public—Major League Eating claimed that he was attempting to disrupt the contest, permanently terminating their involvement with the man who had built them to begin with. He was banned from the 2011 event, removed from their Wall of Fame, and lost his sponsorships from Heinz Ketchup, Pepto-Bismol, and Old Navy. In exchange, the ratings for the next year's contest dipped significantly. Chestnut called him crazy in the press following the altercation, but changed his tune in 2019, saying that it "took strength" and he was "amazed that he was able to walk away."

Kobayashi has endured as a legend after his removal from the sport in America—he began to set hot dog eating records across the city from the contest he was banned from, a community-building tradition he continues to this day. More recently, he's done smaller ad campaigns for pest control company Terminix and filmed customized Cameos, while Chestnut has held down his legacy in addition to larger sponsorships from Raising

Cane's, Dude Wipes (I can't talk to you about Dude Wipes, I'm out of words for the book, but these appear to be wipes for . . . dudes), and a vanity mustard brand in 2022 alone. There is no doubt that Kobayashi was fucked beyond reason during his time in the MLE, removed from a sport he made popular in the US, and replaced by a white American who appears to have found it easier to capitulate to the whims of the insidious marketing Sheas than to point out what he appears to know is right.

"I thought the US was a place where people would be recognized as an American hero because of their achievements," Kobayashi said in 2019, frustrated. "I'd thought that where you come from and what race you are had nothing to do with it."

To this day, there are very few competitive eaters who are able to make their living from the sport. In the mid-2010s, Shea estimated that Joseph was the only person to make a significant living at an estimated $200,000 a year—Kobayashi is thought to have made several million dollars during his time in the sport, and others have built significant followings on YouTube that have created a financially sustainable fan base. Still, the vast majority of people onstage keep their day jobs—even 2021 second-placer Geoffrey Esper is a teacher first, eater second.

Shea's take on Kobayashi's reaction in 2010 remains firmly rooted in marketing impressions. He told *MEL* in 2021: "When Kobayashi stormed the stage, it was phenomenal. Unfortunate in so many ways, but phenomenal for press . . . it was always about free media."

Well, sweetheart, here's some more.

The VIP entrance to Maimonides Park is crowded with eager spectators when we arrive three full hours before the contest begins. One guy in a hat reading LEAH'S DADDY and a shirt reading I ATE MORE HOT DOGS THAN MOST PEOPLE jabbers with a man a full foot shorter than him who's not wearing a shirt at all, while I manage to find one of the myriad masked day gig workers wearing BUN BOY IN TRAINING on a cheap nametag. I mean, my God.

I'm able to get past the press table where they're expecting me, slapping on limp red wristbands labeled FIELD ACCESS that allow us into the bowels of a park best known for minor league baseball. I wander through the long cement hall and hear a voice that almost sounds like—Holy shit, there he is, ten feet from me. It's Joey Chestnut in his signature jersey, the red-and-white shirt with the Nathan's logo and a cartoonish Uncle Sam giving a thumbs-up on the front, CHESTNUT strewn across the back like he's about to play baseball instead of eat seventy-six hot dogs. He's standing next to another legend, one my boyfriend is over the moon about—Eric "Badlands" Booker, who made a name for himself as a champion chugger with a gigantic YouTube following. They've been competing together for years, and I try to play it cool as I slink past their hug and a handwritten sign that points to the Judges' Lounge and into the beating sun where the press pit is assembling.

There's not a ton of quality control going on here—everyone from student reporters to ESP-fucking-N to, yes, me, are assembled without masks in a pack by a sweetheart in a polo shirt, miniskirt, and Hello Kitty backpack named Henry who is being paid exactly enough to give about 40 percent of a shit what's going on. Their main task is to stop us from bothering the competitors and from going into the *real* VIP area, where competitors' family members and local radio contest winners get within Joey's spitting distance. We try to plant ourselves and look normal as an old man in a cowboy hat holding an acoustic guitar soundchecks a simple, potent song that begins:

Hot dogs out on the grill, Joey's in for the kill

He continues to "celebrate the nation's anniversary . . . thankful to be free."

A few feet to his left, three dancers in sundresses practice a synchronized routine they'll perform between musical and eating acts throughout the afternoon. Just as in the WWE events that the contest appears to be modeled on, women's bodies are relied on for entertainment in the form of dancers and counters, crop-topped day gig workers keeping an eye on how many hot dogs each eater has successfully completed to keep score. Yes, women are allowed to compete in the sport, but the contest has been separated by The Two Genders (heavy sigh) since 2011, with the women's competition consistently sidelined.

The women of this contest, presented as the opening act for the Chestnut main event, are not the subject of documentaries in spite of equally intense rivalries and training regimens. This year is particularly interesting in the women's contest—the seventime reigning champion Miki Sudo can't compete because she is pregnant with another hot dog eater's baby.

Not to wave my anthropological know-how in your face, but the most important question when examining any niche community is this—is anyone fucking? Who's fucking? And if they're fucking, how can I know more about the fucking? If this is your only takeaway from this book, I've still provided you with a doctoral education.

Here's another secret—the answer is *always* yes. Someone is always fucking someone else with the same very specific profession as them, whether you're scanning the Olympic Village or backstage at Nathan's Hot Dog Eating Contest. Longtime women's champion Sudo and third-place men's competitor Nick Wehry are the most famous couple at this event, meeting hours before the 2018 contest at a hotel gym and hitting it off. They're far from the only ones—the competitive eating community is full of couples falling in love in an objectively hopeless place. Second-place 2021 women's champion Sarah Rodriguez is married to and trains with fellow competitor Juan Rodriguez; Joey Chestnut was briefly engaged to eater Neslie Ricasa; Randy Santel and Katina DeJarnett are competitive-eating YouTubers who carpooled to a pizza eating contest in Alaska and fell in love at first sight; Rich and Carlene LeFevre were major competitors at the Nathan's competitions of the 2000s, later retiring to Nevada and becoming big supporters of then Las Vegas–based Sudo in her early career. Yes, of *course* there's fucking, and it's one of the many highly exploitable angles the Sheas have emphasized within their sport.

George Shea comes out to hype up the crowd in his, and I hope this sounds condescending, *little hat* before bringing on Badlands Booker and a chugging protégé to entertain the crowd. Back-to-back, Badlands demolishes in a lemonade drinking contest and performs a rap before a *very* tepid local's performance of "God Bless America." The stage is set for the women's contest, and Shea howls to the unmasked masses.

"This is the biggest, most important live in-person event since the pandemic ended, and since New York rose again like a phoenix from the flames to take his position!"

The comparative lack of coverage and interest in the women's contest by the media and the MLE itself is a fact that the league's champions (who win a pink belt, as if you needed to guess) have been extremely vocal about. It is a level of bullshit not often found in a time where most industries have developed a system to, at very least, *pretend* that women are a meaningful part of their sport.

"To be dismissed as an opening act is disappointing," Miki Sudo said before winning her third title in 2016.

Sarah Rodriguez echoed this sentiment in an interview conducted alongside her husband in 2021. "We're on the same stage thirty minutes prior, they literally clean it off and they don't show us [on the same channel]," she said. "We train just the same."

Michelle Lesco said the same in an ESPN interview the day she took good friend Sudo's title. "As a girl growing up in sports, you don't really ever feel like you're gonna have the opportunity to win a big event."

Miki Sudo is a pragmatist, whether it's regarding her own body or how the sport treats her gender. She famously rejected the results of a study that insisted that eating a single hot dog took thirty-six minutes off of her one human life, telling *Inside Edition*, "I will take that study with a grain of salt, and how that grain of salt affects my lifespan is yet to be determined."

Of ESPN and Major League Eating's treatment of her, she is primarily irked at the lack of equal pay for women, telling *TMZ* in 2018 that she didn't "need to get my fifteen seconds of fame, but I *would* like to get paid."

One thing is clear—no matter how equally compelling the rivalries, George Shea and Major League Eating don't have a vested interest in women. It's obvious not just from their contest's placement in the event's runtime, but from Shea's commitment to announcing it, only lending his signature editorial introductions to the top three women competitors in a somewhat less enthusiastic tone. He brings up the correctly assumed winner of the day's event, Arizona's Michelle Lesco (Tucson, AZ / Age: 37 / Weight: 112) onto the stage:

"She has lived her life surrounded by the nimbus of power, for as a child the ancient lightning that destroys the unworthy and anoints the pure came down and touched her on the forehead, and she is ranked number two in the world . . . fierce angel, elegant angel, breathtaking queen, Michelle Lesco!"

In competitive eating, it's uncommon to separate athletes by gender—sure, there are your occasional male wunderkinds like Kobayashi and Chestnut, but there are plenty of women running laps around their counterparts. Most notably, Sudo holds the current women's record at 48.5 hot dogs and buns, a figure that exceeds her fiancé Nick Wehry's personal best. None of that mattered to the MLE, with the women's monetary prize only a quarter of the men's when the league was first separated. This has since been rectified, but only after press and social media outcry—the women's contest itself grew less emphasized in the event and league's coverage on the whole as years passed.

So why? The buck, as with all things Nathan's Hot Dog Eating Contest, stops with George and his brother and business partner, Richard Shea.

"I don't know that the thinking's parochial. It was more embracive," George Shea said in 2011, the first year that women were separated from the main contest.

Among hot dog women, the decision was polarizing—for champions it meant less coverage, but the split did mean that it became easier for new competitors to qualify for the event. Whether one agreed with them or not, the Sheas' intention remained focused on encouraging the controversy, going so far as to throw a tea party at the Plaza Hotel for women the night before the contest to make their new status within the MLE clear.

ESPN is an even larger eraser of the women's contest, airing it all the way in the TV suburbs of ESPN3 since its inception in 2011, with the exception of the unusual 2020 indoor broadcast. Now that the event is live again, the women's event has been nudged back into obscurity. Unlike the heavily publicized Chestnut, the primary way for women to distinguish themselves as public figures in the sport is not just to be good at what they do, but to create the myth around themselves that George Shea happily does on behalf of the male competitors. For years, there was no one better than Sonya "Black Widow" Thomas.

Thomas's career is a uniquely American one—a naturalized citizen by way of South Korea, the "Black Widow" worked as a Burger King manager at Andrews Air Force Base in Maryland and became a fierce competitor in the world of eating in the mid-2000s, when everyone still competed together. Like virtually all competitors at the time, she became motivated to take up the sport after seeing Kobayashi on television in 2002, becoming one of his main threats only two years later.

No one can introduce Thomas better than she can, most recently in an extensive FAQ section on her website in 2018, at which time she still proudly managed the Air Force Burger King and was a big fan of Amy Grant, The Carpenters, and the Backstreet Boys. One of the first things she addressed was her nickname—please enjoy falling in love with her.

"Because like the female black widow spider, it is my desire to eliminate the males," she writes. "In competitive eating I want to eat more or faster than the men. I want to make boys out of them." I'll say it! She sounds like a domme.

The Black Widow first put herself on the map at the 2004 Wing Bowl in Philadelphia (167 wings in thirty-two minutes, thanks for asking) as the first woman ever to win the competition, weighing ninety-nine pounds at the time. She soon set the record for women's hot dog eating in 2005 and was a fierce competitor of Kobayashi's, at one point besting him in the bratwurst category.

After a streak of wins, the success of a then twenty-one-year-old Joey Chestnut left Thomas reassessing her training approach. She was a rival of both Kobayashi and Chestnut in spite of her omission from popular history, at one point holding a strong pound-for-pound lead over Kobayashi in burger eating contests and defeating Chestnut several times over, first edging him out by a single burger, then dominating him at turkey and meatball eating contests in 2005.

While she developed training techniques to suit her body just like any other competitor, Thomas's early success was often dismissed as symptomatic of an eating disorder.

"She's just so small. I wonder how she keeps it all down," commented an associate professor of nutrition and food science at the University of Maryland. "It wouldn't surprise me if she was bulimic. After the time limit has expired, she may just throw it all up."

That's not to say that disordered eating isn't a valid subject to explore within the sport, or its effects on the health of its competitors. The physical toll of eating contests appears to be all but verboten for eaters to discuss in the public sphere, in spite of the deaths of competitors like Stephanie Torres, an ex-MLE eater who died of low potassium levels during an eating contest road trip in 2015, nor the sudden and unexplained passing of ostensibly healthy fifty-four-year-old MLE cranberry sauce eating champion Juliet Lee in 2019. In an interview with FOX 5 following Lee's death, George Shea made a point to mention that "I can say that it certainly had nothing to do with competitive eating."

The discussion of eating disorders and health maintenance shouldn't be avoided—it's just that you don't often see the conversation about it revolving around a man. While Sonya Thomas was randomly speculated to be bulimic, Joey Chestnut was at home choking on air, but I digress.

The thing to remember is that Thomas was once considered as strong a threat to Kobayashi's reign as Joey Chestnut, appearing in a MasterCard commercial with Kobi in 2007 that highlighted their ongoing rivalry with era-appropriate offensive samurai music. She still holds records in asparagus, cheesecake, chicken nuggets, chili, crab cakes, eggs, jambalaya, MoonPies, oysters, pizza, tacos, tater tots, and turducken. The woman is a goddamn legend, and competed alongside Kobayashi and Chestnut from 2004 to 2010 before the contests were separated, placing second in the overall competition in 2005 and holding strong in fourth place the year before she could no longer compete against Chestnut at all.

"She looks so lovely," George Shea said of Thomas as she devoured forty hot dogs in perfect syncopation to "Superbass" by Nicki Minaj during the first women's-only contest. "Not once has she violated table manners, she's absolutely an elegant young lady, and yet she has the jaw of a German shepherd!"

Thomas's changing feelings about the removal of women from the main contest are interesting to track. She explained to food blog Eater in 2011 that she had grown to be supportive of the decision after giving it thought.

"Initially, I felt as if competing in a women's division of the Nathan's finals was an admission of not being able to eat as many hot dogs and buns as men," she said. "But, having finished in the top five or six at the finals every year since I started in 2003 means I've finished ahead of at least two-thirds of the best eaters in the world—men included—so that's pretty good."

Thomas's support of the decision was hinged on the hope that two champions instead of one would mean better endorsement deals, press, and attention for women competitors.

"Unless you win Nathan's July 4th event, no one pays attention to you," she continued. "Having a ladies' division will not only enable its winner to get noticed, the guys will certainly remember us, and the female fans will identify with us too. What better way is there to encourage more women to compete?"

This statement hinged on the assumption that the women's contest would be given equal emphasis by ESPN and Major League Eating—a reality that never materialized. At the time, Thomas attempted to justify the initial cash prize for women, then a quarter of the men's money, by saying it would be offset by increased media attention.

"This is the first year of separating genders, and it would be wrong and greedy of me to expect the same payout for the ladies as the men," she continued. "Once we women rapidly build on our fan base, the purses should grow accordingly."

In 2018, the year after Thomas's last appearance on the Nathan's stage, she reflected on how men received her during her competitive prime on her website when asked how they felt about losing to her.

"When I first started eating competitively in mid-2003, some of the men that I defeated, from time-to-time, had a tough time accepting defeat from a member of the opposite sex, especially a little one like me," she wrote. "Even though I am now looked upon more as one of the guys, much jealousy remains. I suspect it always will."

More than ten years later, the women's contest is still broadcast on ESPN3, and Thomas and Kobayashi no longer compete—even in the silliest American structure, the Joey Chestnuts of the world are given increased opportunity to succeed over others. The Black Widow made the best of the patronizing treatment and easily became the first women's champion to be bestowed with the bright pink Pepto-Bismol belt—nearly identical to the WWE Divas Championship belt of the same era—and the significantly smaller $2,500 prize.

Then came 2014, shortly before Thomas's forty-seventh birthday, as a crop of young women eaters, Miki Sudo and Michelle Lesco included, began to nip at her heels. Sudo rocketed forward from a fourth-place finish to the top, eating 34 hot dogs to Thomas's 27 ¾—Lesco came just behind the Black Widow at 27 even. The Black Widow would continue to compete through her fiftieth year in 2017, but would never recapture the top title.

You cannot convince me that there is anyone more fascinating in competitive hot dog eating than Sonya Thomas.

Following her departure from the sport, Miki Sudo slid into the role of women's champion with ease. Eighteen years Thomas's junior with a charismatic Las Vegas–bred presence, Sudo lived in New York, Tokyo, Hawaii, and California growing up before getting interested in competitive eating in her twenties, beginning as a pho eating wunderkind in 2012. She qualified for the Nathan's contest in 2013 and was on a roll after defeating Chestnut in a ribs eating contest, but had to drop out for an absolutely unhinged reason—she, whoops, threatened to blow up a plane on the anniversary of September 11.

Okay, hear her out, it's pretty funny. As it was presented in the media, Sudo's ex-boyfriend took her credit card to purchase a series of flights back in 2010, a charge that Sudo spent hours on the phone with the airline trying to reverse.

"I did snap. I was swearing. Never at any point did I intend to convey that anybody on any flight was going to be hurt," she told *Las Vegas Weekly* in 2014. Unfortunately, the flight, which was already in the air, had had mechanical issues before takeoff, and Sudo was reported as saying "blow up the plane" multiple times in frustration. She was charged with conveying false information and hoaxes and took a plea deal, ultimately sentenced to ten months in home confinement.

She spent that time becoming, well, extremely fucking good at eating hot dogs, harnessing her stress in the same way Chestnut internalized the end of his relationship a year later to surge forward professionally in a major way. Like Joey, Miki Sudo hasn't lost a Nathan's contest since—she also holds world records in kimchi, ice cream, and wild rice eating.

Sudo and Lesco know each other well, training together for the same contest that Sudo got house-arrested out of participating in, but Sudo remains professional when commentating on ESPN alongside Richard Shea during the 2021 events, noting that her friend hasn't broken her personal best since 2017. As for Rodriguez, Sudo praises her steady progress through the years, but wryly notes that Sarah and Juan Rodriguez are the *second*-most famous hot dog eating couple on Coney Island today.

When the women's contest begins, male models tasked with counting hot dogs consumed keep track of the two favorites in particular, with Lesco and Rodriguez neck and neck for the first several minutes. Lesco thrives on the energy of the crowd, whipping her ponytail around and looking to the crowd for encouragement as she shoves hot dogs into her mouth, moving her body sporadically with a ten-year-refined jumping approach to keep herself limber and energized throughout the ten-minute event. Rodriguez stands firmer, a tall woman with long curly hair who ignores the crowd and wears a pair of bright red headphones to listen to her own soundtrack and filter out the havoc. Halfway in, Rodriguez takes a significant lead over Lesco, though Sudo notes that this doesn't cinch a victory.

"I think Joey and I are the only ones who pick it up in the last few minutes," she says.

Sudo knows her stuff, Rodriguez's lead doesn't last long. As a tall woman who is also sweating, it's hard for me to not root for the deeply charismatic Rodriguez, maybe the most ardent of women's advocates in the sport.

"I bet there's a ton of good eaters out there that are women that would crush it, they're just, you know, we're not seeing them," Rodriguez said in the days before I see her compete. "You don't even see us on the contest, so if I can get women's faces out there and encourage them to show up and try, then—"

On the broadcast, Sudo reacts with her signature indifference, saying she's happy for her former training partner Lesco while noting the count "isn't official yet." The men commentating—Richard Shea included—seem to have no idea what to say, and defer to her opinion on The Woman Stuff.

"2021, year of the woman, Juliana Hatfield touring again, Nicki Minaj very much on the comeback, and I think Michelle is cruising to victory," the ESPN commentator says, sweating through his clothes. Come on, buddy, stick the landing! "Free Britney, bring on the fireworks!"

Am I awake? As Michelle Lesco's mouth corners become the pasty whitish-brown of a hot dog bun, I remember that I *am* awake and it's basically against my will.

Lesco picks up the pace for the victory with a personal best—30.75 hot dogs and buns, her smirk tempered by the fact that she very obviously feels like dogshit. Sarah Rodriguez finishes in second with 24 hot dogs and buns, whipping her headphones off and hair down as George Shea announces, beaming to the crowd, another personal best.

ESPN interviewed Lesco following her win, an unofficial challenge issued to any person who just ate more hot dogs than one should be able to and survive. For a crowd that very much expects the Lescos, Sudos, and Chestnuts of the world to immediately flee the stage and throw up, they need to prove that they can hold it down and drape their championship belt over their shoulder, answering questions from the press without breaking a meat sweat. Lesco looks sickly and grateful, mentioning her close friendship with Miki Sudo before praising herself.

"It was a lot of hard work to get here," she says. "I was doubting myself a little bit leading into it."

Maybe you're a more progressive feminist than I am and don't care what Joey Chestnut thinks about the women's contest. I am not that person—here is what he said while sitting beside Miki Sudo in 2016 right after they won their respective contests.

"It just doesn't seem ladylike," he said. "I hope that will change."

Wow. Thank you, babe.

(Author's note: Miki Sudo returned for her crown in 2022, eclipsing Lesco with forty hot dogs as her own precious tube-o-meat baby cheered her from the front row. Reader, when I tell you I cried, believe me.)

After Kobayashi's departure from the MLE, Joey Chestnut became an American god—not that that excepted him from his own humanity. He won the Nathan's contest eight years in a row after his two Kobayashi defeats until the decade-younger Matt Stonie, who'd made his name as a speed eater on YouTube, began to catch up to his numbers. This quickly translated to professional competition, and Stonie began creeping on Chestnut's record in 2014 when finishing at fifty-six hot dogs to Joseph's winning sixty-one.

Something else happened at the contest in 2014, a legendary moment that George Shea and my unconscious mind constantly reference to this day. Joey Chestnut, now the well-established king of competitive eating, proposed to his longtime girlfriend and trainer Neslie Ricasa *onstage* before winning the contest. It's fucking electric. George Shea is in on the ruse and brings Neslie onstage, talking her up as Joseph enters unseen to her.

"Let me ask you something," Shea says, arm around Ricasa. "Do you think that Joey Chestnut has what it takes to be a man?"

Ricasa raises her fist as Chestnut comes into view, beaming. "Yeah I do, just like everybody here thinks Joey Chestnut has it!"

George Shea pats Joseph on the shoulder and hands him the microphone. Joey regresses to the shyness of his early competition years as he sinks to one knee, mumbling that "this has been the best three years of my life and I can't, I don't want to live without you. You make me better. Will you marry me?"

She says yes and they're so happy, they kiss in the shadow of a roller coaster in front of thousands of freaky nationalists and hot dog fans alike. He wins the contest. He's getting married. 2015 should absolutely have been his year, but the hot dog world giveth and the hot dog world taketh away.

The next year, Joey Chestnut is brought onstage to "Baba O'Riley" by The Who as always, as one with "the courage to stand for a nation when all others turn away," his legacy inscribed into history in every language in the world "including Klingon," as "America itself." As the contest begins, Joseph looks more in his head than usual, his eyes dead, his body language drooping— all the while Stonie is on fire, moving his body to accommodate the dogs. Something feels *weird*.

An ESPN commentator tells us why, screaming the truth mere inches from Chestnut himself. "Last year on this very stage, Joey Chestnut proposed to his longtime girlfriend and eating coach, Neslie," she said. "They have since parted ways and broken up, but he does have a familiar face in his corner today—his brother, Willie."

Chestnut darts a quick glance to the back of the broadcaster's head—he heard everything.

That's the nature of the Nathan's contest—even the champion of the world is not safe from public humiliation if it means more press, a fact that ESPN announcers and George Shea prove over and over throughout the ten-minute contest every year.

"He's fighting through it," an announcer said on national television. "We learned that he did not indeed marry his fiancée, which might have been an emotional . . . challenge for him." After complimenting Chestnut's technique in slamming thirty-nine hot dogs in just over five minutes, he continued, "and yes, he's a single man, he's back to flirting with the girls at Panera Bread after this."

I mean, shit.

Sweet Joseph lost to Matt Stonie 60–62 and took it hard, losing his future wife and defining professional achievement in the space of a few months. This meant a lot was riding on 2016, and he spent it just as his colleague Miki Sudo had while under house arrest for threatening to blow up a commercial airplane—eating a shitload of hot dogs with extreme precision.

Between the 2015 and 2016 contests, Chestnut made sure there would be nothing to make light of, demolishing his own records—he improved by ten full dogs with seventy consumed in 2016, seventy-two in 2017, seventy-four in 2018, and seventy-five at the indoor, audience-free COVID-friendly contest in 2020. Now back in front of the crowd in 2021, the man I walked by in the dugout is here to compete with only himself.

We Are Politely Staring at Joey Chestnut

The way Ernest Hemingway would have.

ESPN is turning over their camera crew in another middle finger to the women's contest—*now* the real event is beginning, and the crowd behind us stand in line to buy hot dogs and beer as we continue to fucking *roast* among the other reporters. It never occurred to me that I might spend the day here starving, but that's what's come to pass as Henry and the other gig workers have nothing to offer us but water bottles and swag bags (Bounty-branded tote bag, sunglasses, a little timer watch, and a bathrobe for some reason). There's not a granola bar in sight while the servants of Nathan warn us that to mix among the hot dog chomping peasants just feet away in the stands is a safety risk.

Fuck 'em—I slip past Henry and the bright red, throbbing Nathan's hot dog mascot being interviewed by a college reporter and into the stands. I need a hot dog, and I need to know who these people are.

The event is free, so there's a fair number of people eager to once again walk maskless among the masses—veterans and front-line workers who got seating preference, a couple kids sneaking sips from their parents' Heinekens, nationalists in head-to-toe

American flag regalia that scans to the average leftist as menacing. Still, *most* of the people are here to see Little Miss Joseph specifically. I talk to groups of young women in Joey tank tops and push-up bras, moms who want to fuck Joey, dads who want to be Joey, kids who watch Joey on YouTube, a man in a cape for no reason, a gay couple whose shared crush on Joey first brought them together. The manic energy of the contest ripples through the bleachers as everyone walks around like the plague never happened. This is sticky and sweaty and familiar, and no one is looking out for themselves in the interest of having a good time.

"It's outside, so, uh," one maskless man tells me. "Can't get it out here." Best of luck!

I bump into a guy named Grayson in the hot dog line, a twenty-something whose hair is tied in a bandana, wearing a T-shirt with Chestnut's image emblazoned across the front. He tells me he's driven here all the way from Tennessee to see Joseph compete for the second time, and has been watching eating competitions "from the time I was born, probably."

"I aspire to try it one day," he tells me. "I admire Joey Chestnut, he's been a role model to me for years but I know I could never measure up."

I bring half a hot dog back down to the press pit in my pocket, hoping Henry is none the wiser to my blatant disregard of the hot dog rules. The field is flooded with unmasked people chanting "Joey! Joey!" as the sun grows hotter, mostly family and friends of competitors and the exhausted press pit. In our midst are more shoddily masked faces, either legacy reporters who delight in the tradition or college-aged stringers who couldn't be more upset to be there. My boyfriend is right where I left him, still talking to the same five-foot-nothing old man in a gray cargo vest, checkered shirt, jeans, and a baseball cap—an outfit that makes the already sweltering heat ten degrees hotter. The man doesn't seem to notice, and that's because the man is Al Freni.

Reader, I need to tell you about Al Freni.

Any New York reporter in the press pit who's been at it for a while knows Al Freni—he's been a veteran photographer in the area since he was a teenager. When two middle-aged writers in polos notice us talking with Al as he weaves tales from four decades before I ever existed and I resist the urge to fact-check him in real time, they corner us.

"We don't want anyone being mean to Al," one says protectively, looking to his friend. I won't learn that Al is nearly ninety years old until much later in the afternoon—you'd never know from how sturdily he stands in the sweltering summer heat. Al is a loudmouth who will tell his life story to anyone who'll listen, but if you had a life like Al's and there wasn't much of it left to live, you would too.

"I shouldn't be doing this, I'm too old to be doing this, but I love doing it," he tells me, gesturing to the stadium. "I've been taking pictures all my life."

Freni was born in Queens in 1933 and has lived there ever since, save the four years he served in the Korean War, and tells us the last time he took a trip was to Washington, DC to be honored for his presidential portraits by the White House. He can tell I'm not convinced right away and laughs, asks me to "do the Google thing to check. Al Freni, Eisenhower."

Reader, Al Freni was not lying. After learning as a ten-year-old that he lived two blocks from *Life* photographer Alfred Eisenstaedt, he bought his first camera for $1.79 and later attended the School of Industrial Art (currently the High School of Art and Design) in Manhattan. In 1951 he was declared the senior "most probably to succeed," and didn't take long to deliver on the promise—after spending about a year as an Air Force mechanic, he began photographing for the military and took his most famous portrait in 1954, at twenty-one years old.

"People say 'baloney.' I say 'don't bet me.'" He laughs, asking if we'd like to bet $1,000 or a car on it as Katy Perry's "Firework" blares in the background.

Freni's sincerity takes me there, all while I'm sweating through the itchy tourist cotton T-shirt I bought when we didn't see *The Thing* in Arizona. It was 1955, and the young Freni was asked to photograph a highly staged setup of Eisenhower golfing, horseback riding, and fishing with his grandson David. Then press secretary James Hagerty had orchestrated the photo op so closely that live trout had been driven in and put into the water so that David would catch it in the shot—but no one was betting that David and his grandfather would wander away. Freni was the only photographer who followed them, capturing a sweet image of the president and David on a short pier, the kid casting his line while his grandpa looked on in a flannel and cowboy hat.

Freni will be the first to tell you the image was one partially staged and hollow, but believes in the affection that comes across in it, and is proud of its legacy. The photo ran in the *Rocky Mountain News* and has been reproduced over and over in textbooks and encyclopedias, including a personal request for forty prints from President Eisenhower himself. Sure, the image is sort of a lie, but what nugget of Americana from "the old days" isn't? The president signed a print for the photographer—"for Alfred Freni, with best wishes, Dwight Eisenhower"—and Freni was promoted to a sergeant in the Air Force as a direct result.

There are little moments that make you want to believe the American dream isn't complete horseshit, aren't there? But a gasp of hot dog air will sober you up.

There are many fucking fascinating things about Al Freni that I learn later—most relevant to my interests is that he took the iconic Pet Rock promotional photo in the '70s—but Freni's takeaway from the Eisenhower photo's success was his own willingness to look at things differently.

"You stick with something long enough, either you're fired or maybe you've got something," he tells me. "Out there in the rain—you're the only guy that showed up in the rain when everyone else is goofing off, and you're in the right place at the right time. That's the whole trip, right there. That's the trip."

I could spend the rest of the afternoon with Al, but the crowd is filtering back into the stands and beginning to froth for Joseph, a person who I completely forgot existed for the half hour during which Al was telling me his life story. Al had a personal studio in the Time-Life Building for decades, he had the second New York press credential ever issued, tells us his ex-wife was born the same date Kennedy was assassinated, has photographed every president from Eisenhower to Trump, remembers all the reporters he's ever met in the pit and asks them how their babies are.

"You never know. I need to shave sometimes. I want to fit right in," he says, observing the crowd. "The minute you start to look like you're above, the door gets closed, you don't get the information you want. You gotta look like you're just doing a job. And I am!"

Then he takes his camera and goes back to work.

At the front of the stadium, George Shea is back on his bullshit, bringing a man onstage to a chorus of loud boos. It's not without reason—the man in question is then New York City mayor Bill de Blasio, he of the failed 2020 presidential campaign and the 37 percent approval rating. The crowd isn't shy about letting him know how they feel, much of it due to his mismanagement of the COVID-19 crisis and his response to the George Floyd protests the previous year, but de Blasio doesn't react and continues to act out the half-hearted skit prepared before presenting Michelle Lesco with the pink Pepto-Bismol belt. A few months later, de Blasio would be ineligible to run for the mayoral election and the hot dog heathens would become the problem of Mayor Eric Adams, who—we don't have time, the contest is beginning.

Because the world of hot dog eating is built to give deference to the men's contest, there is a noticeable *shift* in the energy of the stadium when George Shea poises himself to introduce the competitors he really cares about. As he's teeing up, a failed marriage proposal takes place in the stands—a man in an American flag tank top and cargo shorts gets on one knee as his girlfriend, a blond woman profoundly out of his league in the ugliest Zara maxi dress these eyes have ever seen, rejects him.

She can do two things I could never do—say no to someone she loves, and say no to someone she loves in public. He grasps her hand as she starts to walk up the bleacher seats, and glances over his shoulder as he realizes he's not going to see Joey Chestnut eat seventy-six hot dogs with his future wife after all.*

George Shea brings up the competitors—legends like Crazy Legs Conti and Juan Rodriguez, and Chestnut's closest competitors, Miki Sudo's baby daddy, Nick Wehry, and soft-spoken Massachusetts high school teacher Geoffrey Esper. Then, Joseph comes to the stage as Shea inflates, shouting to the heavens with an introduction that was cowritten by three other people. He lets it rip for the camera:

"In an endless universe of infinite matter and energy, we have been given consciousness to gaze upon it all and understand. What greater fortune have we? To live in America, to stand side by side on the Fourth of July, to behold *this man,* what greater fortune?

"Like the force of life itself, he is written on the world, a belief etched in the shining machinery of our mind. Immune to the vagaries of time, entwined in the trip that binds our arms together, and when history collapses and existence has no meaning, he wants to stand for his obligation—to fight any god for

---

* Jamie's little aside: A year later when I was in the trenches of editing this book, another curveball. My brilliant friend Annie Rauwerda, who curates the Depths of Wikipedia and has chronicled some of the world's most cursed facts, informs me at our first in-person meeting that the woman who turned down the wedding proposal *was her.* The man in the tank top was comedian Johnny Gaffney, whose calling card is, and stay with me here, staging viral failed wedding proposals with people he knows. It was all fake, but standing in the middle of my Fourth of July sweat puddle, it meant something to me. Hi, Annie.

an idea, for a conviction, for freedom! For his is the blood of a nation and his is ever onward, and to the breach, pressing the charge blind to all except the object of his fury and the roar of his assault will sunder the dome of heaven to reach the ears of God himself. The number-one-ranked eater in the world, the Nathan's Famous champion of the world, *Joey Chestnut.*"

I cannot overstate how *in-ter-est-ing* it is for a completely ordinary-looking man to walk onstage after an introduction like that, and the crowd is on *fire*—they want nothing more than to see this man deep-throat a billion hot dogs. The women who just competed drink water at the front of the stage and scream along, supportive of their peers even in the face of the whole, you know, ESPN3 *thing.* Joey wins, of course he wins, he beats his own record by a single hot dog and makes the headlines just like he has thirteen times before (except the one time, but we don't talk about that). Geoffrey Esper would have been a vital competitor for Chestnut ten years ago, but in 2021 Joseph won by *twenty-six hot dogs.* The only question is if he'll win against himself from the previous year.

At the start of the contest, I don't understand the appeal. By the end, I'm in love with him. Here's what it feels like:

Ten minutes to go: Joey comes in hot, falling into a fluid motion that means this will be a good contest. The people in the stands are leaning forward in their foam hats and screaming, looking to their families and back at Joey, covered in sweat, no one able to take a bite of their own hot dog while he is at *work.* I don't understand it—this man is killing himself in front of us on purpose, because we will love him if he does. He'll take in the glory, smile alongside Shea as they declare that forty thousand pounds of hot dog meat will be donated to the less fortunate, and go on a two-day water-and-lemon-juice cleanse to prevent his body from shutting down altogether.

Seven and a half minutes to go: The natural stink of the outdoor stadium forms an invisible mushroom cloud above the masses and I feel myself pulled in. Not everyone in the press pit seems to agree, but I see Al Freni bouncing on his heels between shots and know he feels it too: it's *exciting*. Joseph is pounding dog after dog with absurd focus, and any time absolute sweetheart Esper is referenced by Shea as he live commentates, the crowd pops with a boo almost as hard as they did for their own jagoff mayor. Esper doesn't deserve it, but he's the chosen villain of the operation, Steve Austin versus Joey's The Rock. I can hear the playback broadcast from the tinny speakers of the ESPN production iPads in front of me, and the unhinged excited cadence of the announcers pulls me in further. "Joey Chestnut eats hot dogs the way Hemingway wrote novels," one says, and I . . . agree, I fucking agree. This is *athleticism*.

Five minutes to go: I'm breathing heavily for some reason, why am I breathing like this? George Shea is hollering over the roar of the crowd and the smacking of jaws about Joseph's journey, breezing through his romantic history and failed engagement as Joseph continues to pound food and I feel the hot dog pheromones pulsing from his skin complete their journey from the stage to my nostrils. It all hits at once, I can *fix him*, the titties whipped out in the crowd suddenly make sense, this is a *man* who has *sacrificed* for his *craft* and needs *love,* hey that could be me too, hey this person makes perfect sense, yes, let's talk about it later, I love you Joey, let's get you the fuck out of here.

Two minutes to go: Around fifty-six hot dogs, something in the air changes—the sex chemicals turn to solid meat and fall to the ground, oh shit, oh wait, no, my first instinct was right. This is the most fucked-up thing I've ever seen, and we're killing Joey Chestnut because it's fun to watch. This man is dying. I can see the blood being pushed to the surface of his skin and his breathing change as he pushes his own guts around to accommodate the record the people want. He's going to get to seventy-six if it kills him, and it doesn't today, but surely soon?

Ten seconds: George Shea is foaming at the mouth as Joseph crosses the seventy-five-hot-dog threshold. Joseph is all focus, and I miss the artful touch of Kobayashi as Joseph *grabs* the final dog and "clears" it (nothing hanging out of his mouth) before the buzzer sounds. The crowd loses their shit as the un-suspecting theme park attendees scream in the distance.

He wins. America wins. I love him. I win.

The roar of the crowd fades some five hundred years later and they begin to filter out to a boiling hot afternoon. Still, Joseph has to jump through his final hoop of the day—remaining on-stage for a full forty-five minutes to answer questions from the press, again to prove he doesn't leave the stage and immediately vomit his brains out. The press section is not just allowed but *encouraged* to line up and ask Joey their single question, one after the other, most of them asking how he's feeling in body and spirit. Jo-seph burps up different versions of the same answer with the same crooked smile, glancing over to the Bounty-sponsored tent where he'll get to wipe his mouth and exhale when the crowd disperses.

"What are you gonna ask?" my boyfriend whispers to me. My mind is completely blank as Joey can be heard saying, "Feels *good*!" a few feet away.

Henry approaches. "If you want to ask a question, you should get in line," they say to me softly. I can see the two hours left in their shift reflected in their eyes. I look to Joey, to them, to him. I have no question.

"I have no question," I hear myself saying, in spite of the fact that a reporter has one job and it's to have a question.

They shrug and walk away and I grab my boyfriend's hand, suddenly overwhelmed by a need to get the fuck out of here. We say goodbye to Al, who I assume goes on to live a hundred more years, and nearly walk right into a day gig worker holding an enormous plate of hot dogs that passerby pluck up in one of the most unsanitary event moves I've ever witnessed. I've seen this plate before.

"Is that—" I say.

"Joey's leftovers," the worker confirms, pushing the plate toward us. It's disgusting and of course I take it. It's delicious, I want a second, they really grill those things up nice for him. Moments like this are why I save my meatpacking-industry research for when Hot Dog Summer is over—in moments like this, one can't handle the truth.

As we pass through the bowels of the building, the volume kicks up behind me because Joey's reached the end of the press line and is making a beeline for the bathroom, flanked by a small entourage. The line for the bathroom is long, but the sweaty, beefy men in line know what to do when a living legend needs to shit himself.

"You can get to the front of the line, Joey, it's okay!" Joey smiles at his fans, a thick sheen of sweat covering his body.

"Don't worry about it, guys," he says, nodding into the distance. "I've got my own bathroom." He goes back to the VIP area and presumably throws up seventy-six hot dogs in the same shape they entered his body.

Why did that make me horny? Joseph Chestnut is America, USA; he is gross and complicit and smart and weird and I hate how much I like him in spite of all of it being so hard to watch. I love him. I could fix him. Right?

I forgot to tell you, we're supposed to be meeting someone outside.

We empty out of the stadium's bowels and I find the person I was trying to get in touch with when my phone overheated and I fell in love with Joey Chestnut and forgot entirely. I've worked with this person but never met him before; he's handsome, he and my boyfriend shake hands and I say let's drink, yes I'll take those mushrooms, anything to take the edge off of what I have just seen. I am a dignified and interesting person, I tell myself. I am completely fucking miserable and eating five hundred hot dogs a day. *I* feel bad for *him,* yes, that's it. We get in the gigantic line at the original Nathan's Famous Hot Dogs stand.

Let's get one thing out of the way—the hot dogs here are tourist priced into oblivion, a fact that is made further dystopian by the non-distanced, exhausted staff who desperately try to keep a mob of drunk and disorderly pier-walkers moving toward their seven-dollar chili cheese dog. This summer, the only employees to clear a fifteen-dollar-an-hour wage at Nathan's Famous Hot Dogs are the cooks, and only by sixteen cents, with the lowest-paid making only eleven dollars an hour before taxes in a city where a person with no children would need to make nearly twenty-two dollars an hour to live with a cent of disposable income. The people in line hold up their end of the bargain by blatantly not giving a shit, and I distract myself while standing between two men who are hot to me by looking at the absurdly large Nathan's menu. No one in this line is a fool, no matter how drunk—we're all getting hot dogs—but if we chose chaos, the options range from New York cheesesteak to fish and chips to clam chowder to a thirty-six-dollar lobster roll.

Still mulling over the taste of Joseph's leftovers, I keep things simple and order a chili cheese hot dog, a large Diet Coke, and cheese fries for the table. There's no doubt that the Nathan's dog is a good one—they have the good sense to use nacho cheese and a proprietary beef-blend chili so as not to overwhelm the solid snap of the natural casing on the all-beef dog. We sit among the Coney Island offerings of the day: tense parents on the brink of divorce, packs of twentysomethings blitzed on hallucinogens, the winding line of annoyed teenagers waiting for a Doja Cat concert that will start hours later and have no running water to speak of. I have never been more American. Hell, I can barely taste the ill-gotten coronavirus-era PPP loan Nathan's was forced to return the year before.

I look at my boyfriend after the man from work leaves and wonder if he knows what I'm thinking. "He was nice, right?" I ask.

He looks up at the sunset and nods. "He was really nice," he says, and smiles at me. God, I suck.

That night we head back to Ridgewood and don't go to the rooftop party, sitting next to each other on the fire escape with White Claws and watching the fireworks shoot up in different neighborhoods. It's nice. We are together in the way that we can be. I say sorry, he asks me what for, it's a beautiful night and the hosts said we can drink their beer, our host's brother works at the brewery so it doesn't even cost them anything. Tomorrow, there are more hot dogs to be eaten.

The next morning, my brain chemicals are still coming down from Joey's performance. I imagine where he is now, then remember it's probably in severe pain on a hotel toilet in Brooklyn.

Ten years ago you would call this a Woody Allen day, but now we know better and call it a Nora Ephron day. Another Central Park Sabrett, a long walk through a garden dedicated to someone I've never heard of. Our time is running short, but after we strike out at Crif Dogs (closed) and there are no soft-breaded hot dogs left at the fabulous Chinese joint Dragon Bay Bakery in Brooklyn, there is one other gigantic New York institution those in the know would draw and quarter me for missing.

Gray's Papaya isn't just famous among New Yorkers; it's a soft pop culture touchstone. Matthew Perry, eternally the Vague New York Guy, receives a box of them from Salma Hayek's character in 1997's *Fools Rush In*, as if she would ever. He is overwhelmed by the gesture, beaming at the sight of the logo. "I can't believe you did this!" he says. "This is the most wonderful birthday I've ever had." In the end, they enter a lukewarm marriage and in the 1990s it was considered very romantic for some reason.

Unlike most hot dog institutions, Gray's Papaya has only been around since 1973 and began as a spinoff of an equally successful hot dog franchise—Nicholas Gray, a former partner in the legendary Depression-era Greek joint Papaya King, created the competing business. This was *not okay* with the Papaya Kings, and those in the know consider the rivalry between the two to be active to this day. Papaya King is a local legend with the expected narrative, founded by Greek immigrant Constantine "Gus" Poulos, who began the business in 1932 as a place for fresh tropical juices. He expanded to hot dogs in response to the large German immigrant population in the area and the dish's growing popularity on nearby Coney Island. The original Papaya King has attempted to franchise without much success during its nearly ninety years in business, leaving them to duke it out with the locals.

These days, Gray's Papaya is known as a purveyor of cheap and delicious all-beef franks with a snap cooked right in the front of their flagship standing-only restaurant on Seventy-Second Street, topped with a sticky sauerkraut-and-onion topping in an untoasted Sabrett bun. On the side is their signature papaya fruit drink, a little regional diabetic treat. Still, it's constantly pitted against the business it spun off from—most thrillingly during the Hot Dog War of 1976.

The conflict got quite a bit of publicity in its day, pitting Papaya King, Gray's Papaya, and Nathan's Famous against one another during a time when the three joints were extremely close in proximity. A price war ensued, becoming an endless source of free press and entertainment for cheap-eating locals. For the record, Nathan's lost the war—they folded six months later, and both Papaya King and Gray's Papaya are thriving in their flagship locations today.

The last two decades have seen Gray's slowly edging out its

father company in popularity, employing smart publicity maneuvers ranging from endorsing Obama in the 2008 American presidential election (YES SENATOR OBAMA "WE ARE READY TO BELIEVE AGAIN," read the banner) to a $3.50 "Recession Special" (two hot dogs and a fourteen-ounce papaya drink). For an industry that generally remains politically neutral in its optics, making a statement was a bold move for Gray's—not a single place I went throughout Hot Dog Summer, nor any of the competitive eaters, make a habit of announcing their politics. Still, if the dogs are good, the customers will adjust accordingly.

"I'm here for the hot dogs and the papaya drink," said a fifty-something customer concerning the Obama endorsement in a 2008 *New York Times* piece. "Even if Gray's Papaya were supporting the most deplorable candidate imaginable and there was a big sign about it out front, I'd still be here eating hot dogs."

These days, the Gray's deal isn't what it once was, but it's still pretty damn good. The recession special costs $6.95 in 2021, with additional breakfast deals and as many as twelve hot dogs to go at a given time. The corner business is well-branded, with the signature yellow bamboo Gray's Papaya font displayed proudly above a series of bright red declarations—LET'S BE FRANK, WE WANT YOU TO BUY OUR FURTERS! WHEN YOU'RE HUNGRY, OR BROKE, OR JUST IN A HURRY! NO GIMMICKS! NO BULL! A friendly hot dog in red gloves, booties, and a chef's hat points you inside. The restaurant sings its own praises in the same red-and-yellow fonts in line as you catch the scent of all-beef dogs, with a framed photograph of John Lennon behind the register—it's unclear whether he was a customer or the business is capitalizing on being on the same street where he was murdered in 1980.

Let's not harp on it, reader—the dog snaps, the caramelized, paste-like onion sauce compliments the soft roll, and the whole thing goes down easy over a friendly conversation between you, your boyfriend, and your friend who came along gently suggesting polyamory. The best hot dog in New York? I haven't had a wide enough sampling to tell, but Gray's and Nathan's both strike me as hot dogs that taste more like a person's pleasant childhood memory than the best hot dog I've ever tasted.

We're due back to New England that evening, where another week of family fun (i.e., sleeping in a bedroom with no door, silently fuming) awaits.

A brief epilogue: in 2022, the year after Hot Dog Summer, Joseph returned to the Nathan's stage, now back at the Coney Island storefront that makes for better pictures. I keep my distance from the contest this year, retreating to Central Florida for reasons that are my business, but I follow the event like it's the birth of my own child from the back of a screening of *Minions: The Rise of Gru.* Twitter declared the year's contest to be Joey Chestnut's "flu game" (referencing Michael Jordan's championship game with the Chicago Bulls in 1996) when he arrived at Coney on crutches, having injured his leg several times in the previous year.

2022 was *not* Joseph's flu game—he won by a long shot, but didn't beat his personal best. What it *will* be remembered as is the year of the chokehold, the contest where Joey, already fighting for his life with the crutches, was surprised by a protester wearing a Darth Vader mask rushing the stage while holding a sign that said EXPOSE MITHFIELD EATHSTA. Reacting like an absolute zoo animal, Joey grabbed Vader, pulled him in a chokehold, and (if you were watching on a feed as blurry as mine) appeared to *snap his neck* with George Shea on the assist, then continued eating hot dogs. The moment was not broadcast on ESPN until later in the night, leaving online viewers only to wonder whether the hot dog eating champion of the world had, in fact, killed someone and no one had cared.

Fortunately, he hadn't, and outside of being kind of terrifying for instinctively jumping to self-defense that disarmingly scary, I don't think Joey did anything irredeemably bad. As with many things Nathan's contest, I'm tempted to once again pass the buck to Mr. George Shea—knowing his penchant for allowing his eaters to be put in danger for free spectacle, having security overlook a campily dressed protester in order to stage an extremely "USA! USA!" moment for his favorite livestock doesn't strike me as out of the question. The event has been spun by MLE as more of the pro-Joey same, the "look how scary this man is when he's in the zone" rhetoric that Shea would love.

But since the protester seemed to be okay (and, in classic police-state fashion, was arrested for nonviolent protest instead of simply being kicked out of the event), one must ask—what *is* MITHFIELD EATHSTA? It's a damn shame, is what it is, because in all of the photos of the event, the very worthy message of the protest's subject was obscured by Darth Vader's hand. The sign *should* read EXPOSE SMITHFIELD'S DEATHSTAR, explaining the costume and the company that organizers from Direct Action Everywhere hoped to criticize. Smithfield, Nathan's current distributor, kills an estimated thirty million pigs a year for their products. The specific factory involved, located in Virginia, has been accused of using inhumane gestation crates, and it was Smithfield's CEO who colluded with leadership at Tyson Foods to push forward a COVID-era executive order from former president Trump. Smithfield absolutely has blood on its hands, and not only the animals'.*

Shout out to an effective protest, and what would we have *given* for his thumb to have shifted an inch to the left.

---

* If someone e-mails me to say nice try Jamie, but animals have *paws and hooves*, I will kill myself.

We Are in the Northeast, Right?

Hot dog summer slows to a crawl.

Ten days later, I am suffering from a chronic case of Why Did My Family Never Allow Us to Have Bedroom Doors, Did That Stunt Me Sexually (Yes), and Why Have They Still Not Installed Them Now, It's Still Fucking My Shit Up. The family is kind and doing their best, my boyfriend's doing his best, I'm doing my best, and it's a complete fucking disaster. Once we see Joey Chestnut eat seventy-six hot dogs on Coney Island, it could not be more obvious we need to flee the Northeast as quickly as possible, but I've got priors in the form of New England hot dogs.

First, I return to one of the many teats of my college food trauma—Spike's Junkyard Dogs in Allston.

Allston is many things, the foremost of which is a place virtually overrun with twenty-one-year-old college students who have no idea their parents (lawyers, teachers, owners of small but lucrative businesses) are grossly overpaying for their terrible apartment that has an active overgrown rat problem. I knew many but remained adjacent to them in my time living off of Harvard Avenue one year, Commonwealth Avenue the next, all the way down in Brighton the year after in an act of poverty-stricken social suicide. In addition to not believing in bedroom doors, my parents also could not afford college for my brother or me—

even so, the private institutions who feel comfortable charging a quarter of a million dollars for a degree that boils down to "try an open mic and see how you like it" were happy to take full advantage in the form of predatory loans and a trillion part-time jobs.

Revisiting some of our nation's grimiest streets brings out a little tapeworm in me that I usually manage to Whac-A-Mole back down into my bottomless pit of psychic trauma. The Green Line subway (T, if you're a native, but I can assure you it does not matter) is a trolley tour of places I worked for eight dollars an hour in the early-to-mid-2010s, trying to scrape together enough money to make rent and student loans for a degree I honestly could have googled. There's the radio station I would turn on to play a seven-minute Springsteen song if I needed to take a shit downstairs; there's the bagel shop where I worked the day of the Boston Marathon bombing in 2013, when my manager explained that anyone could use the phone but their bagels were only free if they were actively bleeding; there's the pizza place where I got sick of being told that "tight yoga pants are uniform for counter girls," so I wrote an anonymous Yelp review about all the times we served pizza that had fallen face-first on the floor and the owner told my boyfriend he was going to take a hit out on me; there's the hockey arena where, I can't say it enough, I got fired from a hot dog stand for tweeting "fuck hot dogs." Take the B-line train down to see where I got so drunk I pissed myself for the first time on a brand of rubbing alcohol called Mr. Boston; the grocery store I was banned from for stealing guacamole and caviar; the apartment where something awful happened to me and no one believed it.

Eventually, you'll get to Spike's Junkyard Dogs, where I meet my friend and his fiancée for a hot dog I haven't tasted this side of my current tax bracket. It's a goofy yellow storefront across the street from the best Korean grocery in town, and leans into the dog theme harder than any Southern "dog house" had the energy or interest to. Above the bathroom is a picture of Chairman Spike himself, a white bulldog surrounded by goofily photo-shopped gags and novelty signs—SPIKE RULES!, SPIKE'S PRIME DIRECTIVES: GOOD CLEAN FUN, WARNING: HOT DOG ADDICTION POSSIBLE!

I look over to where I used to sit at one in the morning after getting off a shift at which my supervisor was a twenty-two-year-old in way over her head who'd fallen in love with one of the mob members who ran the place. We called him Roady, and he named every menu item after himself. My college boyfriend worked there as well, his first real job, acquired mainly as an attempt to "relate" with me. "Isn't that nice?" he asked. I hated it. We'd come to Spike's late at night to have arguments about nothing and go back to the apartment where something aw-ful happened, and the food smells like a 2013 argument to this day. I can get past this, I think, no food tastes like an argument forever. I skip their classic Junkyard Dog and opt for my Spike's go-to—the Cheesy Buffalo Dog.

What businesses that choose to print their menu in Comic Sans lack in self-awareness, they make up for in enthusiasm. It's a font so profoundly legible that it crosses into embarrassing, not to be confused with the people who use Papyrus, who I'm con-vinced are a little racist for reasons I don't have the space or lan-guage to express here. Spike's menu employs Comic Sans for the absurd number of specialty dogs for drunk college students to choose from for five bucks and under. There's the R.I. Grinder Dog, topped with Spike's grinder sauce and named for the chain's state of origin; the Samurai Dog with teriyaki sauce and sautéed onions; the Hey Now Dog with Spike's Mustard, barbecue sauce, and a pickle, named with what I'm relatively sure is a reference to a Smash Mouth song. Their signature is a low-rent riff on the Chicago hot dog, featuring a satisfying mix of mustard, tomato, pickle, hot pepper rings, and chopped scallions with the fries that Blackie's in Connecticut were too Catholic to just hand over.

My friend Jake is standing next to me in Allston during

Hot Dog Summer just like he was eight summers ago, but now we're standing with his fiancée, Alex, and I'm not worried about whether I will be able to afford to take the train home. Still, a lot is the same. Jake has been with me through everything, one of my first friends who believed the worst parts of my time in Boston, and sat with me at the IHOP that never closes while I dipped my one over-easy egg into pancake syrup and waited for my debit card to overdraft. He wants me to stay in the relationship I'm in, and I think you can love someone very much and think their advice is better applied to themselves or nobody.

Unlike most hot dog institutions that hold their eating contests once a year, Spike's has the good sense to make one happen whenever a person is brave, drunk, or both enough to declare one themselves. This is the premise of Spike's Kennel Club, an ongoing challenge with four conditions: eat as many hot dogs of your choosing as you can in ninety minutes without leaving the store or using the bathroom and receive the prize of a free T-shirt if you crest six. You can even get your photo in the Kennel Club Hall of Fame and your money back if you unseat a reigning champion. The cardinal rule is at the bottom of the poster: BLOW CHUNKS = DISQUALIFICATION.

The part of me that wants to forget I'm going to be sleeping on an air mattress in my friend's spare room wants to take my chances. The genetic makeup of the all-time champions in the Kennel Club is chilling—the women on the board are all unconscionably hot, and it makes me feel more certain that everyone knows something I don't. The male champion ate twenty-five hot dogs in one sitting, the female champion twelve, and at least one Polaroid features a person who is absolutely blackout drunk. I've debased myself worse for a free T-shirt.

The dog itself fucking rips, just like it always did. Spike's is one of the hot dog joints that taught me the simple act of toasting a bun could be the difference between a forgettable night and a late-night food that kills your hangover just enough to stop you from getting into an argument you'll regret. The all-beef dog is a decent size and generously smothered (do you associate this word more closely with food or with pussy? please report back) with blue cheese, scallions, and buffalo sauce that creates a pleasant little meat canoe on a still lake of artery-destroying thick dressings. I feel especially inclined to this style of food, having grown up nearby in a household that encouraged salad dressing to go on *everything*. In my house, you dip your french fries in Caesar dressing, or dump a bottle of Catalina on a bowl of Doritos and hamburger meat and call it taco salad.

"I want to go to Six Flags so fuckin' bad," Jake says as we eat in his Corolla. "Bet they have hot dogs there."

We don't check; we reserve the tickets and *go*. When we arrive at Six Flags New England in western Massachusetts the next morning along with my boyfriend and brother, they do have hot dogs, among other atrocities. I hadn't been since a trip with my middle school band, when the entire oboe section shit the bed on getting onto Superman: The Ride after I blurted out someone had died on it one time.

It gives me no pleasure to inform you that I am nearly twice the age of the employees at Six Flags. I find no joy in the concept of aging—just as with my adorable "body" "issues," I'm unable to apply the sound logic of treating one's age and body type as facts of life and not grounds for wanting to flip one's body inside out and bronze it like a baby shoe. Body positivity should be accessible to everyone but me, my brain has asserted every morning since I saw how much Mandy Moore "weighed" in *J-14* twenty years ago. Empathy does not apply to me—everyone is beautiful but I should not be allowed to vote. While true, these aren't the reasons that I'm disturbed to feel so old at Six Flags— it's because this means that the employees are *fifteen years old* and running a theme park where, to quote my own eighth-grade statistic, *someone died one time.*

At thirty bucks a head, this is the best deal in theme parks, which is why the company reduces money on the back end by staffing the park exclusively with horny children who stop Jake three different times to tell him that it's "so cool you can grow a beard like that, man." The pizza is fourteen dollars and cold, the soda is twelve dollars and warm, but no one cares—we can hardly believe we aren't still confined to our homes and are willing to play whatever capitalistic game is necessary to keep it that way.

The "guests" at Six Flags are just as full of unmitigated hormonal body odor as the park's employees, a perfect date for a western Mass teenager who wants his crush to know *yes*, my balls *did* drop during the pandemic, I noticed you've leveled up to a B-cup, Sarah (horrific). There are teenagers in *Playboy* jackets balking at fried dough prices, theater kids in oversized shirts reading SUPPORT SONGWRITERS AND INSTRUMENTALISTS foaming over an admittedly sexy statue of Catwoman, kids doing pushups to prove something they couldn't explain to you with a gun to their heads in front of an abandoned stall labeled LOST PARENTS.

This is one of the reasons I love my boyfriend, even when our days are numbered. It's little gestures that become huge things when they disappear—a lean into your ear, "Do you wanna go on that ride? No one will be mad at you if you wanna go on it." The Wicked Cyclone coaster nearly blows my mind out of my ass, and I'm able to bully Jake into getting in line for Superman, the same ride I hall-monitored my way out of boarding in 2005.

Unlike the elite parks—your mouse-themed, your Minions-flanked—Six Flags has no interest in telling you how long you will be waiting in line, most likely because they have no idea. Superman: The Ride is a behemoth, with a 221-foot drop that winds around the line of sweaty fifteen-year-olds and deposits you back in the gift shop with some of the most diabolical fonts known to mankind—cHiCkS DiG bAd BoYs, Catwoman and Harley Quinn proclaim, hands all over the Joker in a shirt designed for a twelve-year-old on a gaming headset.

We snake toward the front of the line, inhaling every scent of teen that I wanted to be but couldn't a decade ago, to the final vestibule, where we are unceremoniously cut off by a pack of no less than twelve middle schoolers.

They storm in front of us like it's Normandy. Twisting their freakishly thin or linebacker-cubic bodies, they blow past every Superman-shaped physical obstacle in their path, around families desperately trying to make it far enough in the day to make it worth the two-hour drive, theme-park vloggers with unforgivably large sets of teeth, teeth made for the lead in a high school musical, screaming at their iPhone 6 about how "THE PAINT JOB IS HOLDING UP REAL WELL ON THIS THING, DO YOU REMEMBER WHEN THIS ROLLER COASTER WAS PURPLE?" The middle schoolers cut us in line like they've done it before because they have, they've been doing it all day. They did it at Taco Bell yesterday too—sure, they fell out of practice while locked in their parents' homes for the last year, but the world is almost open again so they can teleport to the opposite side of a seventy-minute queue at a varsity level like no time's passed. A donut box's worth of stinky Baryshnikovs have entered the room. I think, what can you do, we're already doomed to ride a steel death trap operated by an AP student with maskne, what's another five minutes?

Jake does not see a ballet. He hates to wait, he says. Who *likes* to wait? I don't mind waiting, but only when there's someone who hates to wait nearby for me to observe. He's not gonna take this, he says. I remind him that teenagers run this place and we have no chance—the people who would mitigate this issue are their peers and think we are Fucking Cops.

"We are fifteen minutes from going on this ride," Jake says, and I realize abruptly that we look like a married couple trying to keep things going with Mandatory Fun instead of Interesting Sex. "These *fucking kids* can't just—"

My brilliant friend, my short bearded king, he *taps a fourteen-year-old on the shoulder.*

My body goes stiff. The fourteen-year-old turns, all sweat, and releases a doomsday cloud of vape smoke. He's laughing at us already. He's right. Don't look at me. "Hey, man," the kid says, laughing the entire sentence as his friends echo him, a dozen horny little hyenas capable of absolutely leveling us emotionally in a sentence or less. Jake stiffens his back, why are you doing this, we are grownups.

He says, "Hey, so I'm sure you know what I'm going to say here, but I'll say it. We've been in line for a half hour and you guys just got here. So, uh, if it's all right, we're just gonna take our spot back."

This is not going well. Their leader grows three inches by standing up straight for the first time in his life, then turns his back to Jake as if he'd said nothing. I put a hand on Jake's shoulder to acknowledge the humiliation, but he moves forward again and I feel like throwing up a hot dog I haven't even eaten yet.

"Hey, me again," he says, like it's a video game, like he knows how the scene ends. "I asked real nice before, but I'm not messing around here. We want our spot back. I don't care if you cut *them*"—he gestures at a group of English majors behind us who wish to be left out of the narrative—"but you can't cut *us*."

Five gigantic children keep their heads down to laugh, vape, and clench their fists as the line keeps moving forward. They know what's going to happen to Jake and mercifully are too afraid of grown women, even with hair as bad as mine, to make eye contact. The leader looms over Jake, and he reveals all three hundred of his nubby, half-brushed teeth. He puts his skinny finger right where my friend's heart is and says something you may want to get a glass of water before reading.

"Tough titties, old man."

Tough titties, old man.

Tough titties, old man.

Tough titties, old man.

I don't remember what happened next, exactly, only that the leader turned back to his people and I knew that any of them would die for him. He was the hero who told a man who could "grow a beard like that" *tough titties.* Jake looked like he had just survived a gunshot to the head. He asked if we could get out of line, and I heard myself saying no—this is a part of the punishment, I have enough wits about me to recognize. We can't retreat now; we need to sit next to these kids on the only roller coaster in a park where that guy died one time.

Right when we get to the front of the line, it starts raining and the ride closes for the rest of the day. Tough titties, old man.

All right, fine, I'll get a hot dog.

Theme park hot dogs aren't playing in the same league as your carts, independent joints, and vanity projects. Their purpose is to extort you out of more money than is reasonable, to fill you up just enough but not quite enough, so you'll return a second time and take it too far, and most important, good theme park food at a shitty thrill park will *not* make you throw up.

These are my expectations for Wheeler's Wild Hot Dogs, a stand just outside the Harley Quinn queue that features a sharp-toothed red dog cackling on the signage, the Scrappy Doo to Clifford's Scooby. I set my expectations on the floor and clench my ass as we pay thirteen dollars for a hot dog that is about to get rained on. Unfortunately for Wheeler's, I have a bar set for the theme park hot dog experience.

DON'T PANIC BUT WE'RE IN DISNEYLAND, JUST FOR A SECOND

I don't have many cards to play in this life, but one of them is a little withheld information. This isn't my first theme park hot dog, sweetheart. That distinction belongs to Disneyland, a park I was so thrilled to have an excuse to go to as a business expense that I barely cared when three of the four most popular themed hot dog eateries in the park were closed due to either COVID or lack of interest. This was in May 2021, a precarious and thrilling time for the privileged American who had waited their turn and gotten two doses of the COVID vaccine by mid-spring.

There are certain things that remind me of my destiny to raw dog American capitalism, get the same UTI over and over, and keep going back out of shame and lack of prospects. I skew pretty left, but I *will* wait in line at Space Mountain for an hour and foam at the mouth over the intellectual property of one of the world's vilest conglomerates. Their labor and integration practices are sick, their refusal to produce anything new is obnoxious, and when I see a princess at a theme park who has the same hair color as me, I pass out.

I contain multitudes: I fucking suck *and* I fucking suck. There are three hot dogs of note here.

In the same spirit of their adherence to COVID protocols and child labor laws, Disneyland takes their approach to park food more seriously than Six Flags. This is mainly because Disney tickets tend to run between three and four times the price of the home of "tough titties, old man," and there is a marginal increase in dignity that comes with the fee—the roller coasters aren't as good (and you can quote me on that), but the general feeling of "I am going to get Maced by a theater kid" is far lower. Pluto's Dog House, Angry Dogs, and Corn Dog Castle were closed for business the day my boyfriend and I went and only got into a single argument, but the Star Wars hot dog was very much on the menu.

What can I say about the Star Wars hot dog other than it's a bad idea and I worry a feral pack of Reddit users will assault me for calling it a bad idea? For your reference, the Star Wars hot dog is a grilled pork sausage with coleslaw and peppercorn salad dressing on an oversized pita wrap that costs thirteen dollars. This is a good idea if you are drunk on a weekday and need to create a whiskey sponge quickly, but in the context of a hot dog, you really need to stretch to make the pita worth the dry-mouth

Disney is counting on your lubing up with a thick blue Slushie called Blue Milk (plus ten dollars for branding).

But okay, I'll humor you. The Ronto Wrap, the canonical menu and expanded universe name for this coleslaw hot dog in a pita wrap, is said to consist of ronto meat topped with Clutch (not peppercorn, *Clutch*) sauce, served on the planet of Batuu at the Black Spire Outpost, first seen when a First Order mechanic brought a resistance spy to Ronto Roasters and ordered themselves whatever the Star Wars amount of thirteen fucking dollars is. The recipe took off as the war between the Resistance and the First Order continued to spiral outward, and *that,* my dear child, is why we are eating a coleslaw sausage in the piercing sun while we wait for our group to be called for Rise of the Resistance.

The truth is that the dish was invented for the opening of the Star Wars: Galaxy's Edge park and was worked into a series of comics and audiobooks prior to the park's opening, a relatively harmless bit of vertical integration designed to make food vloggers soil themselves. It's perfectly fine, a pork dog with an actual snap (a snap? at a theme park? you're sick!), and I'd take nearly any opportunity to watch an animatronic pig be repeatedly spit-roasted in the middle of a room. I've tactfully filed it under "good, but would give you a panic attack if served in an ordinary setting."

On the opposite end of the park, Award Wieners is a concept so demented that I have no choice but to love whatever ten-dollar corn dog they fool me into buying, whether there are only two options on the menu or not. Located in the Disney California Adventure section of the park, another of my favorite uncanny valley elements of Southern California theme parks emerges—a whole section that is pretending to be the extremely nearby Hollywood, without all the pesky class chasms and police surveillance. It's here where I find the Academy Award–themed hot dog stand, sporting a fake Oscar with BEST WIENER

IN A SUPPORTING ROLL on the bright red sign. The menu has been pared down during COVID-era mobile ordering, leaving us to choose between the traditional Corn Dog and a Hot Link Corn Dog, both all-beef and freshly battered.

Served with fries, it's fucking incredible. I don't make it a habit to take in a corn dog—while they *do* fit into the parameters of what I define as a hot dog, being an animal-cased shitstorm fighting for its life in a grain-based exterior, it gets too messy to venture this far out of peninsular bun territory. A bun is a hammock and a corn dog casing is a crypt; do you see what I mean?

The two of us have been to Disneyland together before, two days before the park shut down for COVID the first time, and by May 2021 we are happy to be alive and there and holding a corn dog at all, much less a damn good one. I look at pictures of myself clutching an anthropomorphic rodent's head in my hands in March 2020. Everything is different. Our hair is longer, not everyone is alive who was then, everyone surrounding us is choking down whatever is necessary to access a serotonin reserve that may very well be as skunked as the water reserves in our own neighborhood. We are having fun. We are having fun.

For what it's worth, the Disneyland corn dog is an entity all to itself, encased in the same exciting, somewhat overstated mythic weight. The story was rehashed with PR-driven flair in 2010 by a man named Gary Maggetti, then the general manager of food and beverage operations at the California parks. Do *not* underestimate Gary Maggetti—not only did he work his way from jungle skipper and Main Street food-slinger at the parks in college and network his way through thirteen different positions in the food and beverage division to his current job as general manager of Disney California Adventure Park West, he is also hot and I would let him have sex with me. You're right, let me say more on that last part! He has a babyface with an unexpectedly deep voice. I guess that's all I have to say about it!

I want to tell you Gary's little (pejorative) corn dog story. The park's dog has always been the subject of Disney lore, standard off-the-shelf batter mixed with water, hand-dipped in front of the customer to assure what so few corn dog vendors can't—that this food has not been actively rotting for hours on a cafeteria tray. In the late 1990s, an executive chef suggested the batter be reimagined, creating what he describes as "the most expensive corn dog batter in the history of corn dogs."

"He searched the Earth for the incredible ingredients that would go into this batter," Gary continues, looking to the videographer to make sure she's listening (she's *listening*, giggling a little, maybe that was me). "The right honey, the right cornmeal, the right flour, everything was coming together perfectly."

Certain that his millennium corn dog batter would revolutionize park food, Maggetti quickly heard the droves of Disney park-goers complaining that the corn dog did not taste like it did in their memories. The woman holding the camera laughs and says, "Gary, that's the *best* corn dog story I've ever heard," and while he's fucking her with his eyes I think about what he said instead of how he was looking at me when he said it. For every hot dog I've hated in the country, there are fifty people who would riot if their recipe changed, because it did not taste like their memories—regardless of how soggy or undercooked or boring those memories were. I eat boiled hot dogs to this day because they taste like my dad meeting a deadline on a Gateway 2000, just like the adults in Stitch T-shirts screaming into front-facing cameras about how the roller coaster they held their now-dead parent's hand on looks the same as it used to. It's embarrassing when *they* do it, not when I do.

You're not a true hotdogger at Disneyland unless you go to something called the Little Red Wagon, a Disney food institution so quaint and compact that Gary Maggetti couldn't blow my back out in it, even if he wanted to. It's an antique food truck that appears at the end of Main Street, the long, winding, never-really-existed Victorian Americana street that Walt Disney insisted be the first thing guests see when the park opened in 1955. The cart encapsulates the era that Main Street is cast in, an antique font declaring HAND-DIPPED CORN DOGS AND REFRESHING COLD DRINKS in a parked vehicle. The classic Disney corn dog is your only option—hot dogs were much more present at the park in the 1950s, but the years favored the corn dog as the superior scent to tangle with churros and peanuts.

Walt Disney's emphasis was always on encapsulating the memory of something more than reflecting any actual reality—"it will continue to grow as long as there is imagination in the world," he said at the park's opening. In one way, he uses "imagination" as a clever substitute for "disposable income and so-so labor practices," but he also means imagination in its profoundest sense. Main Street is not about history, really; it's about an idyllic American image that sells—it wraps around a kid's synapses like flypaper, saying *this* is how things used to be, except it wasn't and they tell you that at the door.

HERE YOU LEAVE TODAY AND ENTER THE WORLD OF YESTERDAY, TOMORROW, AND FANTASY, a plaque at the front of the park says. What it does not specify is that their yesterday is just as much a fantasy as their tomorrow, a collection of 1900s storefronts hawking merchandise from a movie that came out last year, animatronics deifying Americans who owned slaves and thought their bitch wives shouldn't get to *vote,* how would I get *elected* if my bitch wife could *vote,* and a magic shop that is above criticism.

The corn dog in the Little Red Wagon is, to borrow a phrase, the best wiener in a supporting roll in this fantasy.

Any adult with half a firing brain cell can slam a tooth through the hot, fresh batter that my boyfriend Gary wasn't allowed to change and know the Main Street they're walking down isn't real—it ends in a bubblegum-pink castle where a cartoon princess is comatose in two dimensions. Why didn't you say that the executive chef who designed that doomed corn dog batter was your twin brother, Gary? Is it a fear of nepotism exposure, or a fear of railing me over Radiator Springs while your twin brother the corn dog king watches?

AS I WAS SAYING,

Six Flags does not find itself as weighed down by its own mythology in the summer of 2021, nor by the quality of its hot dog.

Reader, I will say, the teens manning Wheeler's that day did not give me a dog that made me physically ill—it was mostly hot and even, gasp, had a slight snap to it. We dressed it in sugary ketchup because, and I have to remind myself of this stark reality sometimes, *he does not like mustard and will not abide by it,* and finish about half before the rain gets so bad the untoasted bun turns to glue in our hands.

All five of us—Jake, his fianceè Alex, me, my boyfriend, and my extremely tall brother—stand in the middle of a 235-acre theme park soaking wet, daring another person to say we've gotten our money's worth, let's get the fuck out of here. I choose the coward's way, exhaling hot dog breath into the center of the hang.

"Anyone wanna do Pandemonium?" I ask, and my brother shakes his head.

"I need a new pair of fucking pants," he says, and the boys immediately head for the exit as Jake details the closest place to get affordable pants, a fact I cannot wrap my head around his having at the ready two hours from home. We're stopping in the queer-commune-slash-Sylvia-Plath haven of the Northeast in Northampton, Massachusetts, the sort of place where I can buy a pair of wide-legged pants that I'll get compliments on at the airport until I die.

Local Burger is across the street from a Citizens Bank that loves the gays now according to their signage, with an array of vegan options to match the community it serves. Alex is shaking her finger at what she wants me to have—when someone knows about a hot dog you don't, you *have* to know about it, it's the rule. The Captain Crunch Dog she's pitching me sounds like a nightmare, a thick beef hot dog breaded in Captain Crunch cereal, deep fried, then topped with buffalo sauce and bleu cheese. It's a classic case of Too Much Going On, a hot dog inside a novelty corn dog inside a savory dog inside an oversized roasted roll and, holy shit, it's really good.

The car reeks of wet clothes when we pile back in, in full Phish regalia, the smell of deep-fried cereal piling on top of body odor on top of an unseasonably cold wind. Jake and Alex tell us about Jewish musical theater on the way back and I tell my brother that he looks like a dumb asshole smoking cigarettes like that when Dad is having his lung macheted out next month, doesn't he know that? He tells me that he read somewhere that cigarettes aren't addictive until you're twenty-six. He's twenty-four and three-quarters, stay out of it, Jamie, you don't even live here anymore.

If you love someone, you will love where they come from, especially when that place is Brockton, Massachusetts.

I am a third-generation Brocktonian, the first to defect from the city and the only to say, "The school shooting here was not as bad as on *Degrassi*," *and* "The Jonas Brothers are amazing at softball," on local television during the course of 2009. My brother and I grew up on Massasoit land with eight cousins in and out of our house around the corner from where our mother grew up on the south side of the city, down the street from where our grandfather got drafted into the Korean War at twenty and half a mile from where he lived until he was in his eighties. His mother came from Italy by way of Greece, the same way my great-grandma came from East Fuck Nowhere, Italy, and settled in the projects of the North Side so her daughter could one day afford a starter house in the slightly nicer ticky-tacky projects down the road.

Brockton is a city that has always had a diverse, immigrant-heavy population, and has the bad press from the majority-white New England media to match. The headlines surrounding our city are designed to make you Kegel so hard your holes seal— "Brockton Named Second-Most Dangerous City to Live In," says one; "Brockton Man Admits Selling Drugs on the Dark Web," says another; "Brockton Man Among State's Most Wanted Fugitives." In a state known for its penchant for blunt discrimination, it's no surprise this kind of coverage escalated for the entirety of my life, as the makeup in the city shifted from a large, poor Greek, Irish, and Armenian population during my parents' childhoods to an influx of poor Haitian and Cape Verdean immigrants during mine. When I visit in the summer of 2021, the city is around 50 percent Black, 25 percent white, and 10 percent Cape Verdean, with an average income hovering around $21,000 per capita.

We ate boiled hot dogs on the South Side, an indiscretion I will never fully be able to forgive from a family that allegedly loved me. Cheap food can be prepared in a way that isn't cheap—there's a pan right there, throw some butter and oil on the stovetop and split the motherfucking hot dog in half, right? But we're white trash dog boilers, and to deny it would set me back in therapy. It was a meal in which you could have two without feeling bad, ketchup only on an untoasted bun, puréed from rubber and paste into fuel for screaming at your little brother. It was a meal you ate unsupervised when your mom was away for a day or two with a friend, and when your dad had to pay attention to the game for work, you would wake up with your mouth bleeding because your brother body-slammed you in his Pull-Ups to knock out your loose tooth. Dad would have three hot dogs, sometimes four, something that felt decadent and impossible.

The fact that Brockton exists is a miracle. The city adapts, closing its Greek restaurant when the Greeks move away and opening a Cape Verdean restaurant when the community need for seafood soup and Cachupa became overwhelming. The systems adapt around underfunded schools, the ones that look like state prisons but are run like Hogwarts, assigning all five thousand high schoolers a "house" they belong to on the first day of school to make sure you're not walking half a mile through the prison hallways to Algebra II. I was in the azure house (bookish, boring) while lusting after the teens in red (athletic, nearly discernable personalities) and yellow (bad boys, five-foot-four skateboarders I would cut my leg off to be noticed by). Green house was where the affable kids who never lost their virginity after prom ate lunch, and the school kept getting awards for not being as fucked up as it should have been under the circumstances. We had huge productions of *Anything Goes* underwritten by the handful of rich people who lived there once and moved away; inner-city kids were trotted out once a year to tell an audience of parents how learning the French horn kept them off the streets; aren't you proud to be from Brockton, they asked you, and used the taxpayer money to buy a twenty-foot statue of Rocky Marciano instead of social studies textbooks published after 2002.

There's something about a city desperate for you to love it, an insecure teenager who doesn't quite see the reason they make people nervous. The city responds to media coverage of violence by bringing armed cops to the high school and responds to a rise in crime with more cops in areas that need programs and support. It's dogged by the issues that antagonize people who are marginalized by their race and class, by language barriers and by legacy white politicians remaining in power in a city whose needs are out of step with their interest or abilities; it's a place where the attention will always go to what is going wrong and not the million things that are going right. Brockton is special, I tell myself, eating bar pizza and looking at the church where my parents decided to get married but definitely should not have.

Where else can you walk past five different abandoned shoe factories on the way to be gaslit by your favorite auntie? "Who's your favorite auntie?" she'd ask when I was two, the first memory I can put on a scoreboard. I desperately want to see her, to put my boyfriend in front of her and see whether I've gotten it right or not this time, but we can't even argue this summer when she keeps refusing a vaccine. I'm angry about it, I'm sad about it, I love her, I won't get to tell her before she dies the next Christmas. Does this city have a fucking hot dog I can eat or not?

It has to, but the prospect makes me nervous. With all due respect to my homeland, New England hot dogs tend to be dogshit, even with a few canonically cool events like the annual Worcester Hot Dog Safari I have to miss while my dad recovers from surgery. I need to look for a Brockton hot dog while there's still time.

It's not like the food here is bad—yet another sticky untrue idea about Massachusetts is that it's a massive Wahlburgers full of extras from *The Departed*. There's a handful of old food institutions: the clam strips at McMenamy Seafood (hung with a disturbing blue line flag the summer I come home); the Greek salad (my mom's pregnancy food) at Christo's Restaurant, now closed permanently; meatballs the size of your head at the Italian Kitchen (we put a few in my brother's Christmas stocking every year); the roast beef sandwich at Georgio's Roast Beef, Pizza & More (fingered in the parking lot in the middle of a *Saw* movie marathon, 2010), and the bar pizza at Cape Cod Cafe.

This last place in particular holds some familial significance— my uncle worked there as a bartender in the 1990s and had a fatal heart attack after his shift when his daughter, my cousin, had just turned three years old, prompting a moment of remembrance over Diet Cokes every time we come in for a hamburger pizza. There's one guy from Georgia who drives up the coast every year to buy fifty frozen Cape Cod pizzas to eat at home once a week.

"The pizza's just that good!" Dad says. 'Did you know your Uncle Louie died here?" I always do.

On my last night in town before heading to the Midwest, I decide to try the hot dog at Cape Cod Cafe. The suggestion draws some mockery on both sides of the family, who know damn well that coming to CCC without getting a bar pizza is a waste of their money (I offer to pay: "Oh my *God,* Mrs. Hollywood with her own frickin' money, huh," an aunt says before slapping down a Visa with travel points). It *is* overpriced, eight dollars without any description except "hot dog." I choose violence. I order the hot dog.

It's—it's unconscionable at any price. In a bun that's not just untoasted but *cold,* I am served a completely raw dog that has been thrown on a grill for so little time that it may as well be boiled. Beside it are a handful of dill pickles in the process of writing their own suicide notes. I'm shocked. I'm appalled. This great institution serving *shitbag hot dogs?* My auntie laughs, mutters she can't believe we're *fuckin'* paying for this, and reminds me to correctly make note of Cape Cod Cafe's indisputably perfect bar pizza if I want to be able to show my face in this town again.

My cousins make me promise that when I return the next month to oversee my dad's recovery, we'll get a hot dog at the place that shares a bathroom with the strip club next door. You can bring the hot dog into the strip club! they say. That's the appeal.

When I show up a month later, the hot dog joint attached to the strip club is closed—NO ONE WANTS TO WORK, a Sharpie-scrawled sign on the door reads.

I hear this over and over throughout Hot Dog Summer—*why* doesn't anyone *feel* like going to work? As with most words out of a hot dog business owner's mouth, there's a hell of a lot of context missing here. The movement that came to be known as the Great Resignation had been in full swing since early 2021 in the United States, with waves of employees voluntarily leaving jobs where they felt underpaid, underappreciated, and in many cases, not sufficiently protected against a pandemic that had yet to be effectively vaccinated against. Think of it as a soft strike against the American government's notorious refusal to take care of its people through wage stagnation, refusals to freeze rent or reclaim hotels for the unhoused, and paltry $1200 checks individuals were expected to live off of for months.

It makes particular sense that employees at the hot dog places I visited would be impacted—many small businesses paid an uncompetitive wage that could be matched or exceeded by a reliable unemployment check, or did not provide healthcare benefits. While most overworked business owners I spoke with held employees individually accountable for this "refusal," one that would peak in October 2021 when a wave of worker-solidarity protests snowballed into "Striketober," this issue could be resolved with . . . and I don't mean to blow your mind . . . *universal healthcare.*

The Great Resignation may not have happened without the massive layoffs that took place during the 2020 coronavirus lockdown, which resulted in more than twenty million Americans (more than 15 percent of the workforce) being unceremoniously laid off and left with few options during a massive public health crisis. It can be easily argued that mutual aid organizing and community-based efforts did more to protect those affected than the government that relied on their labor until it became inconvenient—and workers didn't forget it, watching as those declared "essential" were repeatedly put at risk in order to keep American capitalism grinding along.

For many, the forced lockdown was a time of both financial and health anxiety *and* one of reflection on the elements of society that had exacerbated the crisis and cost the lives of their own friends and family members. When vaccinations became widely available in the US in the spring of 2021, four million Americans quit their jobs, the majority in food service and retail; more than 40 percent of the workforce considered bailing on jobs where they felt undervalued. This was driven by younger people—millennials and Gen Z cannot agree on the correct cut of pants but they can agree on basic labor rights—and more than half of the latter group expressed dissatisfaction with how they were treated and compensated during their time in the workforce and demanded better conditions. This wave of discontent was matched by the fact that some workers, affected by the lingering symptoms of long COVID, simply *can't* work as they did before.

Hot Dog Summer is one of workers' awakening, of the first time you can see and touch your family that made it through, of the time when you're sure as fuck going to use the last social safety net at your disposal from a government that can't stop reminding you it doesn't matter to them if you live or die. It has to matter to *someone*. Who wants to work at a hot dog stand at a time like this?

We Are in Teeny Tiny
Hot Dog Town

Sorry, the Hairy Arm was outlawed years ago.

"You know, you could just stay here!" My dad says this every time I come home, followed by a no-no-I-don't-mean-it-but-what-if laugh that I can conjure just like the sound of his footsteps coming up the stairs when I need to turn off my flashlight.

"I'll be back in a few weeks," I say, a little disappointed he's not taking to the HBO-whatever-the-fuck I was hoping to get him into. The surgery I came across the country to oversee didn't materialize by the middle of July, and so we decide to resume hot dog business and push toward the Midwest to see my boyfriend's family. The flavor-of-the-month COVID variant is pulsing in California and the one place I cannot go is back to my apartment, so we're heading to Chicago to try what I find to be some of the most vile and aggressive hot dog toppings I've ever encountered before I turn back to Brockton to oversee Dad's surgery.

"I'm just saying," Dad tells me. "It could be nice to have some time apart."

We're leaving in the morning, piling the cocker spaniel and the black cat and an assortment of garbage from my childhood into a rented sedan, and driving five hours to eat our nation's tiniest hot dogs.

One failed attempt to get halfway decent weed before crossing state lines later, and we're three hours away in Troy, New York, the alleged home of Uncle Sam.

I know, I know, you can't just *say* you're the home of a fictional character, but let's hear Troy, New York, out. Andy Cohen aside, Uncle Sam is as close to a mascot as a flop of a country like America has, created as a propaganda tool to stir up jingoistic feelings in potential soldiers during the War of 1812, a personification of the country in the form of an old guy with a little beard pointing his finger at your head while wearing this little outfit and saying, "I Want You," and you're like, Me? Sorry, you are not my type, but he doesn't want you like *that,* he wants you to drone-strike civilians to secure a fossil fuel deal that will kill the planet. Oh! Sorry, still no thank you.

Uncle Sam wasn't the first draft of an American mascot. The first was Columbia (yikes), a white woman in an American flag dress that's telegraphing bad Met Gala moment, who was later retrofitted into the mascot for Columbia Pictures (we love a pivot!). This scrapped draft was followed by Brother Jonathan, an Uncle Sam–adjacent, tall-hat-wearing personification of New England used during the Revolutionary War. Troy, New York, isn't claiming that Jingo Daddy was a real man but was *based* on one, a meatpacker named Samuel Wilson who was contracted by the United States government during the War of 1812, before any of the regulations present in today's factories were put in place. The legend is almost certainly not true, with the character's origin predating Wilson's work by nearly three years. The first claim of Wilson's association with the character wasn't until the 1840s, but the image of a meatpacker preparing rations for soldiers as an everyman mascot for The Cause was potent, and a huge boon for tourism in Troy.

Again, the lie makes no difference. Samuel Wilson was not the inspiration for Uncle Sam, but people believe he was—by 1961, Congress formally adopted the character as the official symbol of the country, saying that "Congress salutes 'Uncle Sam' Wilson of Troy, New York, as the progenitor of America's National symbol of Uncle Sam." The character's proximity to lies and hot dog meat craters my brain, and there is no choice but to put the lie being served up in a tiny bun and suck it down.

Its ties to one of America's fakest daddies aside, the streets of Troy are well-kept with sherbet-colored high-rises and small businesses, but the whole place feels empty. It's a poor and relatively diverse community that hasn't gotten the budget to enter the current decade, so they're making do in a way that would rip your heart out if you were from there. For me, the streets are too quiet. We drive past Uncle Sam Lanes and the Burden Iron Works Museum, a local history museum desperately trying to reckon with its past (*recognizing every face and story,* the website declares, *we're not handing it to the Dutch colonizers anymore, we swear*). Finally, we arrive at Uncle Sam's local hot dog institution, Famous Lunch.

There's knowing that a place is famous for its tiny hot dogs, and then there's the stark image of a gigantic grill overwhelmed by tiny hot dogs. Like the banners on the street that are *still* celebrating local World War II veterans—didn't get anyone into Iraq, Troy?—the lore surrounding Famous Lunch is steeped in jingoism. Their three-inch pork-and-beef hot dogs, manufactured at Troy institution Helmbold's, line up shoulder to shoulder, child armies in the front window, anticipating steamed three-inch Helmbold buns and a light shower of the house "zippy sauce." They're *not* pigs in blankets, the locals will tell you; they are *tiny hot dogs* and meant to be consumed in increments of ten.

I walk past the big blue Famous Lunch block lettering and sit at their bright red counter on a Wednesday afternoon. There is a sacred ritual in progress—the manager's friend's teenage brother is getting trained on the counter, and he's doing a terrible job.

There are three men on deck today—the manager, the cook, and the new guy, all of whom work in plain sight making items from the joint's impressively sized menu, ranging from breakfast options to Depression-era sandwiches with zippy sauce on top. As I've learned is customary at places known for their hot dogs, there's a separate windowside grill specifically for the hot dog youth militia apart from where the zippy burgers and less popular dishes are made. It's a diner where you can smell the last several years' worth of customer sweat in the air, the kind of place where a practice called "the Hairy Arm"—a cook lining his bare arm with tiny buns and dropping mini-dogs into them before sliding everything into a bag to go—was a neighborhood spectacle before being declared unsanitary by the Health Department. It's weird here, but the people have no idea, so *I'm* weird.

An older regular sees a target in the new guy.

"Hey!" he yells at the kid. "TikTok!"

The cook yells over his shoulder, distracted from the zippy burger he's preparing for the same customer. "That's Jack," he tells the teenager. "Stay away from him." The teenager grins.

"No respect!" Jack shouts from the red stool that looks familiar no matter what state you're in—sticky counter, meaty smells. "Too late, I met the kid three days ago."

I order two tiny hot dogs at $1.11 apiece, to the bafflement of the staff. Fuck. The easiest way to blow your cover as a tourist is not living in Troy, New York, for your entire life or believing that Uncle Sam is a real man. The second-easiest way is ordering the incorrect quantity of tiny hot dogs at Famous Lunch with your weird face and your wrong smell.

"Just . . . two?" the cook asks, getting the new guy's attention for the first time—even *he* knows it's wrong, and he doesn't know shit. I panic.

"Yes?"

The cook lets it slide and asks the new guy if he wants to learn how to make a tiny hot dog, to which he replies, "I guess." Do I want a Diet RC Cola while I wait? It's on the house; this is a training shift.

I watch the process from my stool as a divorced-dad regular saunters in wearing a suit that's a little too big for his already big frame. You really do need a trusted partner to tell you when something fits, and he doesn't have one anymore; it's one of the first things he reminds the manager of when he walks in.

"Back on the alimony diet," he says, ordering a zippy burger. The manager knows already, and tells the divorced dad that he took his advice about backpacking from Airbnb to Airbnb on a recent vacation. He'd felt cleansed by it. The divorced dad is a little *too* thrilled to hear about the manager's travels, and the new guy watches the cook at work—the cook says not to worry about being the new guy, hell, he's the manager's friend's brother, you know? The stakes are low. He guides the new guy to the teeny weenie grill and picks one up with a little pitchfork to slide it into a teeny bun and slop on whatever zippy sauce is. The new guy nods, not offering to try it himself, and goes back to texting someone named Cassie, followed by three puppy emojis.

Upstate New York is a reunion with Greek-style hot dogs, a style and a culture that dominates the hot dog scene of the region. Famous Lunch's zippy sauce is an extension of this lineage, still a secret house recipe but rumored to be a mixture of beef suet, onions, hamburger meat, chili powder, mustard, and paprika—*no* tomato. In a classic slip, the only reason this information is publicly available is because a customer of sixty years caught a new guy on a bad day in the 2000s and asked, only for the employee to be scolded by one of the family owners midway through disclosing. This mixture is simmered in water for hours once the onions are cooked and the pink is gone from the burger, then left in a vat on the same grill the hot dogs sit on. I adore each and every one of these vats across our great failed nation—the confidence it takes for a business to proudly display a bowl of diarrhea is unmatched.

In spite of its nearly ninety years in business, Famous Lunch doesn't curate its story on the walls, preferring to do so by word of mouth and in Comics Sans on a fifteen-year-old website. The manager tells me as I sip on Diet RC that the business wasn't *always* called Famous Lunch, did I know that—he's covering for the cook, who just dropped both of the tiny hot dogs I ordered on the floor and can't stop laughing about it. "I fumbled the bag!" he yells, laughing, but I've got time and I want to know what Famous Lunch was called before.

In 1932, the business was established as Quick Lunch at the same location, but its current reputation has everything to do with the summer of 1958. In an overmilitarized myth befitting the town, a Troy native stationed in Moscow special-ordered the tiny hot dogs from Quick Lunch in a fit of homesickness, and they were eventually served at a US ambassador's birthday celebration. The event got a fair amount of press in the days before you could just watch someone have sex online whenever, and the popular "Operation Hot Dogs" story motivated then owner Steve Vasil to change the name of the business to Famous Lunch. Famous continues to serve tiny hot dogs to the community starting at six in the morning, complete with an eating competition that's been dominated by Rensselaer Polytechnic Institute frats since the early 2000s. I appreciate the place's confidence, knowing when to change from the humble Quick to the somewhat overstated Famous.

The dog is tiny as promised, and it's good—the locally sourced pork-beef dog has a snap in spite of its size, and the onions, mustard, and zippy sauce make the meat virtually invisible in a meal I manage to extend to three bites per dog. I was frustrated at the concept of a tiny hot dog at first, then realized this is maybe the only appropriate serving size for a dog with chili on it. Given the absolute havoc this same style has wrought on my one and only ass, the option to reassess every few bites was a welcome one, the zippy sauce itself thick and fresh in defiance of the shit bucket from whence it had come, the bun so small that it didn't need additional grilling to tie the whole thing together.

Jack the regular turns his attention to me as the new guy plops a zippy burger in front of him.

"First time?" he asks me.

"Leave her *alone,* Jack," the cook says, not looking up from the divorced dad's alimony-diet zippy burger.

"Suit yourself," Jack says, turning back to his plate. "Suit your*self.*"

There are plenty of other tiny hot dog vendors in this area with their own meatpacking shops of choice, their own Uncle Sams waiting to be turned into a symbol. One of them is Hot Dog Charlie's, relocated after yet another grease fire took down their original Troy location established back in 1922—the same three-generation legacy, the same Greek lineage, the same Helmbold's mini-dogs, and the innovators of the Hairy Arm system. Remember, from before health codes encouraged businesses not to choose carnival showmanship over hygiene?

I order the equivalent of a tiny hot dog charcuterie board— one with sauerkraut, one with nacho cheese sauce (violence, Jamie, violence), and one with the signature Hot Dog Charlie's chili sauce with mustard and onions. Besides being the blueprint ostensibly ripped off by Famous Lunch, Hot Dog Charlie's shit bucket is full of a markedly different chili. The recipe is sold by the jar in-store, but sleuthing fans have determined that it likely includes ground beef, onions, and a hell of a lot of spices—chili powder, paprika, celery salt, pepper, cinnamon, cumin, ginger, nutmeg, and a tablespoon of tomato paste for good measure.

I walk back out to the rental car, where my boyfriend tells me he has "truly no interest" in another tiny hot dog as sheets of rain come down, preventing us from completing the tiny hot dog trifecta by visiting Gus's Hot Dogs nearby. We've only got so much time to get to Rochester, where I've got a date with a garbage plate.

The weather is awful but I'm feeling peppy for the four hours it takes us to get to Rochester from gloomy Troy, more than happy to trade in Uncle Sam's alleged home for the more laid-back college town where we will, once and for all, learn how to distinguish a white hot from a red hot. There is some relief to returning to the road after a few weeks too close to my child-hood bedroom. The mission is simple: flee tiny hot dog country for somewhere different.

At Dogtown in Rochester, New York, the tiny hot dog creed is gone—these dogs are *large* and served on a thick bed of fries (home or french), macaroni salad, baked beans, or coleslaw and smothered in as much mustard, Dogtown meat sauce, and what-ever other texture you care to add that isn't ketchup (will you people *relax*). This is a calorie-dense X Games of hotdogging, a Rochester signature called the garbage plate. The city itself is fascinating to me—it was a hotbed of mid-nineteenth-century progressivism where Frederick Douglass's paper *The North Star* advocated for slavery abolition and the Seneca Falls Conven-tion kicked off the first wave of feminism in America, and it was the home of a favorite of mine, American spiritualism (or, where two teenage sisters told their parents they could talk to ghosts and like two months later it was a full-blown religion). And what do progressives love? Plates of elegant garbage.

Unlike some more forced hot dog vocabulary terms that own-ers push to take off, the concept of the garbage plate was named by kids in varying states of sobriety who were eating them in the third-densest student population in the country. Its origins lie in a business we narrowly miss the chance to visit—Nick Tahou Hots, a century-old institution whose signature dish was "hots and po-tots," the heaping pile of home fries, beans, hot dogs, onions, mustard, and chili that makes for the wettest hot dog dish since 4 Way Lunch in Georgia. Throughout the 1980s, kids would come to Nick's near closing time and ask for "that plate with all the garbage on it." The business trademarked the term in 1992, but no one can trademark the idea of a split hot dog surrounded by three thousand calories of other shit, and so local businesses began to catch on.

Enter Dogtown, a business that opened in the 2000s with comparable prices and a series of specialty dogs that sets it apart from the East Coast Great Depression eterna-stands that wouldn't order an avocado with a harpoon to their heads. They don't *completely* reject tradition though—their red and white hots, the two hot dog variants closely associated with the area, are ordered from regional German American hot dog manufacturer Zweigle's. With the expansive meaty and meatless menus necessary for the college set, it's not that their fancier dogs aren't tempting, with each named for a different breed of dog in one of the most intense commitments to theme I've ever seen. It's one of the only joints on our nationwide route that encourages us to bring our cocker spaniel inside, and the cashier cheerfully notes that he looks identical to the cartoon puppy chowing down on a classic red hot on the Dogtown sign. She's right. I miss my dog. That's not what the book is about though.

Dogtown doesn't, or maybe legally cannot, identify their pile of slop as a garbage plate, instead tastefully referencing the local phenomenon as a "Junkyard Plate." For the first time at the end of a long hot dog day, I actually arrive a little hungry—a day's worth of tiny hot dogs have gone down easy, and the prospect of bodily punishment is almost exciting. I choose the classic "Dog Plate," one red hot and one white hot on a bed of fries, macaroni salad, chili, onions, and mustard with two rolls on the side to scoop up any residual damage. Yes, this is a punishment I can handle.

I hesitate to enter the red-hot-versus-white-hot discourse, itself a hotbed of debate among foodies who are already fuming that I've wasted so much real estate talking about my little feelings. What they don't know about me is that I'm a hot dog reporter with nothing to lose.

Here is what you need to know—in Rochester, both red and white hots are made by Zweigle's, a family butcher shop begun by German immigrants in the 1880s that quickly became known for its "Old World" sausages and hot dogs, which are produced in-house. Today, the fifth-generation company is best known for their "pop-open" red hots, a variation on the Texas hots that are most popular in the New York and New Jersey regions and have nothing to do with Texas at all. The pop-opens are named for the snap of their casing, with a juicy pork-beef combination classic hot dog inside. At Dogtown, they split the damn thing in half and grill it before tossing it onto a ball pit of noodles and potatoes for you to massacre with your plastic fork or not.

White hots are the real only-in-Rochester experience on hand here, a dish so specific to the region that most people outside of western New York wouldn't even think to ask for it. It's a thick, beige dog that reminds me of, well never mind, a dish first brought to the region in the 1920s that's a blend of unsmoked and uncured pork, beef, and veal. Because it's not smoked, the frank keeps its pale, fleshy exterior while retaining a fair amount of flavor. I order one of each for my Junkyard Plate, and the cook splits and tastefully scissors them like a middle school boy's fantasy before putting the crammed-full Styrofoam container in my hands to keep from the cocker spaniel I love so much.

A love letter to the white hot—this is a hot dog so good that people will sometimes serve it cold. This is a hot dog that can be your breakfast, lunch, or dinner, a dog that is objectively ugly to look at, whose grilling evokes a castration fantasy that's never quite resonated with me (I prefer to imagine giving someone a fatal bonk to the head, the dubious bonk) but whose taste manages to overpower the too-sweet macaroni. Maybe it's the addition of the baby cow flesh, I could not say. The pop-open pairs well with the fries and pasta, its pork casing peeling right off the dog like my cousins and I used to do to Thanksgiving turkeys while dressed up like little Pilgrims, believing everything we read in our social studies books.

The garbage plate is a dish best served to a twenty-one-year-old going through a breakup, to the entire softball team we're sitting next to who are debating whether Elon Musk can be "fixed," to a lifelong Rochester native coming home to see their parents for the first time since lockdown. I'm not its target audience and good lord is there no way I'm finishing this fucking thing, but I find myself grazing on it for the next twelve hours in our hotel room while I frantically try to finish a podcast episode so I can pay my bills. Garbage plates are a dish served for sustenance, and the farthest eight bucks can get you en route to Buffalo as a lightning storm that wouldn't have been environmentally possible ten years ago ravages the sky. Is this safe, I ask. Probably not, my boyfriend says, but we're already behind schedule.

We sneak the pets in through the back entrance, one of my favorite acts of intimacy: Okay, can the desk clerk see us from this angle? Take the cat's collar off or they'll hear. Will the kennel fit through this revolving door? No, we're going to have to risk it. I have the twenty dollars to pay for a pet deposit, but that's not the point—this is where we're at our best, on a useless mission that makes us laugh. It's amazing what you can overlook when there's a little hot blood beneath your skin, running down a hotel hallway with a rug so thoroughly trampled that the floor is cement again. It's fun, it's funny, I love it, we sleep in separate beds again. My generational trauma is that my parents were roommates who enjoyed each other's company. Plus all the other stuff.

I don't think it's controversial to say I've never experienced the feminine urge to "go to Buffalo." By all accounts, it's a miserable place to be, and it's a miserable place where you can find extremely good food.

I have one last Upstate New York Greek-owned hot dog empire to try before we swivel into the Midwest. The downtown location of Ted's Hot Dogs is double-closed for business—first because of COVID indoor-dining restrictions, and also because of the eternal construction that seems to be taking place across Buffalo in spite of a pretty steadily declining population. Ted's was opened in 1927 by Greek immigrant Theodore Spiro Liaros, who'd cut his teeth in the hot dog world at a horse-drawn cart that primarily sold dogs to construction workers at the nearby building site of the Peace Bridge that now connects the US and Canada. Once the bridge was finished, the foreman's sister offered to sell him a centrally located tool shed for $100 to open his own business. The shed barely held together, but the charcoal-broiled hot dogs were a hit and Liaros was able to expand his business before passing the franchise down to his children.

Ted's is as close as Buffalo comes to a solid hot dog tradition, with a loyal following that trickles outside the mostly fenced-off industrial park the afternoon I place a mobile order for a hardwood charcoal–cooked dog with the works. Here, that means mustard, onions, a dill pickle spear, secret hot sauce, and holy shit, *ketchup* on a toasted bun. The local preference is to burn the dogs on the grill, my absolute favorite, and I slip in and out of the sterile location socially distanced from city employees panicking at the possibility that their midday Polish sausage may not be ready in time for them to clock back in.

For all the urgency and abundance of precautions Ted's takes around COVID—something I honestly forgot a hot dog business was capable of—the food itself is remarkable, the first dog I polish off voluntarily in days. There aren't many hot dogs across the county that include hot sauce in their signature make, and Ted's (alleged) combination of tomato sauce, red- and green-pepper sauce, lemon juice, margarine, and Sweet'N Low (two teaspoons of liquid smoke optional) has a sweetness and kick to it that doesn't overwhelm the well-cooked snap of the dog itself.

I slip the last bite, supported by a perfectly toasted bun, to our cocker spaniel. My boyfriend wants to scold me but we decide now's not the time to get into it; his patience with my bullshit is slipping; we'll talk about it *later*.

WE NEED MORE WOMEN PRIESTS! a billboard declares a few miles outside of Buffalo, a new cursed addition to a folder in my Google Drive called "feminism except not really."

We Are in the Midwest

"Suicide is painless." —hot dog bun I saw

There is something about a Midwestern gas station that makes you feel held. The moment you cross into the region, right past that massive Denny's billboard built right into the side of a mountain, the hot food gets hotter, the booze aisle gets longer, the prices get cheaper, and the attendants actually *notice* that you're only getting mashed potatoes and a White Claw for the car. We manage to wait until we cross into Ohio to refuel and don't regret it—it's at this gas station that I find the single most thrilling piece of roadside tourist detritus I've ever bought, a mood ring in the shape of Ohio. I pretend Ohio is proposing to me and say yes, watching its deep blue curdle into a nervous amber.

There's no shortage of hot dog culture in Ohio, with two extremely different styles dominating in Cincinnati and Cleveland, respectively. Cincinnati specializes in Coney dogs, the dog nestled in a grilled bun and topped with chili and a metric ton of shredded cheese—most popularly at Skyline Chili locations across the state, where the chili is spiked with cinnamon for an extra kick. Coneys, even the good ones, can be gotten almost anywhere, though, and I judiciously decide to go for the Only in Ohio options for the final twenty-four hours of an egregious car rental price on a research budget that has yet to hit my limping bank account.

Cleveland takes the edge here, focusing on gigantic kielbasa Polish boys (just call him po'boy, Jamie, you're friends). That area is marked by institutions like Seti's Polish Boys, Cleveland's first food truck, which slings Polish sausages topped with slaw, fries, and barbecue sauce; or Banter, a bougier affair that offers their own Polish and a specialty sausage called a Cleveland, a kielbasa topped with pierogi, sauerkraut, and ballpark mustard.

But I want the best of what the state has to offer that's reasonably on our route, and that lies in Toledo at Tony Packo's. We've moved out of Greece, skirted around Poland, and landed smack in the middle of Hungary, where the most unhinged hot dog experience of our five thousand miles is waiting.

YOU WILL DO BETTER IN TOLEDO, a bright blue sign, both optimistic and ominous, tells us as we pull up to one of Tony Packo's franchise locations in Maumee, a distinction I make only because it affects the fossilized array of celebrity-signed hot dog buns on display.

ÜDVÖZÖLJÜK! the door greets you into a cafeteria space, much different from the bar-style flagship location. This is a spot most often frequented by University of Toledo students, something the man at the counter is about to give us an earful about. Let's get him in the mix.

"Well, WELL!" he says from behind the counter, projecting an enthusiasm for my sunken eyes and dehydrated skin that he doesn't know I desperately need today. "You're here!"

There's no denying we're here, and what "here" constitutes is pretty interesting. To get to the man who knows we are here, we have to walk past approximately 150 hot dog buns autographed by celebrities of varying degrees of fame dating back to the 1970s. The tradition began when the son of *the* Tony Packo asked Burt Reynolds, the first Person of Note to pass through Packo doors, to sign a bun for posterity. This quickly became the chain's calling card, to the extent that the buns that today's big names sign while passing through are custom-made foam replicas that can cycle in and out of different locations. The Good Shit is kept at the flagship location, but we still get a hell of a show upon looking closer— the Maumee location houses signed sort-of-buns from the likes of (inhale) Herbie Hancock, Tito Puente, Pat Benatar, Jimmy Carter, Tommy Lee, BB King, Jerry Springer, Mr. T, Rosemary Clooney, George Carlin, Glenn Beck *and* Tucker Carlson, Debbie Reynolds, Leslie Odom Jr., Carlos Mencia, The Four Tops, The Monkees, and an Olympic soccer player who signed his name *and* the terrifying phrase "Suicide is Painless." Thank you, king! (You may exhale.)

"Pretty cool, huh?" the guy behind the counter asks, prompting his teenage ward to roll his eyes. The older guy *does* think it's cool, and takes a break from teaching the teenager how to use the Packo's register to tell us that he, as manager, gets to decide who is a bun-caliber celebrity and who is not. "I'm good about it though. I let the valedictorian of the high school sign one when the whole cadaver class came down a few weeks ago." I desperately need to know what a cadaver class is and why it is being taught in high school and why they are taking hot dog field trips, but he's already moved on to the next thing. "Can I get you a Hungarian hot dog? Best in the city. Wait, did you see behind you?"

Reader, it gives me no pleasure to inform you that behind me was a floor-to-ceiling display, *museum,* of Tony Packo's–branded gender pickles—and no, not *those* gender pickles. There is a second brand of gender pickles, and they are even hornier. It absolutely wrenches my guts to let you know that after ordering the Hungarian hot dog, which I will foreshadow is terrific, I carefully inspected every aggressively anthropomorphized heterosexual pickle, pepper, sausage, and tomato. It makes me sick to know it is my duty as the sole chronicler of This Sort of Thing to disclose what I have learned. It feels awful to share that there appears to be a *storyline* to this wall of pickles and mustard, a love story I will retell as faithfully as possible. With deepest regrets, this is the story of how the Tony Packo's pickle and the Tony Packo's pepper fucked each other and had a baby.

 **She catches his eye on the Sweet Hot Jalapeños jar.** In the grand tradition of Van Holten's Hot Mama, Tony Packo's jalapeño chanteuse *is* wearing a wig of human hair, but is serving something closer to Ms. Green of M&Ms fame. She's got a bright blond Marilyn bob, winking at someone out of sight in high-heeled red shoes and twirling a pink feather boa in her hand, something jalapeños famously have. OOHLALA! the jar reads below the curtains of the stage where she's performing, an otherwise completely nude showgirl trying to make it in the big city of Toledo. We can't know who she's winking at, but I'd be willing to make a bet.

 **They meet on the Sweet Hot Pickles & Peppers jar.** It is rare to see love at first sight on a pickle jar, but here we are—our jalapeño is seen on this label running in a field toward the pickle man, who is wearing big brown shoes and is covered in masculine pickle warts, if I'm being generous. It's the music swelling in Tchaikovsky's *Romeo and Juliet*, it's a Taylor Swift music video from 2008, they have their anthropomorphic arms outstretched and eyes locked with bright pink x's and o's raining between them. This doesn't happen every day, the jar says, you're gonna want to drain these peppery pickles and come back for more.

 **They go on a date on the Pickles & Peppers Relish jar.** Something that complicates the world of this couple, whose heads are pressed together as the pepper shyly turns her eyes downward at a romantic picnic, is that they eat . . . hot dogs. How big are these hot dogs? What precludes hot

dogs from being anthropomorphized in this world? The pickle man looks at his jalapeño beloved with a sneaky look in his eye, holding a hot dog in one fist and a jar of something in the other—is he holding a jar of Tony Packo's pickles? These two have to be fire signs, this is unhinged. It's intimate and weird and their friends aren't going to be able to talk them out of it; they are twin flames.

 **They fall in love on the Sweet Mix Pickles & Peppers jar.** It's rare that a pickle brand really takes its time in telling you their perverted love story, but Packo's has the variety of toppings to really let you sit in the second act. Here we see their relationship deepen further in a reverse image of their first meeting, running to each other with a gigantic half-crescent moon looming behind them. They can't stay away from each other; her friends are saying to have some self-respect and make him wait but it's not 1952, she says, his friends aren't telling *him* that.

 **They get married on the Thin Sliced Pickles & Peppers jar.** Their first dance as husband and wife is at a Tropicana club somewhere in No-where, Ohio, with a bright blue tile floor, peeling orange paint on the walls, and fake plants that make you feel like you're in the rainforest as long as you don't get too close. Her eyes are cast down as they slow dance and he is looking at her again, he is always looking at her and she is always looking down and blushing, and I don't know if she's thinking about something or is just happy to be seen. Look up, babe, you're missing it; things are so good.

 **They get … pregnant … on the Original Pickles & Peppers jar.** I will engage with a rigidly hetero couple of anthropomorphic pickles … to a point. Our happily married couple are holding hands—a less charitable interpretation is *shaking hands*—after fucking in their marital bed. She

is *really* blushing with the corners of her red lips turned upward, on account of just having had her brains fucked out by the pickle man, who wears a little red stocking cap to let the world know that he's done for the night. He looks intently at his wife in that pickle man way of his—I wouldn't like being looked at like *that* quite so much, but that is why there are so many types of people and pickles to fall in love with. They've really done some work in this bed, and while I first think that it's seven in the morning after a long night of produce fucking, it's clear that something *else* is happening here.

 **They have a baby and the baby is a tomato and their baby is named Brittany Tomatoes.** I honestly don't know what to tell you here. They have a baby, and the baby is a tomato, and their baby is named Brittany Tomatoes. Brittany is, I regret to inform you, a baby with a gigantic tomato head and a muscular little pink body and a cloth diaper sucking on her tomato thumb in a crate-of-tomatoes bed. Based on the energy of Tony Packo's, I am genuinely not sure if the Tonys past and present intend for me to imagine the C-section of a whole tomato being taken out of the jalapeño pepper; I would say they used a surrogate except I *saw* the jalapeño get pregnant. Brittany has a little bow in her tomato baby hair because these people are so sick. I'm rooting for you, Brittany, they're not going to make this life easy.

 **There is an expanded universe of their friends, former lovers, and colleagues.** There is the pickle in a tuxedo looking at me like he's going to go down on me for a full episode of *Ghost Hunters* on the jar of Gourmet Bread & Butter Pickles; there is the couple of absolute swingers looking for a third on the Sweet Hot Skinnies jar; there are the four banana pepper Rockettes on the Hungarian Banana Peppers jar, labeled as THE HOT LINEUP; there is a deeply insen-

sitive drawing of two Mexican peppers on the Hungarian Salsa jar that I won't subject you to a description of. Most importantly, this is proof positive to me that the team over at Tony Packo's *is* heavily influenced by the Dutch Van Holten gender pickles, because they feature a version of buff Ken doll husband-stealer Joe Garlic. On the Packo's Really Chunky Dills with Garlic jar, a bodybuilding pickle man flexes his left bicep while holding a garlic dumbbell in the other fist. The disrespect. I hope Joe Garlic sued.

 **And I'm so sorry to tell you about the Tangy & Sweet Mustard Relish jar.** Reader, this is an image so disturbing that I had no choice but to purchase it to prove it existed. It sits in my refrigerator as I type this, and, if I'm being honest, I use it frequently. It's a good mustard-relish mix, one I'd never tasted before, but there's this scene happening on the label, one that says A TOUCH OF HEAT! beneath these characters that we see only here and never again. There is a *human woman* on this jar, a blonde with huge naturals wearing a pale pink bikini, *rubbing mustard sunscreen onto a pale, white hot dog man.* Yes, they are at the beach. Yes, they are locking eyes to confirm that this is consensual foreplay. Yes, this *human woman* is about to fuck this *flesh-colored hot dog* on the *beach.* Babe! Babe. It's the worst thing I've ever seen. I buy it immediately.

Either two minutes or two hours later, I turn away from the pickle wall and back to the manager, who has a Hungarian hot dog waiting for me, and it doesn't disappoint. The kolbász Packo's uses is a split-in-half pork dog with the house sauce— beef, garlic, brown sugar, chili powder, Hungarian paprika— and onions and mustard. Should I ask about the cadaver class? I ask him. The kolbász is thick and delicious, I get mine Coney-style with a fistful of shredded cheese on top.

It's an intense and chaotic hot dog that matches the energy of its intense and chaotic founding family.

A few things set Tony Packo's apart from the traditional Depression-fueled hot dog origin story—begun in 1932 like a million others, Packo's is one of the only legacy joints to be started by a first-generation American hotdogger, the son of Hungarian immigrants. In a very American move, the "Hungarian hot dog" the place became famous for in the ensuing century doesn't come from the old country at all, but was a recipe that the elder Packo finessed over his time running the shop in the Hungarian-dominant Birmingham neighborhood. Packo evolved the pseudo-Old-World dish from a traditional "sausage-and-sauce sandwich" on rye bread using a Hungarian kolbász—let's call it kielbasa-adjacent, about twice the thickness of your average hot dog—and repackaged it as a bunned behemoth with mustard, onions, and Packo's signature sauce. The man was an inventor, and his family took to the excitement of being Toledo royalty.

After seventy years, this led to the hot dog equivalent of *Dynasty*. After Tony Senior died in 1962, his children Nancy Packo Horvath and Tony Jr. ran and grew their father's business for years, expanding to packaged foods in 1980. In 2002, the kids turned on each other—Nancy and her son Robin sued Tony Jr. and *his* son Tony Jr. Jr. for libel, breach of duty, and attempting to force Nancy out of the family business. The Tonys swiftly countersued and attempted to dissolve the business altogether in retaliation. Eventually, the family reconciled and in the season finale, Nancy was diagnosed with cancer and died by April of the next year.

Season two—the family mourns Nancy, and her son Robin finds a raging second wind in the summer of 2006. He claims that the Tonys Jr. and Jr. Jr., his uncle and cousin, had spent more than $400,000 in company money on personal construction fees and golf expenses, which the Tonys vehemently denied. Horvath went broke trying to prove his point, which led to the company's court-ordered sale in 2011 for $5 million to an unrelated man who had grown a series of Burger King franchises in Toledo, removing the frothing familial mess that had almost sunk the business. Robin continued to sue his cousin, going to court in 2012 and openly admitting that he'd been sneaking into the office late at night to look for his cousin's receipts. The house he bought next to the original Packo's was foreclosed on and sold in 2016 to the company that had purchased his grand-father's business. What does justice look like in the world of hot dogs? I want Robin to be okay. Of course, he is not.

"What'd you think?" the manager yells over from the counter, about to try to upsell us on some objectively hideous local art. I tell him it was perfect, and the teenager rolls their eyes again. As you are reading this, someone somewhere is training a teenager how to work at a hot dog place against their will, and they are hating every second of it. I take my gender pickles and go.

That night we get to my boyfriend's home in Wisconsin, where his family is thrilled and he is upset with me and wants every-body to know he is upset with me. We are spending the next two weeks in his grandmother's basement, working and walking and waiting for it to be safe to oversee my dad's lung extraction. I want to go home, to sleep in my bed and feel the punishing Southern California heat, but the latest plague flavor is pulsing in our neighborhood and there's no way. The basement it is, Ohio pressed against my ring finger, dark gray.

I love a Midwestern bar, and I am able to summon enough of my little personality to make my boyfriend love me for a whole PBR when a guy named Connor asks me to play bar dice. Con-nor starts by flirting with me, then immediately gets annoyed when I'm not fucked up, single, or attracted to him enough to flirt back *and* lack the basic competence to play a game of bar dice. His friends laugh when I start winning and Connor turns on me. "Is that your boyfriend?" he asks, pointing to the man sitting next to me who is, in fact, my boyfriend. Connor shakes his head and starts to eat meatballs out of a plastic cylinder he's brought from home; is that even allowed?

"That's the weirdest fuckin' bar snack I've ever seen," the bartender says. She is the one who can get us weed, a girl my boyfriend kissed when he was fifteen and now she's thirty and engaged to another bartender, she loves him, the other bartender's name is Kevin. It's a very incestuous scene out here, did I know that? She met her boyfriend at a different bar a few blocks down where "shit really blew up," and now they spend their nights smoking and drinking sangria with their upstairs neighbors and will get married in the spring. I get swept up in her the way I do, wonder how someone can have two-tone bangs and be so in love. She is perfect when she tells me that that *guy,* the one with the red neckbeard, has a twenty-dollar outstanding bar tab and keeps asking her and Kevin about having a threesome. He doesn't respect her establishment or her relationship, she says, lending the bar dice to another couple. The guy receiving the dice is wearing a shirt that says I CAN'T ADULT TODAY, and orders two PBRs—I ask my boyfriend if he wants to try playing, but he's tired and already knows how.

I beat Connor at bar dice once and for all and he has to buy us all green tea shots—they make me feel sick on top of the metric ton of laxatives I took that morning, but when someone puts something in your hand and says you won it, it goes in your body and you see what happens. Connor is *fuming.* I use the five bucks I win to pick music for the jukebox: two classic rock songs, one Rina, one Rihanna, and something from the *SpongeBob* soundtrack. I'm about to implement one of my more effective I've-accidentally-angered-a-guy-named-Connor-at-a-bar schemes.

This is a system I've been perfecting since I started sneaking tallboys back in Allston. First you wait for some fuckin' guy, the Connor of the moment, to get a little mad at you—maybe you beat him at dice without knowing how to play dice, maybe you used a word with too many syllables, maybe you didn't want a *third* Miller in twenty minutes. He's pissed and you don't want to get yelled at, so you excuse yourself to "go to the bathroom" (stand in a stall and check Twitter, then realize you actually *do* have to pee), then come back out and put on a little show.

"Could you tell me how this game really works?" I ask, putting my hand on his back for a moment. He looks up from his meat tube, thrilled I've asked him to explain something to me. He spends the next ten minutes explaining drunk arithmetic, and the bartender laughs. The most interesting women in the world are tending bar in Wisconsin, telling you to find a song on the jukebox that sounds better than a Sunday afternoon golf tournament, wearing three pairs of earrings and a crop top and the same pair of shorts every time I see them, and it's my job to tell you that. I like her, she likes me, we won't meet again.

Let's not forget that Wisconsin has hot dogs of its own—some of the best, with some of the ugliest names known to man.

There's no better example than Dogs & Cream, a one-floor shop in a red, white, and blue–painted brick building in Racine. It's only been open for three years when we stop by, but owner Eric Robinson has made it his mission to make it feel like it's been open for fifty. Its menu features eleven signature dogs from around the country, the Chicago to the New York to the Hot-lanta, and the one I try on the recommendation of the bartender my boyfriend's kissed and I fell in love with for two hours—the Pretzel Dog, served with sweet potato fries, marshmallow dipping sauce, and a gigantic orange Dreamsicle Float.

This is the Wisconsin trick, so much dairy that you forget that your life is a fucking disaster. It works like a charm, and I would like to declare the hideously named business with an equally menacing mascot, a toothless hot dog with a nose looking into the middle distance with a gummy, leering grin, one of my favorites in the country. The pretzel bun is an inspired idea that I can hardly believe it took us a full month to encounter for the first time, the beef hot dog is well grilled, and the only other topping to speak of is a matter-of-fact cum-wash of classic nacho cheese. Paired with sweet potato fries and marshmallow sauce, it's easily the best ten dollars I've spent in weeks.

Every day for the rest of July I walk five miles under tall trees, play bar dice with men who respect me about 40 percent, work for twelve hours buzzing on Adderall in a grandma's basement while my boyfriend waits for Grandma to fall asleep and then goes to sleep somewhere else. I think back to when we came here last summer, all wrapped in plastic back when it was the plague and we cared, not like now when it's the plague and we're tired of the plague and each other. We went to the tippity top of the state, the Upper Peninsula; there is no beauty greater and no argument louder than where no one can hear you. Didn't we agree it was over then too? It's over still now, I know that, but we have nowhere to go, and so I stay in the basement and keep working and walking beneath the trees. I fucked up plenty, myself. It's over but we love each other, over but neither of us can go home, my dad's surgery in flux and the house we share in California on sale and full of disease. So again, I stay, because it's the end of the world and there's nowhere else to go.

My friend Melissa is the one I ask about these things. She visited last spring and asked if I was okay; she had left the person who made her look like I did lately, did I need anything? I said she was nuts, and two months later I say she's right. I tell her we don't want to be together anymore, and she says, "Okay, but don't you have two hundred hot dogs to eat first?"

Tomorrow is Chicago.

We Are in Fucking Chicago

No, I get it, you all aren't into ketchup.

The pizza in Chicago is soup and the hot dogs in Chicago are salad but I'm happy for them. It's fine, I'm from Boston and our "signature soup" looks like the cum of a very sick person. If one more person gives me a lecture on ketchup, I'll stick a fork in my fucking eye, I swear to God; don't tell me to leave if I don't like it, I'll not like your shitty little rule wherever I can.

Okay, I'm being defensive. It's hard not to be around someone aggressively defending a Chicago hot dog because they're *so sure* they're right that they've written books about it.

Hot Dog Chicago by Rich Bowen and Dick Fay is something of a biblical text to hotdoggers, a 1983 book in which two psychology professors from Loyola University Chicago did anonymous, blind taste tests of the hundreds of hot dog establishments open in the city at the time and reviewed them at length.

"If you have to ask the price of a hot dog, you can't afford it," they warn in the book's opening.

I'll let them explain the Chicago hot dog to you—yes, they oscillate between all-beef and beef-and-pork blends, but what do these absolute freaks mean when they say their hot dog has been "dragged through the garden"?

"What makes a Chicago hot dog totally unique is the 'everything' that it comes from," the boys explain. "Of course a Chicago hot dog has mustard, relish, and chopped onion . . . but a basic hot dog also comes with a pickle spear, tomato slices, hot sport peppers, and a sprinkling of celery salt. The extravagant 'garden on a bun' Chicago school of hot dog thought specifies the addition of lettuce, cucumber slices, and pieces of green pepper."

What I'm saying is it's a *lot,* and Chicagoans don't like hearing that it may, in fact, be *too much.*

The Vienna Beef Factory is a thrumming center of Chicago hot dog culture, the company most closely associated with the city's signature preparation. It's through this company that I'll get my thorough, overwhelming one-day education at Hot Dog University a few months later, the one that spearheaded a thrilling local contest to see how many Vienna Beef stands a single Chicagoan could visit in five weeks (367 is the answer—*three hundred and sixty-seven*). They've only just moved their factory and adjoining restaurant to the West Side of the city after years in the Bucktown area, and I am once again denied the sick compulsion to tour a hot dog factory for what I'm told are safety reasons. Sure, but I am equally convinced it is because of the trouble it takes to make a hot dog factory look like a safe and sanitary place to work. I make the call to forsake the discourse surrounding the famous Chicago Polish sausage, the only tubular meal that sparks conversations of equal vigor to the Hot Dog Discourse itself.

We walk past the pale concrete factory to the Factory Store next door—one floor with a simple yellow-thatched roof, flanked with what I'll realize are signature yellow Vienna Beef flags and red picnic tables in the back for dining. The store is quiet the morning we arrive and is about as heavily branded as a place can be, with the company's logo emblazoned across the floor, on the walls, and across the large refrigerators, where fans and businesses alike can buy their favorite all-beef dogs in bulk from the source. It's at the front of the store that one of the great pieces of hot dog art is screen-printed, a hyper-realistic illustration of an *enormous* Chicago-style Vienna Beef dog floating in the middle of the city's Navy Pier, right up against the shore of Chicago itself. You can see all five hundred of the qualifying ingredients down to the smallest detail on the signature poppy-seed bun, and I walk up to nervously order the four-dollar (not bad!) Chicago-style dog from the source before sitting at one of the storefront's bright red stools. There, I can gaze across the street at the factory and consider the ethical implications of my breakfast.

Bowen and Fay have already primed me on the history of Vienna Beef, one the city is equally protective of. The company was founded in 1893 by Austrian Hungarian immigrants Samuel Ladany and Emil Reichel, and its mythology involves a debut of their signature frankfurter recipe at the World's Columbian Exposition of 1893, which is central to many of Big Hot Dog's greatest origin stories. This led to a Chicago storefront the following year, distribution at the turn of the century, and a critical inflection point during the Great Depression, at which point the company could tout their Chicago-style dogs as having a "salad on top," providing two full meals for the price of a nickel to down-on-their-luck locals. That's not to say that the company *invented* the Chicago style—that distinction is said to belong to Fluky's, a significantly diminished name in hot dogs whose only current location is inside a Walmart in Niles, Illinois.

The trajectory of Vienna Beef was markedly different—as of this writing, they're the primary hot dog manufacturer across Chicago and have had a fair amount of profit distributing around the country as well. In the city, they're still best known for their sheepskin-cased, all-beef hot dog, but have better success with the child-friendly skinless variety in distribution. My name's called, my dog is ready. I buy a T-shirt. I bite. I don't like it.

Here's what I'll say—I have not found a single defender of the Chicago hot dog who did not grow up with or have an otherwise strong emotional connection to it, nor a single person who has never lived there say, "Hey, that sounds good and I want one." For me, it falls firmly under the category of the Baltimore deep-fried-bologna variety, one that I understand the historical significance of but have no interest in furthering the narrative.

At the Vienna Beef Factory Store, the poppy-seed bun is soggy. The snap of the hot dog is hampered by the wetness of the salad on top, the pepper slipped off, the entire dill pickle was egregious and impossible to keep balanced, the two thick tomato slices slippery and tasteless and yes, okay, the showmanship of the lime green relish is pretty cool. It's not that I don't like it, it's that I hate it, that I deeply resent a good beef dog with a snap showered in unnecessary garnish that watches me as I eat it, oh fuck you. I bring the baggage of the thousands of words you've already read to the sticky table, but my God—Chicago is wonderful and their signature hot dog is *not good*.

I'm much more optimistic about our next stop on the South Side, one that has only a year's worth of business against Vienna Beef's century-plus and isn't hampered by the tradition of feeding me like I'm wearing a goddamn newsboy cap. We've been sent here by the couple who will usher us around Hot Dog Chicago for the remainder of the day—my dear friend Nina and her fiancé, David. She is a music writer and fell in love with one too, a staunch lover of hot dogs, ice cream, baseball, and obscure emo music who insists I grab her something from The Hot Dog Box before heading over.

The business lives up to its name—it is, indeed, a hot dog joint in a bright red shipping container, run by father-and-daughter team Bobby and Brooklyn Morelli since 2020. For the first time on our journey, we've found a business whose origin story and success is tied to a national disaster of *this* century.

The story goes like this. Before The Hot Dog Box, Bobby

Morelli was an R&B artist who paid the bills with a small marketing and web design company that cratered along with a series of planned tour dates when the pandemic lockdown began in March 2020. Morelli is the rare artist who *doesn't* suck at business, and quickly made a plan to lease one of the storage unit business rentals at the local Boxville outdoor mall for a cookies-and-ice-cream business, only for his business partner to bail three weeks before the opening. Now left with no cookies and no partner, Morelli pivoted *again*—this time, to a hot dog business (Vienna Beef, of course) with his nine-year-old daughter, Brooklyn. Bored out of her mind with online classes, she began by helping take orders, appeared in videos on Instagram, and played on the oversized Connect Four board just outside the four-hundred-square-foot shipping container where her dad began improvising an ever-changing hot dog specialty menu. By the time we visit, she's a crucial player in the business, taking our order while her dad cooks their now-signature Bronzeville Bourbon filet mignon steak dog—absurdly priced at nearly thirteen dollars, but it includes chips and a drink and a chat with the nicest fifth-grader on the planet.

Today, according to their Instagram, is the first time the father-daughter team are wearing big novelty hot dog hats. After our wait in a considerable line at the buzzing half-tourist, half-local outdoor mall, Brooklyn's dad looks after her as she takes each order and quietly corrects her if there's a problem. By and large, the confident kid controls the transaction.

"Welcome to Hot Dog Box, what can I get ya?" she asks with a big smile. I miss being a kid like this, enthusiasm with a slight overbite—and I was far from the young entrepreneur that Brooklyn very much is.

I order their Bronzeville Bourbon, natural-casing with steak and *actual* filet mignon, bitch, topped with a "cabbage and carrots medley," crumbled bacon, an in-house bourbon barbecue sauce developed by Morelli and his wife, and hot sport peppers on a baked bun. Nina's had the Bronzeville a few times over and opts for the rotating specialty dog, this week the "Sweet Kickin Buffalo Steak Dog" with a full strip of bacon cruising down the center.

Brooklyn puts my order into an iPad and takes my number down to text when it's ready, saying it will take about twenty minutes. Bobby turns from the food prep area and gently corrects her—"It'll be ten."

While we wait, we take a walk around the pop-up store district that The Hot Dog Box is nestled into—a community area called Boxville, all Black-owned businesses (including the Morellis) in the historically Black neighborhood of Bronzeville. This summer, the site has grown to include seventeen businesses but began with a single container in 2014, with the Bronzeville Bike Box quickly becoming a neighborhood go-to for bike repairs and sales in a community that used them frequently. By 2017, founder and longtime Bronzeville business booster and advocate Bernard Lloyd had identified fifteen businesses to run out of old shipping containers in the shadow of the Fifty-First Street Green Line station and brought a surge of energy, attention, and new customers to the area.

As always, the reality of an operation like Boxville remains mired in the rules of American capitalism. Lloyd has worked for notorious Chicago villain Rahm Emmanuel as a member of the former mayor's Green Ribbon Committee and is the founder of Urban Juncture, a company that has reinvigorated local business in the Bronzeville area but is also a for-profit real estate venture, albeit a more ethical one than most, according to local press. The neighborhood has been subject to a series of "urban renewal" projects that ultimately displaced people and wealth in decades past, with a large portion of the Black middle- and upper-middle-class families in the Mecca Flats complex in the 1950s evicted by the expanding campus of the Illinois Institute of Technology. The community organized and campaigned against the institution, and were ultimately unsuccessful—another setback that benefitted white Chicago, something Bernard Lloyd is determined to fight.

Lloyd struggled for years to secure consistent funding to develop a Black-owned food district that was missing in the city, much of which can be attributed to real estate racism—when the professional (majority white) class left the Bronzeville neighborhood, the area was deemed "too dangerous" to put any serious money into. What followed was a long period of trial, error, and investment that led to Boxville over the course of a decade.

Upon opening in 2017, the impact the development had was huge, becoming the nucleus of a $10 million initiative called Build Bronzeville, the culmination of fifteen-plus years of Lloyd's efforts. Food has always been the main thrust of business, an intentional move by Lloyd.

"We're not there yet, but I think folks are recognizing that we cannot have healthy neighborhoods without a vibrant local commerce," he told *Chicago Business* in November 2021. "In order to do that we have to start with entrepreneurs who have an interesting concept, who may not have all the assets but [need] a leg up to get to first base."

The Hot Dog Box fits in perfectly with Boxville's initiative, and isn't the only storage container to have a winding line on a day that is sunny for now. We get our hot dogs to go, and I wonder what the whole, you know, child labor deal is with Brooklyn—there's a soft echo of the Bluth banana stand ringing through the metal walls of The Hot Dog Box, but what do I know? They make a hell of a hot dog and will have another location open by the beginning of the following year.

Our guides, Nina and David, are in love and we peek around at their apartment full of records and framed things whose origins I don't know. We catch up and talk about the two years we've had, a nightmare marked by fortune because we could stay inside, like so many others couldn't. She was able to find some peace with herself she did not have in the Before Times and is so gentle and kind.

No one is polite about digging into their Bronzeville Bourbons, and I'm grateful—they're unbelievable, worth every penny in the way that a chic, inflated-price hot dog rarely is. It may not surprise you to know I can't speak to what filet mignon tastes like, but I trust that it's the too-nice-for-me steak that Bobby prepared while Brooklyn kept guard of the iPad—an extra shout-out to the homemade barbecue sauce and perfectly toasted bun that holds a few too many ingredients with ease. I show Nina my list of places to go and she looks at the sky, warning me that we only have so much time until it opens on us.

We choose Fatso's Last Stand, a fifteen-minute walk away and one of the best-regarded purveyors of the char-dog on the planet, complete with a signature cross-cut style that makes the flavor and texture damn near perfect. Another Vienna Beef purveyor, the place was founded by beloved local Phil Ashbach as Phil's Last Stand originally, but later changed the name to Fatso's in honor of . . . well, yeah. Don't cancel me, he approved it.

"I'm a four-hundred-pound Jew, and I'm bald. I'm the easiest guy to make fun of," he'd say to customers, and was known for popping into the flagship Ukrainian Village joint close to midnight and verbally abusing anyone trying to put ketchup on one of the char-dogs. Brain cancer took his life at sixty-six back in 2014, but his presence is still felt in the spirit of the place the afternoon we walk up to the painted red bricks advertising the dogs, fried shrimp, and famous Fatso burgers. The staff is brusque and efficient, not the types to waste time with pleasantries in a way that sucks Nina and me into the tortoiseshells of social anxiety we were born into. We sorely miss the fidgety magnets that customers used to play with on the Fatso's counter before coronavirus made it too dangerous to fidget with your sweetest friend.

The standard dog at Fatso's is served Chicago style, to my dismay, but it's a marked improvement over the soggy mess from the Vienna Beef Factory Store—the artful cross-cut at the tip of each dog's end creates a super-snap event that manages to cut through the pile of absurdity on top of it, with a poppy-seed bun far better equipped for the job and greasy fries to absorb any other doubts I was having. It's made better by the people sitting across from me on the back patio, where we take pictures in a glorious face-in-hole stand of a hot dog in a suit and a slutty cheeseburger. I remind myself to compare it against pictures of us in college to see if we look old, and we don't.

A small militia of Vienna Beef umbrellas protects us from what Nina correctly predicted would be an unwelcome summer rainstorm, and we flee the scene only to find that we're in the only five city blocks that God is taking a helicopter piss on. Our clothes are soaked through and our shoes stink and Nina's eyeliner is running like a goth seventh grader's after seeing *The Phantom of the Opera* for the first time. Our Fatso's leftovers turn to a thick, paper-meat glob in our hands as we try to outrun the storm, but it's no use—we're laughing because everyone else in the street decides that's the only way to get through it. It's an in-the-flesh experience I would have slit someone's throat for a year ago, so I decide to love that it's happening instead of thinking how the Subaru will smell two hours from now. My beautiful friend is laughing and has someone she loves to toss her a towel in a few blocks and we're okay. Her laugh reminds me of the awful electronic concert from 2012 where we were having fun until someone overdosed and the lead singer tried to lure us into a trailer because being a nineteen-year-old with enthusiasm can be a death sentence if you don't have your wits about you, and sometimes even if you do. Today we are wet and happy and the hot dog was good; we hug goodbye so they can be dry and in love and we can be wet and on the way to more hot dogs outside the storm.

Our final stand in Chicago comes after a sorely missed stop to The Wiener's Circle, the emotionally charged home of performative verbal abuse that's closed for renovations when we swing by, substituting a welcome quick bite at a cartoony joint called Wolfy's. We're four dogs deep in the day, but there's one more place I'm determined to hit by sundown, and we head over to the Norwood Park neighborhood on Milwaukee Avenue. Right on the edge of town is a legacy business that has the best merch and the most menacing gendered hot dog sculptures in the country—welcome to Superdawg Drive-In.

We happen to be pulling in around twilight after I spotted the place from a mile away by the two enormous hot dog sculptures on the roof of the campy black building with blue-and-yellow diamond cutouts, complete with the rare and always satisfying we-come-to-you carhop component that places deeper in the city don't have the accommodations for. Again, with the gendered foods, my God—the male-coded red hot wears a leopard-print Borat bathing suit dick-sling, flexes his huge biceps, and, I am so sorry about this, shows off his honking thick thighs. The woman-coded red hot beside him is too shy to meet her virile counterpart's terrifying muscle mass, gazing downward in a blue poodle skirt, bow, and sleeves, but no top? She's tits-out, but she's shy. At this point, nothing on the planet can trigger my fight-or-flight response, and I squeal so loudly on seeing them that my boyfriend nearly crashes the car.

This is a stark enough image in the light of day, but the business stays open well into the night and roof lights keep the horny heterosexuals in view. For some fucking reason, both statues have glowing red eyes that pierce into your soul and remove years from your life. As the sun sets, I see the exact *moment* the man-dog's eyes turn him from a Mogwai into a Gremlin, and it makes me grateful that at least the hot dog is good.

The gendered hot dogs are supposed to make more sense when you know the business's backstory, but I'll let you make your own assessment. Superdawg was opened in 1948 by not just a married couple, but a married couple with rhyming names—Maurie and Flaurie Berman, who the roof statues are named for. They were high school sweethearts who married when Maurie returned from GI service after World War II, with Flaurie working as a public school teacher in Chicago while Maurie studied at Northwestern. The business began as a summer endeavor that rejected the traditional franks and wieners for their own model, the Superdawg—the pure-beef dog and crinkle-cut fries were an immediate hit and the place was opened year-round, with Flaurie serving as its inaugural carhop. Maurie designed and expanded the building over the years, fashioning hot dogs that remind locals that they have seven days to live.

The carhop service has always been a core component, with the signature Stepford-sweet greeting, "Hiya, thanks for stopping. May I take your order now?" that we hear over the tinny metallic ordering box. I keep it real and order the signature Superdawg, served in an aesthetically perfect blue box with a Tarzan-outfitted Maurie gendered dog smiling peacefully, reclining in a beach chair. "Your Superdawg lounges inside," the box says in a 1950s diner font, "contentedly cushioned in Superfries."

The hot dog itself is a good one, made better by the crinkle fries—the fact that this is my fourth try on a hot dog style I deeply dislike, and I'm enjoying the beef-snap, is impressive in itself. Of all the car parks we've been to, I feel most immersed in the American lie here as the sun sets on the hat I couldn't help buying and the satanic eyes of the looming anthropomorphic dogs. Maybe there's something to them, our urge to see ourselves in everything we love, even when it tips into the weird. Maybe I'm not afraid of them, after all. Then, they blink, and I know that I am.

There are virtually hundreds of hot dog stands in Chicago and, by that logic, hundreds we missed on the one day we had to see them, but dear Chicagoans—do not email me. There are only so many chances I will give a decent hot dog topped with a salad unworthy of the 7–Eleven day-old shelf. I will rudely and correctly imply that I get your drift and I love the aesthetic, the culture, the infrastructure, and the enthusiasm, but the real innovation taking place is at stands like The Hot Dog Box, the ones that make an active effort to explore hot dog preparation outside of the Great Depression standby of the city. Why is everyone so desperate for it to still be the culinary Great Depression? Please. Haven't we been through enough this lifetime?

Yes, reader—the best hot dog in Chicago is prepared by a father-daughter team with less than a year in the business. I think that's a beautiful thing.

A Word on Baseball

I understand baseball and I can prove it at any time, ha ha no seriously.

Look, I'm as American as anyone, and I don't know what I mean when I say that but I know how I *feel,* and it's insecure with a throbbing need to prove something. I've been to a baseball game, *okay?* A wealth of city funds were used in Brockton to establish a minor-minor-league team where I once sang the national anthem the summer after 9/11 so, uh, yeah—I *get* it. I invented baseball. I am the only American. In fact, I'm going to tell you about the hot dogs at three ballparks across a nation once effectively publicized as being great. Let's take them, and the myths they're burdened with, in order.

I. CLOSE ENCOUNTER WITH THE DODGER DOG

The 2021 baseball season went like this—the season began with thirty teams and ended with one, an abnormal-but-more-normal adjustment to an abridged 2020 season that was shortened and ravaged by scandal during the lockdown. The 2021 season brought some of the same, but also moments that make baseball such a clickable American sport, from Trey Mancini returning to the sport after a full stage III colon cancer recovery to a highly publicized *Field of Dreams*–style game to Angels player

Shohei Ohtani shattering Babe Ruth's records and the Atlanta Braves taking the championship. I know exactly none of this when we head to Dodger Stadium in Los Angeles in May 2021 in pursuit of a Dodger Dog.

Unfortunately, we've *just* missed the time it was good to be a Dodger Dog fan. I want to be completely up front with you here and say that I have sourced information about the three teams whose stadiums and hot dogs of choice I sampled—the Dodgers, the Brewers, and the Red Sox—from people who know what they're talking about, which is how I am able to tell you things like "The Dodgers made probably the worst decision in recent history by signing Trevor Bauer" and "Our minor-league call-ups mostly did not perform well and showed just how much of our depth we had to sacrifice for big-name trades," followed by things like "Everybody had to watch Donald Trump gleefully doing the Tomahawk Chop with the Braves' sizable racist faction of their fan base, but mostly everyone was glad to see Atlanta beat the loathsome cheating Astros." I trust my sources, will not name them for their own protection, and refuse to fact-check their claims.

Here's the thing about the Dodger Dog—it sucks now. It's shit. It's garbage. It's an insult to the history of the hot dog, one that's as rooted in lore as the myths that explicitly tie the birth of the hot dog to the early days of baseball.

The Dodger Dog originated in 1962, just four years after the franchise moved from Brooklyn to Los Angeles. The legend attributes the dog to a Dodger Stadium food concession manager named Thomas Arthur, who'd been selling a ten-inch dog as a "footlong" and decided to rebrand it, getting permission from majority team owner Walter O'Malley to start calling it by its rightful name. It was a hit, and the stadium eventually switched distributors from the John Morrell & Co. meat brand to Farmer John, the Vernon, California–based meat plant that became associated with the Dodger Dog's signature all-pork flavor starting in 1972. (If you're an all-beef purist who wants your dog grilled and not plopped the way ours were, hop in the adjacent line for the slightly more expensive Super Dodger Dog, $7.75 to the pork variant's $6.75). Just six weeks before my first Dodgers game in June 2021, Farmer John and the Dodgers formally terminated a relationship that was said to sell more than twenty-five thousand hot dogs per game, and fans were *not* pleased.

While Los Angeles isn't the loudest about their hot dog fixation, we are a city that is doing *the work,* consuming the most hot dogs per capita in the entire country and not once, *once,* telling you what you can and cannot put on it. I've grown to deeply love the city that adopted me over the better part of a decade, and the passive indifference for whatever it is you're doing along with it. That's not to say that Dodgers fans aren't intense—they can froth harder than any fan base I've seen—but they're not *scary* until you fuck with the Dodger Dog.

"It's affecting the way the team is playing, need Farmer John dogs," a user waxed poetic on Instagram shortly after the distributor switch. A *Los Angeles Times* sportswriter lightly implied that the change could be blamed for a recent losing streak.

The truth may be that the dog was never great to begin with, with more fans still saying they couldn't taste the difference when shelling out six bucks for what was, on my day seeing the Dodgers face off against the Phillies, a room-temperature pork tube. Foodies, not fans, will tell you that this has always been the make of the dog, more a success in marketing than in culinary prowess—for a shitty hot dog, there's a *ton* of merchandising and signage dedicated to selling you on the idea that this might be edible. I fall for it and get two plush Dodger Dogs, one of whom stares at me across the room right now, *daring* me to say something cruel about it. And I will.

Dodger Dogs are characterized by their long, thin teen-boy-at-the-mall-with-greasy-hair look, topped however you like with an inch of tubed meat hanging out both sides of a steamed bun.

This is my first hot dog outing to research this book, which was meant to be a valiant kickoff to *Raw Dog* Industries, and I frantically try to make it work in spite of the not-grilled, barely warm, diarrhea-colored meat begging me to get those nachos that come in the honking collectible hat instead. I slather the thing in mustard, add relish—yes, you freaks, I throw on some ketchup—and bite in to find—pink. *Pink?* Pink. The meat paste being pumped into the new pork Dodger Dogs by the also Vernon-based Papa Cantella's is a lukewarm pink with no snap.

There's no way around the Dodger Dog being, with all due respect, a crock of shit, but the story behind the distributor switch has more gray area to navigate. Farmer John's contract with Dodger Stadium terminated back in the spring of 2021 after nearly fifty years, with top brass at the meat factory claiming they "were unable to come to an agreement that was beneficial for both parties." The reality is more likely tied to a coronavirus shitstorm tied directly to the Farmer John factory, where the now Smithfield Foods–owned brand—yes, that of the Smithfield Deathstar and the executive order push—was the site of two state investigations and became one of the few plants to be cited for mishandling the initial outbreak.

Even in the torrid world of the meatpacking industry, Farmer John did an exceptionally poor job. In the months leading up to Hot Dog Summer, five plant workers died and nearly eight hundred were infected, numbers that doubled over the year since the virus became a subject of global cautionary measures. This would go down in an already tortured chapter of history as one of the largest outbreaks in the industry. Beginning in May 2020, the company stopped reporting the number of infections to local health officials following then president Trump's executive order to keep meat processing plants open—you know, the one advocated for by Smithfield and Tyson execs. This quickly led to more than three hundred unreported cases, in addition to the company failing to test or require quarantine for employees who had been exposed to the virus.

By the time the deal with Dodger Stadium fell through, Farmer John had fucked over their employees and public image completely. They racked up the largest fine in meatpacking for safety violations at a time when working in the industry was considered a near certainty of illness, with more than fifty-seven thousand employees contracting the coronavirus and nearly three hundred dying. No such human rights violations hung over the head of fellow Vernon plant Papa Cantella's, and they made just as shitty a hot dog.

That's the story of the Dodger Dog—it's okay to have a *little* blood of the working class on your hands, but not so much that it's bad PR.

The Dodgers win against the Phillies the night Hot Dog Summer kicks off, and I celebrate by taking a series of unflattering pictures with an enormous statue of the Dodger Dog, standing tall since the mid-2010s with its Farmer John branding quietly painted over. It doesn't give me much faith in the sport that claims to be the founding father of hot dog culture on our first outing, but I'm reminded the next day where the Good Shit is: just *outside* the stadiums, sold by independent vendors who the city makes it their business to try to destroy in favor of their seven-dollar shit tubes.

I have the good fortune of walking past the Staples Center (now the Crypto.com Arena, the only rename more embarrassing than being named after an office supply store) and getting a street dog, bacon-wrapped and four dollars. It's a million times better. It's *actually* American.

I return to Dodger Stadium three months later in the early autumn, seeking out comfort with three of my closest friends, one of whom is deeply unsettled by the fact that I get along with the others—never mix your chaos friends with your steady friends. It's the only night of baseball I can be expected to show up for with my whole chest: Hello Kitty night, a critical crossover event that is intended to bring absolute heathens like me back to the fold with the promise of a knitted beanie. There is no boyfriend with me this time because, like I told you, Hot Dog Summer giveth and it taketh away.

This time, I opt for something called the Xtreme Bacon-Wrapped Hot Dog, another dish wordlessly updated from a Farmer John's frank to Papa Cantella's well-grilled, quarter-pound, all-beef variant. It extends beyond the (also grilled!) bun in the expected fashion, wrapped in two slices of bacon with grilled peppers and onions and slathered in mustard and mayonnaise. For an absurd price, the portions are generous and the dog is far more satisfying than the lower-priced original. Two friends leave because of social anxiety. One stays with me in seats that are not ours, mercifully quiet about the fact that my hair is doing that thing where it's a triangle.

Being a Dodgers hot dog consumer is much like being a Los Angeles resident—if you've got a little extra to spend, the entire world bends to you in a way that feels wrong and tastes better. It could be worse though. You could be watching racist sausages beating the shit out of each other in the Midwest.

II. THE BREWERS AND THE ITALIAN SAUSAGE

Sure, I could tell you *something* about the Milwaukee Brewers' 2021 season, I suppose. I could say something like, Hey, that pitcher two years younger than me sure did beat those records, huh, or Remember that blowout game against the Dodgers in May? and feel those who *know* have their squishy little eyeballs roll back into their heads in ecstasy. All of these things are true, just as true as the fact that the Brewers will finish first in their division this season, but that's not why I've brought you to my office today, is it?

Milwaukee is a weird city, the sort that will push you away with its catering to white residents' interests and chaotically unsafe coronavirus protocols, then attempt to lure you back in with its stunning culture of functional alcoholics and baseball tailgating so organized you wish they'd help your workplace unionize. After a season of tailgating at a COVID-induced standstill, the parking lots in front of the Brewers' American Family Field are once again flooded with children sneaking spiked seltzers and parents blacked out on Millers before the sun hits the horizon, cooking the brats the area is known for on portable grills. For every family having a good old-fashioned time grilling in the parking lot, there's a party bus full of sports fans living on the residual glow of the Milwaukee Bucks winning the NBA championship a few days before, speeding past Frank Lloyd Wright houses with yard signs alternating between BACK THE BLUE and VOTE BLUE NO MATTER WHO.

We walk through the meat smells on our way into the stadium and it's glorious—a critical rule of thumb we already learned outside Dodger Stadium is that the cheap dogs being cooked outside a sports arena are always, *always* better than what they're charging ten bucks for inside and almost never legal to sell. This is one area in which Wisconsin stands out, with Brewers President of Business Operations Rick Schlesinger in full support of tailgating culture, saying that "Tailgating is a Wisconsin tradition, and how we begin our day at the ballpark."

American Family Field doesn't have the historic legacy of the spectacularly updated Dodger Stadium or the aesthetically pleasing historic Fenway Pahhhk. It was built between 1996 and 2001 with $290 million in public funds (a controversial move to fund a stadium for a privately owned team), and there was tragic bloodshed when three construction workers were killed by a crane while the park was being constructed in 1999. The crane was scrapped and a statue erected in the victims' honor, and the park opened in 2001 with the Milwaukee-based Klement's

Sausage Company meat products populating the park—only to be abruptly replaced in 2018 by much-larger local business Johnsonville Sausages, another joint that had plants shut down due to coronavirus. With no formal hot dog in their lineup, Hebrew National's all-beef kosher dogs became the official make of the stadium, and no matter the distributor, the presence of sausages at Am-Fam Field comes with a tradition just as bizarre and tone-deaf as the city itself can be.

Let's discuss the five meat-tube elephants in the room—the Sausage Race.

If you're not familiar with the ritual, that means you're not into baseball or from Wisconsin, and I can relate. The first time I heard of the Sausage Race was casually, as if I should have known already—five people in seven-foot-three mascot suits vaguely shaped like sausages in various cultural outfits and named just as offhandedly. Each and every home game, this band of hastily constructed freaks comes down to the field during the seventh-inning stretch to race against each other. For an equally inscrutable reason, the Sausages tag off to miniature versions of the same costumed characters, called the Little Weenies, during Sunday afternoon Am-Fam Field home games. Look, I can't account for it either, but the running of the Broad Cultural Stereotypes is a tradition among Brewers fans.

I'd better introduce you to our racers, all of whom are coded male but very much subscribe to the anthropomorphic logic of the gender pickles—they are scary, they look more like seven-foot-tall rectangular humans than sausages, some of them are arguably racist, and fans are unreasonably attached to them out of the financially predatory late-capitalist illness called nostalgia. Meet your runners:

Polish, a seven-foot-tall Caucasian man wearing a red-and-blue-striped T-shirt and sunglasses that we are supposed to believe is a sausage. Each sausage has a biography on the MLB website and Polish is said to have begun racing as one of the original three in the nineties lineup "after years of coaching high school cross-country" for some reason, with slow starts in races whose gaps he closes toward the end. He is from Warsaw and is canonically shy, like a sausage is.

Italian, a sausage my boyfriend insists is offensive but I, having just learned that my family is Greek and *not* Italian as we'd spent half a century thinking, don't feel qualified to comment at this time. Referred to as the "suave one of the bunch" with a "spicy personality," he's an original racer who has a twirly mustache and a white chef's uniform. He's also said to be a failed actor, previously appearing in low-budget movies like *Sausages Are a Butcher's Best Friend* and *Sausages, Sausages, and More Sausages.* Am I awake? Let's keep going. He's the narcissist of the bunch, thriving on attention and fixated on his looks. He makes me horny, and that makes me a Cultural Problem.

Brat, a mustachioed German sausage in a Brewers-emblazoned green alpine hat and lederhosen, who, according to his statistics page, is "intimidating to the other participants with his muscular physique." One of the original three, he's said to be a strong starter who loses steam at the end of the race and has weak ankles. You know . . . sausage ankles. I feel sick?

Hot Dog, a later addition to the party and the winner of the race we see from as far away as one possibly could without leaving the stadium entirely. I cannot emphasize how little this thing looks like a hot dog, I'm sorry—he's tubular and dressed like a Brewers player with war paint and lips I *think* I'm supposed to want to kiss, but ultimately he looks like a seven-foot-tall white guy in white sneakers. Why? He was introduced onto the field in the 2000s "after being recognized in his three successful completions of the Boston Marathon" with his relatives including the cheese, chili, Chicago-style, and corn dogs, attributed with the boot-strappy qualities associated with the great American myth. "People cannot help but to love Hot Dog."

Chorizo, the last and perhaps most controversially depicted sausage, first appeared in the race in 2006 in an attempt to acknowledge Latin contributions to baseball and include the Latin fan base in Wisconsin. Chorizo has been a permanent competitor since 2007, but not without criticism—the mascot appears in a sombrero meant to represent the *entire* Latin population, and has the lowest number of wins of the entire bunch. He debuted on Cerveceros Day, an Am-Fam Field tradition hosted in conjunction with the Hispanic Chamber of Commerce in Wisconsin, and "While his exact workout regimen is kept a secret, it is known that Chorizo has spent time training in the hills of central Mexico, hiking the mountains of the volcanic region of Guatemala," his official profile says, "rock climbing in Puerto Rico, and has even been seen running with the bulls in Pamplona, Spain, all with the goal of someday making it to the big league."

Uh, okay—I guess I don't expect the Am-Fam team to have a nuanced understanding of anything, but there are *notes* to be made here. Chorizo is said to have been sent back to the Mexican League for "further seasoning" before joining the race full time, and that fans "love the strong and spicy kick he gives to everything he does . . . the way he wears his sombrero, and even the salsa dancing he does before games to loosen up for that evening's race."

I don't believe that the Sausages were created to hurt anyone's feelings and were hopefully intended as tributes, not mockery, but they're fucking weird. This season, Hot Dog takes first prize by a long shot, with twenty-seven wins to Polish in second place (nineteen), followed by Italian (sixteen), Brat (eleven), and Chorizo (eight). There's no evidence that races have ever been rigged, but there has to be something to Hot Dog's reign, I'm convinced—Chorizo's sombrero isn't just leaning into a cultural stereotype; it also serves as a floppy drag chute to leave him at the back of the pack. The five Sausages start at the dugout during the seventh-inning stretch, rounding home base running *much* faster than you want to see a seven-foot-tall hot dog running toward you, bumping up against one another as children scream at the Jumbotron for their favorite runner. The whole thing takes twenty-five seconds, and Hot Dog's gorgeous lips and ghostly pallor appear onscreen in celebration, brought to you by some insurance company. The Wisconsinites love it, and I have no reason to take it from them.

For better and for worse, the Sausage Race is a part of the culture at American Family Field. Hell, a visiting Pittsburgh player even attacked the Sausages with a baseball bat out of sheer frustration and got arrested. Offending player Randall Simon later made amends with Mandy Block, the woman in the Italian sausage costume he'd assaulted, accepting a three-game suspension and a fine. He did two things as penance—autographed the bat he hit her with, and gifted her a trip to his home island of Curaçao. For Block's part, she was unharmed and thrilled for the free vacation.

The Sausages make appearances at local events and run a 5K for charity every year, with family members of the Brewers frequently making guest appearances in the suits even when the team members themselves don't always understand the appeal. Imitators have cropped up, with other teams racing US presidents and pierogi, but no one can match the sausage and bratwurst's inherent connection to the Wisconsin area, and no one is eager to phase it out. The races were inspired by a simple animation shown at games and were done in the flesh sporadically in the nineties, becoming so popular that by the turn of the century they were a fixture of every home game and now are plastered across merchandise and statues for fans to pose with on their way out of the park. Critical disclosure: I am now the owner of a novelty magnet and an Italian sausage plushie.

We've got nosebleed seats at this Brewers game, just behind a masked family with a cranky nine-year-old and her embarrassed thirteen-year-old brother wearing a gold plastic Flavor

Flav chain, and directly in front of a group of wildly drunk twentysomethings in the dead-last-row seats they sell at fourteen dollars a pop. I've got my fist tightly wrapped around an all-beef hot dog, served grilled and bare in a steamed bun and wrapped in foil. Dressed with ketchup and mustard—the prejudice against sugary tomato topping isn't felt as strongly here as in nearby Chicago—the Johnsonville hot dog runs fucking *laps* around the mealy Dodger Dog, almost but not quite managing to snap as I argue with my boyfriend about which sausages are racist and which are just weird. As we're really getting into it, the announcers begin the second most American ritual of any baseball game on the planet, asking local veterans to stand for a moment of raucous applause. Yes, yes, thank you for your service, but is this Italian sausage culturally insensitive and what does that say about the animatronic Chef Pasqually at Chuck E. Cheese?

We cannot ask the Sausages what they think—Brewers officials have gone on the record that "the Sausages don't talk . . . it's one of the basic rules of racing meat."

The Brewers beat the Chicago White Sox in a 7–1 landslide, giving me enough time to take a thumbs-up picture with the Italian sausage that I don't know if I should be documenting my time with or not. What are the rules with Italians? Have I been Rachel Dolezal-ing being Italian for the better part of thirty years? Please send help. I decide to honor the only stadium in the country where sausages outsell the traditional hot dog by snagging a Johnsonville brat for the road, topped with a signature Miracle Mile Smokey Mustard and a well-toasted bun. It's damn good, though my boyfriend tells me that by local standards it isn't even in the fiftieth percentile of what's possible. This isn't a sausage book, so I decide to accept the stomachache and his word for it. After all, Hot Dog won the race.

As we leave the stadium, a line of free party buses flank the streets to bring fans to nearby bars, where they'll continue to spend the disposable incomes it's easier to hold on to in the Midwest. We drive home behind a drunk driver with the license plate DELIMAN, and I quietly hope it's the sexy narcissistic Italian sausage in the driver's seat.

III. YOU DON'T WANT TO HAND IT TO FENWAY PARK UNDER ANY CIRCUMSTANCES, BUT...

My final baseball dog is on my turf, a place best confronted alone. The Fenway area in Boston is sacred to foaming locals, ones I closely associate with the Bruegger's Bagels I worked at in college, sucking down at least a full quart of clam chowder and cold brew apiece each shift. I didn't grow up in a Red Sox family—my dad was a writer who most often covered the Boston Bruins for thirty years, and he trained my brother and me to have disdain for the fan base around the Sox. We are *journalists,* we Loftuses, observers and not fans. We're assholes, is what I'm saying. I'm not expecting to have a life-affirming experience, is what I'm saying. I'm dead wrong, is what I'm saying.

When you're from Boston, you end up at Fenway Park one way or another, and on the thick, hot August night I leave my dad recuperating from surgery to attend a game alone, I find I've retained more about the place's history than I thought.

Fenway gets the edge over many of its ballpark peers on the strength of legacy and intensity alone—its capacity isn't impressive and, for a long time, neither was its team, but it's a cultural landmark that held its first game the week after the *Titanic* sank and holds massive mythic power. It's the home of the Green Monster, a thirty-seven-foot ballpark wall that inspired their Muppet-like mascot, Wally; it's where one seat is painted red to mark where Ted Williams hit a 502-foot home run in 1946; it has a quirky layout that emphasizes its earliness to the sport, with a shorter outfield and a deeper centerfield. It's a stadium with a theme song ("Sweet Caroline," if you know you know), where everything from boxing to Gaelic football to Bruce Springsteen concerts have taken place, where the surrounding bars are built to service drunk fans (shout out to Cask 'n Flagon, which I hear is great and I wouldn't go inside for any amount of money). The mainway leading to the stadium is an Irish white uncle–infested tribute to its most famous dish, the Fenway Frank.

Oh, come on, you knew where this was going. Before entering Fenway proper to the garbage seat I've secured last-minute, I take in the outdoor cart culture: a number of Italian sausage carts line the sidewalk in keeping with the cartoonishly Irish Italianness of the area, along with beer stands and plenty of BOSTON STRONG imagery that's been marketed so heavily as to become completely meaningless. Originally a hollow message meant to be a balm to the city during the fallout of the Boston Marathon bombing in 2013, the phrase has since mellowed into a regional equivalent of the "USA!" chanted at Joey Chestnut on Coney Island.

I wear an N95 mask to protect my dad, and I'm deeply in the minority. By August of Hot Dog Summer, the national attitude toward the eighteen months of COVID-induced pressure to behave well has transformed into a flagrant disregard for anyone's safety in the pursuit of feeling *anything*. The park, much like every other I attend during the summer, does not require that attendees wear masks, and they follow through in typical white Bostonian fashion by not doing it. I'm not bothered by crowds, but the low ceilings of Fenway and an unmasked, sports-loving mob push me into the beer line earlier than I expected just to take the edge off. A benevolent auntie imparts advice to the college student standing in front of me.

"Here's a *pro tip*," she says. "Get a water bottle and a vodka lemonade, then dilute it and have a good fuckin' time."

They take her advice and I don't. I grab a gigantic Bud Light in a can because I respect the culture and head to a Fenway Franks stand, its sign pulsing across the stadium with bright red letters. Call me a sucker, but I love the Fenway Frank. Sold at the park from the year it opened, the Fenway Frank is as close as I can get to a nostalgic connection to my filthy, sticky, fucked-up homeland, boiled and then grilled in a split-bread bun and topped with whatever the fuck you want, not my fuckin' business, it's your hot dog, Jame.

In traditional hot dog fashion, its manufacturing history is full of drama. The beef-and-pork frank was distributed by local meatpacking plant Colonial Provision Company for decades, but the company was subsumed by a Michigan-based company in 1986, risking layoffs for more than six hundred Boston employees. City Council got involved in an attempt to declare eminent domain and keep manufacturing local, and then councilman Joseph Tierney spoke in embarrassingly regional terms on the controversy in an interview with the *New York Times* after being the only official to vote against the motion.

"I don't want those people to lose their jobs, but this is not the way to save them," he said in 1986. "The mayor is full of beans, and the council is full of beans."

Bean rhetoric or no, Tierney's prediction panned out—the meat plant closed after half a century in business, even after ten union advocates snuck into the plant the day it was set to close and vowed to stay until they were thrown out. More than six hundred full- and part-time workers sang and chanted in support of the union as the plant was closed before their eyes, after months of buying billboard space, packing City Council meetings, and leading Boston-based boycotts of Colonial products.

"We had a program to save jobs, but the city didn't have the courage to move forward with it: that was the eminent domain takeover of Colonial," said meatpacking union organizer Brian Lang upon the plant's closure in the spring of 1986. Manufacturing would later shift to the Sara Lee–owned Kahn's brand.

Just as in Los Angeles and Milwaukee, Boston has done a major overhaul of their signature dog since the turn of the century, shifting back to locally owned business Kayem Foods in

2009 after a long battle of internal taste-testing among some of the country's largest meat manufacturers (Armour and Hillshire Farms among them). The Chelsea, Massachusetts–based plant won big on the distribution contract with a signature smoked garlic, onion, and mustard-spiked taste to their dogs that has gone over well with Red Sox fans in the subsequent decade. It's a return to form in hot dog lore—Kayem's is a century-old business founded by Polish immigrant Kazimierz Monkiewicz that remains in the family to this day, now boasting more than five hundred employees and no coronavirus scandals (that have been reported at the time of this writing, to be clear).

Now, holding a steamed bun and boiled-then-grilled dog at a well-priced $5.50, I wander around in pursuit of not the seat I've been assigned, but the one I'm *supposed* to be in. I love to wander a crowded area alone, and have never quite gotten the appeal of inviting a plus-one to a dissonant situation like, for example, not caring about baseball but needing to eat an extremely specific hot dog. I walk up, past the frat bros in polos who are deep-throating lobster rolls, past the married couples, past the community garden and indoor playgrounds, to the top deck, where it's cheap and, on this night, quiet. My seat is waiting for me right behind an older gay couple who are here for fun, one invested in the game and the other reading a pulpy paperback while the Red Sox *cream* the Tampa Bay Rays. Personally, I attribute it to the National Anthem singer really going for the high-school-soprano "freee-EEEEEE" at the beginning of the night.

That's not to say the environment is completely gentle—there are at least three men with flesh-colored hair within earshot of me yelling "FOCK YOU!" at the team, their friend, or possibly themselves—but the mood is mellow for the region. I start to scroll on my phone and fire off an objective truth, which is that Lady Gaga's "Born This Way" *hits* on a ballpark organ.

This sets off an exciting sequence of events. In an interaction that only happens to the embarrassingly online, a follower quickly makes the connection that I've been a guest on the same podcast as the ballpark organist for the Red Sox, and that he *happens* to take requests during games if I wanted to give it a shot from the nosebleeds. I'm Bud Light buzzed and decide to shoot my shot, tweeting that I'd love to hear the one request I'm certain no one would ever play—"Stars Are Blind" by Paris Hilton, a single so bad-good that she never felt the need to release another.

I was not prepared for the one true gem of Boston—Red Sox organist Josh Kantor.

Kantor's success is due to his remarkable talent and dedication, because most Red Sox fans wouldn't accept a non-native fan as their organist du jour. Inspired by *his* local ballpark organist—the legend, the Chicago White Sox's own Nancy Faust—Kantor kept the profession in the back of his mind after moving to the Boston area to attend Brandeis University, honing his niche skills by accompanying comedy groups in college. By 2003, he'd clinched an audition for the Red Sox.

The rest is history—Kantor didn't miss a single game during his first twelve years on the job, developing a close collaborative relationship with former Fenway *and* now Gillette Stadium DJ TJ Connelly and modernizing Faust's request system to Twitter. Now, fans can request more obscure songs days in advance for Kantor to add to his queue and give him time to prepare. It's an idea he got after hearing a Yo La Tengo fundraiser on New Jersey Public Radio, and a system that remains in place right through the night when I'm sitting at an absurd height behind a guy reading a paperback novel.

"i hope i live long enough to hear 'stars are blind' at a baseball game someday," I tweet, with a hot dog emoji to show I'm a fucking professional. I don't expect to hear back but feel at peace, watching what is undoubtedly a handful of people I went to high school with lose their shit while I feel the Fenway Frank slowly digest. I can't stay for the whole game, but I make it to the seventh-inning stretch before heading down the infinity steel staircases to the park's exit, where I plan to sprint onto Commonwealth Avenue and book it to make the final commuter rail of the night back to Brockton. I'm on the first floor and ready to power walk when something stops me—the opening fucking bars to "Stars Are Blind" on a ballpark organ.

I don't remember how my legs got from the gate back to the field so fast but I'm there in two seconds listening to a song that came out when I was in middle school, played by my new favorite Sox player, Josh Kantor. I start taking video as the organ clanks through Paris Hilton's greatest creative achievement (every American gets to be a secret fan of one hideous billionaire and she is mine) and I feel incredible—thousands of Bostonians are waiting on a Red Sox win and listening to a song I asked for. It's a song about low standards that I'm trying not to have, about dreaming of falling in love with a guy who doesn't constantly talk about killing himself and that's what makes him hot.

I stop for a sausage outside the stadium, a twelve-dollar footlong monstrosity made with pale pork in a grilled bun split down the middle, with peppers and onions to keep myself warm for the run. It's my favorite run in the world. It tastes like home, and diarrhea I'll have in the morning in the same toilet in which I have had, historically, many diarrheas before. It's the toilet I thought I had diarrhea in once but it was my period but I didn't know what a period was because sex ed had been defunded in Brockton, a decision that directly led to the city establishing a full-time daycare in our high school's basement. I am home.

I Am in Massachusetts

What do you think, Jame, any good?

My night on the town is thrown back into focus by the Task at Hand—the surgery is done. I visit my dad in the hospital a few times a day and watch Elvis movies while quietly gossiping about Dad's roommate, the red-pilled senior. At night, I go home and look up household remedies to tobacco smoke removal—a vinegar mixture on the old leather couch, a modified recipe for the walls, five hundred washes that threaten to send our ancient washing machine interstellar. For good measure, I boil a hot dog or two between air-fried fish sticks.

The time here disappears in a way that feels familiar—my aunt and uncle walk by the house every day, sometimes with hot food on a ceramic plate. It's been a long month of doctor's appointments, nicotine withdrawal, cleaning out the house I used to love and wiping down the walls one by one. It's a skeleton of the place in all of the videos I spent months of the pandemic digitizing, all exposed walls and holes punched by teenagers and wet spots and areas we agree not to talk about. I want to fix it, but you cannot make someone fix something they don't want to, short of growing a disease on it and ripping it out of their chest. His lung is out on my birthday and I get drunk with my best friend from high school near the library where I dried out after getting caught in the rain. He's okay. I'm okay. I'm inching closer to an age where This Shit Is Getting Embarrassing and know that if he is okay, I need to go back to California and not make the same mistakes my parents did.

When Dad's well enough to come home, I succeed in keeping him under house arrest for a total of two days before his sister agrees we're safe to come to the yard for a cookout. We're not, but I'm exhausted and hope his ribcage doesn't topple out due to my lapse of judgment. Sunday lunch with my aunt and cousins has become a tradition for him out of lockdown, and it's unspoken that the Child Who Left does not get a say in what is and isn't okay.

My cousins are smart and choose every battle against my uncle, whose silent protest in the form of a BLUE LIVES MAT-TER sticker on his reusable water bottle in a house full of leftist women means he will not experience a moment of peace. For once, I don't have to jump on the landmine—everyone else has been at it for months.

"Jame, check this out," my uncle says, putting an egregiously grilled hot dog down in front of me. I forget to ask for the brand because I don't want to interrupt the description of my cousin's wedding on Mahtha's Vineyid, can you fuckin' *believe* Emma got married there, it's lucky her wife's family paid for it because *shit*!

They don't toast the buns at my Auntie Jane and Uncle Butch's house, but they do send me home with a gallon-sized Ziploc bag full of lukewarm spaghetti to eat later. The hot dog I'm served is grill-cremated, covered in a thick, black, rubbery skin like an Irish bog body. Rutt's Hut would never, strictly because of the health risk, but beneath the football-leather snap is some of the sweetest hot dog meat on the planet. There are no rules here, so I dress it myself—yellow mustard, sweet pickle relish, and a thick pile of second-day-period slightly expired ketchup slopped beside to dip the remaining bread and potato chips.

We've silently agreed not to take it personally that I haven't seen this side of my family for years, when I left for Los Angeles with a lump sum of money I'd gotten from *The Boston Globe* after getting fired without due cause. You can't get fired for saying you "cum so hard you bleed" and so I got $5,000, isn't that nice? It wasn't. I moved across the country for someone who never picked me up from the airport. Isn't that nice? I wouldn't do it differently, but it definitely was not nice.

Six years later, my uncle presents me with a hot dog.

"What do you think, Jame, any good?" I slap a chip into store-brand ketchup and use my thick back teeth to tear through the skin.

"It's good." I tell them I'll see them soon, and I'm not even lying.

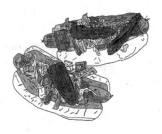

I Am in Los Angeles

A tale of the pups.

There are many things of interest to me in Los Angeles—the cats my neighbor Minda catches, neuters, and releases to gossip with indoor cats like mine; emotionally stunted freaks I'm keeping an eye on; and hot dogs, to name a few. To that last point, you've got your classic street dogs, you've got your strip mall gentrification jobs, you've got your celebrity brands, you've got your holes in walls, and you've got the politician photo ops with hot dogs that are profoundly overrated.

Let's start with that last one. Pink's Hot Dogs is tied with the Dodger Dog for the most famous game in town, and similarly weighted down with an inferior product and sketchy backstory. (I can feel Los Angeles natives clenching their assholes, but hear me out.)

Pink's has a Hollywood twist on the traditional hot dog origin story. It was opened by local couple Paul and Betty Pink in 1939, the same year as *The Wizard of Oz* and *Gone with the Wind*. Pink's was just a pushcart then, a Great Depression business solution that weaponized Betty's signature chili sauce alongside mustard, onions, steamed buns, and all-beef Hoffy hot dogs for a ten-cent meal that quickly became popular.

It wasn't until the business's second generation took over that its reputation as the hot dog provider to the stars calcified—the Pink siblings, Beverly and Richard, took over with Richard's wife, Gloria, in the mid-eighties and expanded the menu considerably to make reference to the Hollywood neighborhood they'd been in for nearly half a century. The Boomer Pinks were industrious, encouraging stars from the nearby Universal, Disney, and Paramount lots to the stand to have their photo taken with the owners and a Pink's hot dog to create a celebrity endorsement wall the likes of which can't be found anywhere else. The several times I visited their original Hollywood stand I caught the carefully posed likenesses of celebrities I like (Johnny Knoxville, T-Boz and Chilli, Guy Fieri, Steve Martin, Whoopi Goldberg, Miss Piggy), many I'm ambivalent toward (I'm *serious,* Jimmy Fallon has dined at every hot dog joint in the country and it makes him look very weird), and a series of celebrities that make me sick to think about (Dr. Phil and then mayor Eric Garcetti).

This connection to celebrity is why there's a line down the block at the Pink's stand on La Brea and Melrose most days. It's a place where legend trumps taste, where you can stand in line for upward of an hour on the strength of your conviction that Orson Welles was said to have eaten eighteen Pink's dogs in a single sitting there, a feat we are supposed to applaud and not attribute to his dark years. It's the place from which Aretha Franklin had food specially flown to her birthday party in Detroit, where Michael J. Fox referred to as "his office," and where the business has named hot dogs after celebrities ranging from Rosie O'Donnell to Martha Stewart to Huell Howser to Drew Barrymore. They've got a flavor variant on *everything.*

One thing Pink's Hot Dogs does not have is a decent hot dog, and that's just the God's honest truth. The Hoffy dog itself is a solid one, prepared on-site by steam system with a decent snap, but for the wait and price you pay for a simple hot dog— $6 for their signature chili dog and up to $13.50 for specials—

it's all style and little substance, paired with personal politics that trouble a leftist hot dog consumer's soul. I've had their chili dog, I've had the Mulholland Drive Dog (grilled onions and mushrooms with nacho cheese and bacon on a stretch dog), I've had the Mushroom Swiss Cheese Dog, I've had the Pastrami Reuben Dog, hell, I've had the Tamale Sundae (a diarrhea pile of chili, cheese, onions, and sour cream sans dog that ruined my body for five days) and it's all *okay*. The snap is okay, the price is okay, and the reliance on the cultural clout of the joint makes me feel *weird*.

There are two things that make Pink's Hot Dogs either especially American, despicable, or both, depending on where you stand on things. First, the hot dogs are just fine, and second, they *love* cops.

Allow me to unpack the latter, a stance primarily connected to second-generation co-owner Richard Pink. It's not unusual for small businesses to feel pressure to lend their local credibility to the powers that be, but the Pink family goes out of their way, taking every opportunity to declare their allegiance with the LAPD and city government. Not by coincidence, the local politicians they tend to support are known to fail the unhoused people living on their own street, and their policies target independent street vendors.

"What goes better than a combination of a pink patrol car and Pink's hot dogs?" Richard Pink asked an audience in 2018. The Los Angeles Police Department has killed 951 civilians since 2000. The Los Angeles Sheriff's Department has a network of internally sanctioned gangs who have knowingly executed hundreds more on the public's dime. During the Black Lives Matter protests of 2020, Pink's made no statement—that's not to say that it's the responsibility of a hot dog business to address systemic inequality, but one that is vocally supportive of American policing not commenting when that same institution is under massive cultural criticism is, well . . . you know.

Richard Pink is a known contributor to local politicians like Mitch O'Farrell, a city councilor famous for displacing an encampment of hundreds of unhoused people by erecting a hideous fence in the middle of a pandemic, finding the time to arrest quite a few of my friends for protesting. Pink has also supported groups lobbying in support of increased policing in their area through money and hot dog donations alike, the same groups targeting local street vendors for a lack of licensing—a problem that would have plagued *their own business* back in the 1940s, had the laws been as aggressively enforced as they are now against immigrant-owned businesses.

When it comes to Los Angeles local politics, it's personal—I love my adopted city, and feel the need to protect a place commonly depicted as full of shit from people who really are. Los Angeles has more character, history, and kindness than the rest of the world gives it credit for, just as my homeland of Brockton is more diverse, complicated, and worthy of introspection than any garden-variety Mark Wahlberg movie allows you to believe. Businesses like Pink's have no interest in expanding the public's view of what their community *really* is, their systemic struggles or their often-erased history—that marketing is too complicated, so it's cops and celebrities to keep people lined up around the block for something they could get better and cheaper around the corner.

It doesn't matter what I think—Pink's is now run by a third generation of the family and other locations are open in eight other states across the US. They are an American institution, and American institutions with inferior products *need* cops and carefully Botoxed marketing to stay afloat. Have I learned nothing from the Dodger Dog?

I know I'm being a little harsh—there's no shortage of prestigious hot dogs in LA, many of them leaning into the celebrity dining culture that's been a part of the city and the industry that has defined it for well over a century. It's a part of the way the city runs, always another famous person taking a check to endorse some of the world's gnarliest food. My personal favorite remains "Mickey Rooney's Weenie World," a failed franchise of fifty-two hot dog joints with *hamburger-shaped hot dogs* and specialty dishes like Erich Von Weenie and relish called "McLish." More recently, Snoop Dogg declared his intentions to enter the Expanded Hot Dog Universe, trademarking the "Snoop Doggs" brand after publicly expressing distress about how they're made on Jimmy Kimmel in 2016.

"If that's how they make hot dogs, I don't want one," he told the host. "I'm good."

For a celebrity as enterprising as Snoop or his Pinks-loving friend Martha Stewart, no one is ever truly *good*. Sometimes, a marketing concept that strong is just too good to pass up, even if you find the product objectively disgusting.

This brings me to the first of the luxe, gentrification-heavy Los Angeles hot dogs that will put a dent in your pocket in a way the dish was never intended to. We'll start with Dirt Dog, a joint in downtown LA that literally features a menu item named for Snoop. Founded by former real estate man Timothy Cam, the franchise's first location was inspired at best, lifted for personal gain at worst—a young Cam fell in love with the bacon hot dogs sold by "a nice Hispanic lady" out of a shopping cart rigged to be a hot dog stand. His mother noticed that cars would kick dirt onto the hot dog cart, its owner, and her product, and told her son to "stop eating dirt."

It's from this childhood anecdote—one that Cam doesn't appear to realize is a long-winded way of saying he monetized an idea lifted from a minority-owned street business whose owner was mistreated by locals—that Dirt Dogs sprang in 2012. The franchise has been remarkably successful, with five locations in Southern California and Las Vegas, developing a large menu of bacon-wrapped, grilled, and slathered dogs with a lighthearted disregard for its customers' arteries and a gigantic social media following.

Dirt Dog is a gentrifier's scam at heart, built with real estate money in an area of Los Angeles that is both dear to the owner and historically gentrified by white real estate men like Cam himself. Which is why it brings me no pleasure whatsoever to inform you that the hot dog is fucking *good*. Shit. Fuck. I'm— look, I'm not thrilled either.

Here's how a Dirt Dog is made. An all-beef, thick Nathan's Famous 5/1 dog is wrapped in bacon and thrown on the grill, while rolls are drenched in butter and thrown on the same grill beside them, split to get the inside nice and toasty. From there, it depends on the monstrosity of your choosing—the popular Elote Dog features seasoned corn, lime mayo, and cotija; the Patty Melt Dog is topped with fries, a honking chunk of cheddar, and chipotle aioli; and ordering a Snoop's Dog brings a helping of what was once referred to as Grandma's Slaw, barbecue sauce, "Billionaire Bacon," and "Gin & Juice Ketchup." "I'm good," indeed.

When I hit their Pasadena outdoor mall location, I opt for their House Dog, the bacon-wrapped Nathan's grilled in what some early reports of the business say is *Thousand Island dressing* with Dirt Dog's tangy house sauce, green chile, mayonnaise, in-house mustard, ketchup (!), bacon bits, and a paste of grilled veggies lining the bun for good measure. I mean, you have to hand it to them.

I don't eat for a full sixteen hours after finishing the billion-calorie, eight-dollar mega-dog, and I mean that in a good way— it's the kind of place where you can see the dog made from top to bottom. Every item on the menu costs less than ten dollars, unlike their peers at Pink's, and the snap of the Nathan's 5/1 pairs well with the buttered-and-grilled bun. Chicago readers please shut your eyes, because I love how ketchup, mayo, and bacon bits interact on an oversized dog, the perfect sweet and tangy textures that give you a stomachache after two bites. I feel guilt loving the gentri-dog this much, but here I am—Timmy Cam, your landlord ass got me.

And yet. The undeniably damn-good dogs served here still ring dissonant when you have a better understanding of who's selling them. Dirt Dog leans pretty heavily on Black culture in order to move product—the location in majority-white and wealthy Pasadena features a mural with Tupac and Biggie waiting in line for a Dirt Dog (they were both dead when the place was founded), a massive Kobe Bryant memorial painting stands next to the bathroom, and general lukewarm, hot dog–themed graffiti flanks the brick walls. Here you can get a ten-dollar hot dog, hit a Warby Parker, and take a stroll down Big Bang Theory Way in the same twenty minutes. It's a good product in a hollow package.

I course correct at a bizarro local joint—Vicious Dogs in North Hollywood, a place that sports one of the most unwell menus I have seen this side of a Taco Bell, and I mean that as a compliment.

Vicious Dogs has operated in the North Hollywood Arts District since 2007, the same year a $1.3 billion investment from the Metropolitan Transportation Authority began to rapidly gentrify the area—the most expensive private development venture in the city's history. At the time of the deal, the concept behind the "NoHo Art Wave" was to build a 1.72-million-square-foot complex near the NoHo Red Line station for retail, entertainment, luxury apartments, and parking lots, with the theoretical idea of "revitalizing" and "resurging" the arts in the area. As with any use of words like "revitalize" out of the mouth of a developer, this meant displacement for many who had lived in the area for generations, the majority of whom are Hispanic.

Conflicts of interest haunted the project and punished local residents, with eleven out of thirteen MTA board members who voted in favor of the gigantic development revealed to have accepted campaign contributions from developers. In turn, these same members refused to disclose how much money they'd accepted and built the multimillion-dollar lofts anyway. For art, though, right?

Swept up in this tempest is a little hot dog store run by Willy Fedail, who opened the store after finally managing to impress his ailing, elderly mother with one of his eccentric hot dog recipes after years of effort.

"I felt like, 'If I can get my mom on board with this, I can conquer anything in the world,'" he told the Airbnb blog in 2017. This venue for an interview with Fedail, a Latin man raised in the area, is an interesting one—the Silicon Valley–operated Airbnb has caused controversy among local residents in the last ten years for cratering the rental market and driving prices up.

Still, drinking the Silicon Valley Kool-Aid does push tourists to local gems like Vicious Dogs, and Fedail has played ball. He spoke frankly about his dislike of activists pushing back on Airbnb's encroachment on the already heavily gentrified NoHo Arts District.

"America is the land of opportunity," he told the Airbnb blog, "and for a while, we were drifting away from that. But now, thanks to these new companies like Airbnb, people are able to benefit from things like travel in a way they never were before. Don't get in the way of that."

Fedail is very much a local boy making good in a predatory environment where his business is not being set up to succeed, and I suspect the pressure to make nice with the powers that be is part of the reason the business is able to exist at all. He opened shop in the center of the arts district, flanked by a Laemmle movie theater, Dave's Hot Chicken, 24 Hour Fitness, and

Panda Express, and has taken careful effort to cultivate a vibe at Vicious Dogs that hearkens back to a "simpler time." Inside, it's more closely identified with the NoHo of the '80s and '90s, featuring a logo with a Bettie Page–like pinup girl hoisting a Chicago hot dog above her head.

It's fucking complicated. But what of the dogs?

With items ranging from four to twelve dollars and using Vienna Beef Dogs exclusively, Fedail's menu can get *weird*. I skip over the more conservative slaw dogs and regional makes and go for the two freakiest picks—the Peanut Butter Dog and the Mac Daddy. A PB&J dog, even with the snap of a Vienna and a tastefully grilled bun, is a classic example of "just because you can doesn't mean you should." It's needed confirmation that a hot dog is, indeed, a sandwich, but the taste overwhelms the meat and sticks to the roof of my mouth.

The Mac Daddy is a more serious contender—wrapped in bacon and topped with barbecue sauce, mustard, and baked mac 'n' cheese, the flavors are far better matched, and Fedail's experimental mind is in a sounder place here. It's a cool idea, and if the area is doomed to become a sprawling Southwestern mall, I'm glad they have the good sense to make space for a mad scientist's hot dog laboratory.

I keep eating the meat in California. There are plenty of places to choose from—Comfy Pup is an excellent pop-up whose owner is incredibly kind; Walt's Bar in Eagle Rock has *the* bar hot dog in the country (tied with Lion's Head Tavern in Manhattan); the reopening of the legendary Tail o' the Pup on Santa Monica after nearly two decades closed brought a tear to my eye, I fear. But my favorite hot dogs are the ones that seek me out, the kind I walk by and stop in my tracks because I'm supposed to know *everything* about this goddamn dish and I don't know *this* one.

The best place to find a hot dog in LA is where it always was—right on the sidewalk. To find one means walking past the independently owned carts in front of the then Staples Center, where the Lakers and the Kings play. Majority Mexican immigrants prepare the bacon-wrapped, grilled-onion-and-pepper-topped Sonoran-adjacent grilled dogs that cost a fraction of the price and are forty times better than the ones that can be found inside. Some stands have a formal grill, but others are more ingenious—one guy has a butane stove burner rigged up to a small cart heating a baking sheet, where dogs, onions, and peppers grill right beside where buns are toasted.

Because they have the best hot dogs *and* their profits don't filter up to a white billionaire, the street vendors of Los Angeles have been fighting with the city to legalize their businesses in spite of the more moneyed brick-and-mortars blatantly ripping off the food culture the vendors popularized in the first place (looking at you, Dirt Dog). It's a time-honored tradition in the city, going back to the nineteenth century when the LAPD and officials displaced "tamale wagons" in this same area. The risk to many vendors was extremely high—until 2013, street vending was a considered a criminal act that could lead to an undocumented seller's deportation. Still, decriminalization didn't deter the LAPD and a number of security firms from intimidating and abusing immigrant vendors, using an already insidious policy regarding "the storage of bulky items on sidewalks," primarily used to target unhoused encampments. (I will here direct the reader to unhoused Los Angeles resident Theo Henderson's wonderful podcast *We The Unhoused,* a project that has documented the unhoused community in LA for years and offers just as many joyful profiles of residents as it does flagrant abuses and failures of those in power.)

Street vendors knew their work defined the food culture of Los Angeles—after all, food giants like Roy Choi began in their position—and began to make more noise to have their businesses legalized and unhassled beginning in the late 2000s. A 2008 conflict, locally dubbed the Taco Truck War, concerned

Choi's business—and reached its final blows when the Los Angeles Board of Supervisors office aggressively implemented a law that required local taco trucks move every hour or face anything from a $1,000 fine to jail time. The question is, of course, for fucking what? Business owners and activists asked for it long and loud enough, but it didn't neutralize the century-long war waged between the city and the vendors who made the city worth visiting.

The fight dragged as Los Angeles continued to deport immigrants at an increasing rate in an evil chef's salad effort among entities like (inhale): the Obama and Trump administrations; the bafflingly still legal Immigration and Customs Enforcement; vote-blue-no-matter-who centrist Democratic governorship under Jerry Brown and Gavin Newsom; and careless at best, malicious at worst city leadership that allowed police and sheriff's departments to terrorize business owners whose work had been decriminalized for years.

In 2018 there was some relief after a decade—a unanimous LA City Council vote to legalize sidewalk carts the week after Thanksgiving, just two months after the state of California decriminalized vendors. The day of the decision, the council specified that this legalization did *not* apply to vendors who wanted to open shop in the areas with the highest foot traffic. This included Dodger Stadium, Hollywood Boulevard, and the Staples (sorry, let me clear the phlegm from my throat, *crypto-dot-com ar-ee-nah*) Center.

By the time I eat my street dog in late 2021, the only thing that's changed is the name of the $400 million stadium built by working-class laborers back in the late 1990s. It's not the first time a massive construction project has vowed to uplift the city as a whole and turned out to be an empty promise, and it certainly won't be the last—the Crypto.com Arena will be the site of basketball events for the 2028 Olympics, for which there are major construction projects underway across the city promising to displace poor and unhoused people in favor of stadiums and a police budget increase. The phenomenon is repeating as I chew the best hot dog I've eaten in weeks outside the Staples Center, in the spot where the city's convention center made that same vague "revitalizing the neighborhood" promise for the downtown area during the 1970s. Here's how the revitalization played out—a stadium was built, and 250 mostly Latin low-income residents, including children, were uprooted to make way for it.

Older immigrants in the area used to live in affordable, if crowded, housing in the space now filled with restaurants for the upper middle class to hit before a Lakers game, along with an oversized movie theater where I once saw *I, Tonya* three times in a week during a deep depression. Local officials took advantage of the language barrier between residents and themselves when aiming to develop the area, not informing them of their rights and uprooting entire communities without any budget for relocation. The logic was that if the city wanted you gone, it was *your* financial burden to manage, something that holds true today.

"There were a lot of people who knew each other in that community," downtown resident and activist Richard Garcia told writer Gann Matsuda in 2009, concerning his parents' experience being displaced from downtown in the 1970s. "But when the Convention Center came in, it broke up the community and those relationships ended there. When you're in a close-knit community, it's kind of a shock to be suddenly removed from that."

In a different decade, it might have been possible for street vendors to afford to live here, but the streets are lined with lofts and condos, with encampments for the rest. In June of Hot Dog Summer, the vendors who fought for a decade to be legalized were shut down at MacArthur Park's Guatemalan Night Market by Department of Public Health officials and LAPD officers, who took food from vendors and threw it away without explanation. With the coronavirus pandemic came additional hoops for vendors to jump through to meet sanitation standards without financial assistance, with no sustainable, code-meeting cart in existence at the time of the DPH MacArthur Park descent.

For the ten thousand vendors operational in the city, the few able to meet the hastily placed health standards could spend as much as 18 percent of their income on city permits. By August of Hot Dog Summer, the Community Economic Development Clinic at UCLA Law released a report declaring that LA street vendors were still thought of as "functionally illegal," and treated by the city in a way that "perpetuates an unending cycle of criminalization and poverty."

"When SB 946 passed in June of 2018, we were so excited because we thought, 'Finally the abuse is going to end here,'" activist Merlin Alvarado said at a June 2021 press conference. "The street vendors at Hollywood and Highland and on the Walk of Fame have been working for years, but we continue to suffer abuse and harassment at the hands of law enforcement every day."

It's a fantastic fucking hot dog, perfectly grilled. I hope it's still here when I come back.

I Am Tying Up Loose Ends

Do you know everything about hot dogs yet, Loftus?

I go back to Philadelphia on Halloween, after a million things change. I'm taking the trip you take when you can afford the time and the flight and feeling like Ms. Schtick Fleisch in your friend's bedroom. My boyfriend and I broke up, which you probably guessed around page thirty but it was surprising to us, honestly. I threw up all over myself at the movies at one in the afternoon even though I hadn't eaten in three days. Living alone allowed my eating disorder to take up space, as the girlies say. I lost ten pounds, gained fifteen back, got raw-dogged by my crush and the most boring man alive (What if they were the same person? They weren't) and I stopped, stopped, stopped eating hot dogs. For a while. Now, my job was to sit in the house where we used to live together and write about a trip where we ate several hundred hot dogs together and "get over it" and "take some space" and "move on," three things that are categorically impossible given my only source of income is reliving the end over and over. And it was my idea. *And* I was right.

So I go back to Philadelphia, a city we completely fumbled during Hot Dog Summer, where I'm hopeful I can pull off something cleaner solo.

My friend Rose is the queen of the world, a genius who does not care that she is a genius and knows how to talk to everyone. She has been married for a million years, is secretly in her mid-forties except she tells people all the time, and she wants to get a hot dog with me. We're going to Johnny's Hots, a place that's famous for the only spin on a hot dog Philly has to offer—a big old fish cake belly flopped on top of a dog in the Fishtown district.

Johnny's Hots is planted right in the middle of a two-lane highway in an increasingly gentrified area, looking out of place in a neighborhood where a working-class fish stick hot dog would have fit seamlessly fifteen years ago. Stolen from the Lenape tribe, Fishtown was named for its proximity to the docks and the white working class that once lived there. We pull in to Johnny's Hots shortly before its three o'clock closure, but that isn't to say that second-generation owner John Danze is lazy—he opens the joint at five in the morning for a largely working-class clientele, construction workers and police officers and EMTs who've been loyal customers for decades.

Danze is the first to admit that Johnny's Hots, one of the last stands in what was once a relatively thriving Philadelphia hot dog scene, borrowed heavily from its now-folded competitors when his father started the business as a 1950s-era lunch truck. This truck grew into a shack that moved to their current location in the early 2000s, and the place is still hopping when Rose and I walk up planning on the $5.75 Hot Dog Fish Cake Combo.

Mr. Danze himself is on-site, and Rose leans directly into the stand where the hot dogs are split and thrown on a griddle and says, "Hey, can I ask you something?" Fortunately, he is more than happy to talk with us as we mow down yet another Depression-era meal that is intended to be an entire day's food for a laborer on one (ungrilled, come *on*) bun. He's candid about the family business, telling us that the pepper hash was lifted from local joint Lenny's at a persistent regular customer's insistence.

"I kind of blew him off, and he kept comin' and he kept buggin' us," he tells us in a thick Philadelphia accent. "I tell him, 'If you want it so bad, then you bring a recipe for it.' I thought he'd never come back, but he brought a recipe and gave it to my wife and she tweaked it. We've been selling it ever since."

When it comes to putting an unrelated meat on top of a grilled hot dog, Philadelphia's fish cake takes the edge over Baltimore's bologna. The fish is fresh and doesn't overwhelm the slight snap of the dog, matching the bun's texture more closely than that of its competing meat and doesn't haunt the body in quite the same way. For all of her annoyance at having to prepare it by the tubload, Danze's wife makes the hell out of a pepper relish, cushioning the meat, tomato, and tartar sauce I order to go on a surprisingly sturdy bun. It's starting to get cold now, and the last few construction workers disperse with the same special I ordered. The seasons are changing and I'm still eating hot dogs, but it's good, it's nice, they change and so do I.

The plague has a new title now, like a season of *Survivor*—this time the name sounds like a friendly cartoon robot, and I won't include it here for fear that there will be six others between this Google document and your hands. I hope we made it.

A week before the plague returns and Christmas is canceled, I go to Portland, Oregon, to see an old friend and meet a new one. The old friend, Robert, lives on an anarchist compound, which is hot but complicated, and the new friend, Sarah, lives across the street from her childhood best friend. She's coming from where she had uprooted her life to train sled dogs in the Midwest, which is both aspirational and ultimately a bad idea. This is the last corner of the country I've missed in pursuit of a more perfect hot dog, and I'll admit that I'm cheating—the full job requires a stop in Seattle, but I'm short on time and the country is short on safety.

The night I land, I wander around Sarah's home—where I'm staying before we've even met—and look at her bookshelves like a Victorian ghost who used to be in love with her. To remedy this terrifying behavior, I decide to take in the legacy hot dogs the city has to offer. First up is Nick's Famous Coney Island, a nearly ninety-year-old business saved from a local buyer after fighting for its life through the pandemic. I order the Seattle Dog, a well-grilled confection longer than the length of the toasted bun that's been slathered in cream cheese—the Northwestern specialty—on its underbelly like it's butter, then topped to an absurd degree with hot sauerkraut, diced, then grilled onions, and brown mustard.

Here's something you can take or leave—hot cream cheese is basically mayonnaise, and I mostly mean that as a compliment. The hot dog itself is terrific, and has a snap surrounded by—okay, yes, that is the hot cum flavor of cream cheese and beef. The guys at the bar are watching football and I pretend to not be more exhausted than I've been in years, breaking my own rules again by eating the whole thing in one sitting.

More important than the taste, it's served to me by an absolutely sick subject of anthropological study—a Guy Who Lives in Portland. While they come in many breeds and variants, your average specimen is pretty good-looking but carries himself either like he is the most or least gorgeous person on earth with no middle ground whatsoever. Common but not guaranteed features: fetishized poverty / lawyer parents, forty-five minute anecdote about something called WWOOFing that I don't have time to get into here, bad music about ex-girlfriend who makes better music, and worst of all, "barcade regular." There are many things about Los Angeles I don't like, but at least hot people don't bother to talk to me there.

The second Portland joint I drag my unsuited-for-winter

shoes into is Zach's Shack, a younger local business that specializes in all-beef Red Hot Chicago dogs served to me by the other classic strain of Portland man, a white guy with dreads. In keeping with the theme of "Zach," every hot dog on the menu that isn't regional (New York, Chicago, etc.) is named after one of his personal favorite bands—the Los Lobos Dog has black olives and jalapeños; the Sgt. Peppers Dog has peperoncini and sport peppers; the Dylan Dog has cream cheese, onion, and tomato.

"Sure you don't wanna hang?" the white guy with dreads asks with complete sincerity when I order Zach's Favorite (brown mustard, red relish, sport peppers, onion, pickle slices, and celery salt), and I'm honestly not sure. There's a table with a *Pac-Man* game going in the middle, and a big sign that reads THIS IS SPECIAL. LIFE IS SHORT. BE COOL. I resent it from a New England perspective in the same way I resent all of Portland—don't you fuckin' tell *me* to calm down, look how *you're* living.

"Do you know everything about hot dogs yet, Loftus?" Robert asks me over our five hundredth glass of red wine in his suspiciously vast home. It's disorienting to see what your friends would do if they suddenly had the money to do it, and Robert has always wanted a compound—all the food we're eating was grown on the land he and his neighbors share, I meet the ram named Hitler he needs to kill, there is a comrade living in a geodesic dome in the middle of the yard. The duck on my plate tastes very recently alive.

"I don't think so," I say.

"Fuck it," he says, pats me on the knee, and returns to the conversation he and his friends are having about how to deal with post-traumatic stress after witnessing daily police brutality for nearly one hundred nights. Robert heroically covered the Portland uprisings of 2020 on the ground every night with the people in this room while I watched from Los Angeles, where I was reporting on land misappropriation at the VA. A year later I'm sitting at the compound, worried about hot dogs and a picture of a quail egg I sent to a man ten hours ago.

"Jamie, I'm telling you, you've *gotta* just start microdosing," Robert continues. "Or just kratom." I love when my friend holds his elderly cat and gives me the worst advice he can think of.

There's one more hot dog I need to tell you about. There is no overstating the pleasures of a Korean hot dog—I'd already tried a Korean corn dog variant at Chungchun Rice Hotdogs in LA, but the specialty on offer at Portland's Kim Jong Grillin deserves its own category altogether. Begun in 2011 by chef Han Ly Hwang, the cart burned down (the sign, as we know, of a good stand) and was resurrected in 2014. Kim Jong Grillin is most famous for Hwang's take on traditional Korean cuisine like bulgogi, galbi, and japchae, with a distinctive kimchi recipe. It doesn't hurt that the place has a conscience too—they served free meals to unemployed restaurant workers during the first wave of the plague.

Behold, the KJG Hotdog, prepared fresh in a food truck on Southeast Division street while you and your new friends—Sarah, who came home and was everything you hoped, Alex and Carolyn, who made the trip summer camp in the late fall—stamp your feet in the cold. It is worth your wait. The meat, recently changed from local all-pork footlongs from Olympia Provisions to the 80 percent pork, 20 percent beef mix at competing Portland butchery Zenner's Sausage Company, is placed in a banh mi baguette and topped with sesame sprouts, spicy daikon, kimchi mayonnaise, and pickled mango. The dog itself is grilled for around ten minutes, guaranteeing a slight char and a hard snap in spite of it being a footlong, and the banh mi bread should become standard practice across the country for bread that won't, you know, fucking fall apart at the first sign of moisture.

It is a perfect hot dog to end a perfect trip to close out a year that a part of me would like to forget entirely. Those ordering the KJG Hotdog are advised to manually move some of the top- pings onto the side of the banh mi roll—the teen preparing ours heaped them all on top of the meat when the mango and daikon is best enjoyed all the way around. All four of us see who can eat the fastest, blasting the heat in Sarah's mother's sensible sedan and playing a local radio station with a penchant for later Elvis. I lose the contest by a mile, but the hot dog is good and the voices are starting to sound familiar.

"I am very glad I met you," I say to Sarah when we hug good- bye, a real Scarecrow-and-Dorothy situation. I am. I go home.

But Before I Leave You: Who Is Fucking on the Wienermobile?

The answer, as you already know, is everyone.

I get a message from my friend Carlye just before Thanksgiving. "Relevant to your interests: did you know the WIENERMO-BILE is in LA on Friday?!?!?!"

Reader, I did not, but in a way . . . I always knew. If you stay in the hot dog game long enough, the Oscar Mayer Wiener-mobile *will* find you, and my only mistake was looking for it instead of letting her—the feminine penis on wheels—find *me*.

Perhaps you know of her. The 'Mobile was first introduced in 1936 by the nephew of the German immigrant that the compa-ny's named for, Mayer, but this came after decades of establish-ing themselves as the *family* hot dog (as opposed to a slutty hot dog, which I will carelessly speculate includes the brand Hoffy's) The company's founder had begun working at a meat market in Detroit and then Chicago, eventually opening his own shop in the latter city and participating in the 1893 World's Colum-bian Exposition. His business grew at a steady clip in the way that hot dog businesses did in that day, and Mayer made the smart move of quickly adapting to Food Safety and Inspec-tion Service standards after Upton Sinclair's *The Jungle* gave the meatpacking industry a shakeup. This secured the promise of quality onto the smartly marketed product's image, as a yellow band of assurance was added to its signature red packaging and Mayer skinless wieners became the go-to hot dogs for kids.

How do you market to kids? According to Mayer's nephew Carl, with a big sexy hot dog on wheels with five hundred whistles inside. Originally, the thirteen-foot-long metal hot dog monstrosity was used as a chariot for the company's now-defunct and extremely dated mascot "Little Oscar, World's Smallest Chef." The character was played by actor Meinhardt Raabe, best known for playing the Coroner Munchkin in *The Wizard of Oz*—as coroner, he must aver, he thoroughly examined her, you know the guy. He began traveling in the Wienermobile beginning in 1937 and well into the World War II years, later joining the Civil Air Patrol and getting his master's in business administration from Drexel University.

Raabe's part then went to actor George Molchan, who met Raabe and was encouraged to get his degree as well. He worked as a bookkeeper at Pepsi for many years before the Mayer company expanded its Wienermobile fleet in 1951 and began casting additional Little Oscars. For some time, Raabe and Molchan played the same role in different areas of the country and Molchan continued after Raabe moved on, traveling the US in the Wienermobile for twenty years. It was Molchan who popularized the ritual of giving away Wiener Whistles, which still exist today and make me foam at the mouth to think of receiving one. The whistles are miniature versions of the vehicle itself and recipients are encouraged to hum the Oscar Mayer theme song upon getting theirs (and if the Wienermobile drivers *really* like you, they have some glow-in-the-dark ones too). It's a near certainty you know the jingle I'm talking about, which debuted on television in 1963 after composer Richard Trentlage submitted lyrics in a contest and quickly became connected to both Little Oscar and the Wienermobile itself. Don't leave me hanging here:

Oh, I wish I were an Oscar Mayer Wiener

And if you don't know the rest, you are not a true American.

By 1976, the Wienermobiles had been on the road for forty years and the company elected to retire the program in favor of allocating marketing money to TV ads. Molchan remained employed by the company after the vehicles were taken off the road, moving to Orlando to hold court as Little Oscar at a branded location at Disney World. When he died in 2005, the Mayer company sent the Wienermobile to his funeral, where mourners hummed, "Oh, I wish I were an Oscar Mayer Wiener," and whistled along on the toys that he'd made his living giving to Americans.

Interestingly, Little Oscar is barely referenced on Oscar Mayer's website today, possibly due to concerns about how the character's portrayal of little people has aged. Point well taken, but it feels unfair to erase Raabe's and Molchan's significant contributions to the company.

By 1988, the public demand for the Wienermobile was high enough that the company commissioned and sent out an updated fleet of six new vehicles across the country, piloted by recent college graduates with souped-up additions like microwaves and stereo systems that played twenty-one variations on the Oscar Mayer theme. It was updated again in the '90s and 2000s before leaning into the online culture surrounding it. Today, you can track where the six Wienermobiles are across the country, piloted by two specially trained drivers apiece, and the people still mob them—anywhere from a formal parade to the random grocery store parking lot I find myself wandering into to meet Little Link Lauren and Nacho Dog Nicholas in November 2021. Their fans are a bizarro mix of older people with Wiener Whistle nostalgia and younger people who know the chokehold the Wienermobile holds when posted to main.

So, reader: Are the people on the Wienermobile fucking?

The short answer is yes, but it's complicated. The Wiener-mobile drivers I meet and exercise my never-caused-me-a-problem-before anxious attachment style upon are *not* fucking, but the month I spend talking to Lauren and Nick is well worth the absurd mental gymnastics.

But I'm getting ahead of myself. Our story begins in the last hour of a Wienermobile's dedicated shift at a Culver City grocery store, where two people in their early twenties wearing signature red-and-yellow Oscar Mayer uniforms quietly talk in the warm womb of the Wiener, with a screen flashing fun facts around which one has hung a wreath of plasticky-fake autumn leaves to remind visitors what month it is. One is Lauren ("Fun Fact: I once sat in the front row of *The Tonight Show* and got a high five from Jimmy Fallon"), a petite girl from rural Georgia with stick-straight brown hair, a middle part, and a cheek-smile combination designed to sell back-to-school clothes in a catalog. She's an excellent driver and the first to let you know it, having begun her driving career on a tractor back home. She sits beside Nick, who I never see without his bright red wiener-emblazoned bomber jacket. A central California import ("Fun Fact: I won a scholarship in high school for winning a hot dog eating con-test!"), he stands several heads above his fellow driver, his black hair slicked over, and has the loud, warm voice of a college orientation advisor who looks at and through you simulta-neously. It does not surprise me to learn that he's *very* into Disneyland, which sounds like a value judgement unless you know I keep having that recurring sex dream about having my back blown out above Radiator Springs.

Let me describe the ungodly feat of American marketing they drive every day. She stands at eleven feet (twenty-four hot dogs) high, twenty-seven feet (sixty hot dogs) long, and eight feet (eighteen hot dogs) wide. She weighs the equivalent of 140,500 wieners minus the two pilots who've been steering her around the country for the last six months, and has more features than any car that anyone in my family has ever owned. An assortment: six-speed transmission, a gigantic resin hot dog on the dash, a ceiling painted like a bright blue sky with cumulus clouds, bright yellow walls with velvet seating (burgundy, with yellow leather and embroidered hot dogs to match), a massive sound system, a roof that lifts, and a horn that plays the jingle that they swear they're not completely sick of. It's fucking magnificent, and Lauren and Nick really had to lobby to get the gig.

The pair had extremely different approaches to securing the job—they make sure to mention that fewer people have driven the Wienermobile than have been to the moon (not true), and that it's statistically harder to secure employment in a gigantic hot dog than it is to get into Harvard. These are all lines pulled directly from the company's website, but hey, these kids are working in public relations. I am the public, and I'm sucking it down like a skinless frank.

Both met the basic qualifications to apply for the yearlong position (a 3.0-plus GPA and a valid driver's license), which involves a two-week training in Wisconsin and two legs of driving of six months apiece, with a change in regional assignment and driving partner midway through the year. Hotdoggers live a functional paid yearlong sabbatical, living out of hotels and short-term housing between long driving stints, between which they're expected to show up to a series of press events and are empowered to arrange their own public appearances.

This has been the process for Hotdoggers since the post-college processed-meat gap-year program began in 1988, and it's had a huge impact on those who've participated, whether they ended up fucking each other or not. One of my favorite examples is Robin Gelfenbien, a woman who worked for the program between 1993 and 1994 and was so affected by it she wrote a one-woman show on the subject fifteen years later called *My Salvation Has a First Name (A Wienermobile Journey)* at the New York Fringe Festival.

"I went to school at Syracuse. The Wienermobile came, and I fell in love with it," she told *New York* magazine when the show debuted. "It was a low point in my life, and I knew I wanted to drive it. I did everything I could, including making up songs and tap dancing at the Oscar Mayer headquarters. I got the job."

Little Link Lauren is the outlier here—initially a type-A Wienermobile skeptic, she describes her journey to the "Hot Dog Highways" from her hometown of Toccoa, Georgia, as almost divinely determined.

"For me, if the pandemic hadn't happened I definitely wouldn't be here," she tells me.

Still, the hot dog pursued her. After she had applied to a series of post-grad jobs, Oscar Mayer came to recruit Hotdoggers at the University of Georgia for the first time in years, and Lauren decided it was a sign—she applied that day and promptly forgot about it. And then she got an interview. And another. And another, and suddenly Little Link Lauren was in the final twenty-four job applicants in a pool that's said to include as many as twenty-five thousand in any given year. My pragmatic queen was shocked.

Nacho Dog Nick had a more classically Gen Z route to the Wienermobile, first learning of the Hotdogger program in a *BuzzFeed* piece and going in deep on its lore. Oscar Mayer doesn't carry the same cultural clout in central California that it does in the Midwest, but Nick was already a shrewd social media operator and threw in his lot with Big Hot Dog by submitting a hot-dog-themed parody video to the tune of Olivia Rodrigo's "drivers license." When I meet them, Lauren is on a journey to see something west of Alabama in the Wienermobile, but Nick is firmly planted in the importance of the vehicle itself—he repeatedly references its history, how people react to it, and where he sees Lauren and himself fitting into its legacy.

"People are obsessed with it—any type of family, class, race, status, we have come in contact with everyone in between," he tells me. "We've met vegans who are like, I love the Wienermobile! It's amazing, there's nothing like it."

While it gives me no pleasure to inform you that Nacho Dog Nick and Little Link Lauren aren't fucking, it at least sounds like they're an exception to the rule. Once training begins, things start to get horny. Before they take to the road, the twelve Hotdoggers-in-training spend two weeks at headquarters in Madison, Wisconsin, in a truly demented adult summer camp called Hot Dog High.

Of course, there are plenty of logistical things the team needs to learn in the two weeks when they're sharing every meal, moment, and scent with the people they will be randomly assigned to spend the next six months with. There are extensive driving lessons with retired police chiefs from Madison that test employees on their ability to navigate a massive hot dog over narrow bridges, into difficult parking spaces, and onto ferry boats that culminates in a test required to graduate. There are full days on public relations and marketing training, how to interact with the public in a way that will best represent the company that once found it appropriate to have a representative named Little Oscar, lessons on best practices to plan events independently, and a half day on hot dog puns alone. This last part is particularly vile—the way that Hotdoggers smugly tell you how the cops conducting their driving lessons "sat shotbun" and that they are "really relishing" this experience makes me feel physically ill. There is a Freemason-style graduation ceremony where the twelve apostles of the skinless frank place their hand on an all-beef dog and pledge their loyalty to the company before leaving with their newly arranged spouse the next morning.

Then there are the more intimate aspects of training, which I later learn happen in conjunction with the Planters Nutmobile team. This is exactly what it sounds like—a rip-off of the Wienermobile from the Planters company that emerged in the late 1990s, owned by the same Kraft Heinz parent company until just a few months before Hot Dog Summer commences. The Nutmobile is far less popular—Lauren says this is due to a handful of cases of children with peanut allergies passing out when getting too close—and only employs three people full-time to the Wienermobile's twelve. Please forgive me for what I am about to say, but what *you* need to know is that the twenty-somethings in the Nutmobile *fuck*. They, uh, they nut. They don't work for the Nutmobile for nothing, and they nut into Wienermobile employees more than they nut into the other Nutmobilers. These are the facts as they've been presented to me, and you can't be happy to know them.

Little Link Lauren and Nacho Dog Nick cannot vouch for why there are so many Nutmobile drivers who fall in love with Wienermobile drivers, only that they firmly believe *they* belong to the superior caste.

"This sounds mean, but most people want to drive the Wienermobile," Lauren says. "Not the . . . well, you know."

That doesn't mean there isn't significant cross-genital pollination in the world of Wienermobile driving pairs. Hotdoggers roll *deep*. When I see the two again in Los Angeles in December, Lauren laughs as she tells me that 50 percent of the Hotdoggers on the road during the peak of the pandemic in 2020 ended up dating, and that at least one couple is engaged so far. That's proportionally higher than most years, and Lauren explains it has everything to do with the pandemic restraints placed on the program. This restricted pairs mainly to drive-bys at hospitals and nursing homes, the rest of their time spent alone in hotel rooms and the honking dog itself to, well . . . six of them are in relationships, you tell me. They were *fucking*, reader. They were fucking, in the hot dog.

Before they drive back where they're staying with Nacho Dog Nick's family, I resolve to shoot my shot. Am I capable of asserting myself in relationships? Absolutely not, run me over with a Zamboni. Am I capable of asking for what I want in a professional setting? Never, pay me twelve dollars and revoke my right to vote. Can I ask a couple of college kids to come to my favorite comedy theater in a big-ass hot dog? Yes. *This* I can do.

"Do you guys like comedy shows?" I ask, a dead ringer for every street barker I've either hated or felt bad for or been over the years.

"Oh my God, *yeah*," Nick says in a voice that's almost convincing. Still, I go in for the kill, knowing that bringing the motherfucking Wienermobile to my community will secure at least three weeks of love and respect from my peers, the thing I want and desire more than my one human life.

So fine, they're not fucking, I *guess*, whatever. They're *so* not fucking, in fact, that he and Lauren tell me they're going to see the woman that Nick is in love with right after their shift ends so Nick can give her a hand-painted ornament asking her to be his girlfriend. Lauren giggles as she shows me the painted snow-capped mountains and Nick's boyish scrawl: "Meet me at the Swiss Alps . . . but first will you be my girlfriend?"

Nick smiles and it's a real one this time, not the gumless marketer's grin he's given me for the past hour. It's their running joke, he explains, because she can't see him on the road so they might as well be in the Alps.

"He's been pining for her for two years," Lauren says, goading him on.

Nick looks at me and puts the ornament away, a little embarrassed. "You can roast me at the comedy show," he says. "You can be like, 'I met this simp that drives a hot dog.'"

So what *do* you do with someone you barely know for six uninterrupted months?

Little Link Lauren sighs. "It's most similar to an arranged marriage if I'm being real," she tells me. "Thankfully we get along. We're like brother and sister, we bicker and are like, 'I'm gonna kill you if you play that song one more time!'"

This is something that's on her mind a *lot*. There's something amiss in the AUX cord etiquette between these two—something that's difficult even when you *are* in love, not to mention when you're in what you are quick to identify as an *arranged marriage*. Lauren and Nick have similar taste in top-forty music and say that most days, there's barely any distinguishing between their individual playlists. And then there's the Zac Brown Band issue.

Lauren is gorgeously passive aggressive on this matter, something Nick is less skilled at hiding. He *loves* the Zac Brown Band, a group I refuse to learn a single thing about but who he describes as having a "very different vibe" from a different terrible band he loves called The 1975.

He fixes his eyes on Lauren. "But we love them *both*."

Lauren refuses to meet his gaze, looking down the barrel of my skull. "I no longer like the Zac Brown Band," she says simply, prompting a silence so long that I decide to see if the three of us will just die here. Finally, Nick sucks parking lot air through his teeth and changes the subject.

"Did we tell you that people have been making Wienermobile mixes since the nineties?"

Lauren is visibly relieved. "*Yes!*" She rushes to the back of the Wienermobile where the aging sound system looms over the seats and comes back with a binder full of burned mix CDs that makes me feel like I'm in seventh grade. "Each pair of Hotdoggers used to make a mix of the songs they listened to the most together and leave it here for the next group. Kind of a history thing."

I look at the big, looping Sharpie handwriting that reminds me of my cousin before her husband died. Their titles are goofy and all ring a little bit west of softcore porn titles: "#thunderstruck," "Schnitzel Itzel Ketchup Kyle XXIIV," "Too Cool for Cornfields #Wisconsin," "Bumpin' Through the Bun Roof," "Hottie Hotdoggers Volume One," "Buns and Kisses! Tailgaitin' Traci."

Are Lauren and Nick going to make a mix? I realize the

microsecond after asking that I've hit the same Zac Brown–shaped nerve.

"There'd probably only be one song on it," she says, and Nick rolls his eyes. The girls are fighting! I want them to fight. I'm rude.

I tell Nick I'll reach out soon about a Wienermobile visit to the comedy theater, and he excuses himself to pee at the Del Taco across the lot. I feel bad keeping them for so long and tell Lauren I'll let them be, but she seems a little relieved to be alone with me. Maybe it's the rare feeling of being unsupervised after a long time, or more likely it's the feeling of *not* being around the world's biggest Zac Brown Band fan.

We haven't talked much about the danger, which sounds ridiculous but isn't. A woman and a brown man traveling through the country in a gigantic hot dog is a beautiful thing, but it's a dangerous one—even now, only two of the Hotdoggers in their class are not white, and the company doesn't allow two women to drive a Wienermobile alone in this area of the country.

"Which I know sounds messed up," Lauren says, "but I think they're right."

The sun is going down in the almost-winter sky and she tells me about times they've been scared, times that usually start with the interactions they were excited to tell me about when I first arrived.

"People just get hyped with the Wienermobile, which makes them do crazy things." Nick laughed earlier, but the things that are done are worth examining. Most of the time, the Crimes Against Large Hot Dog happen while neither of the drivers is there—Hotdoggers have an emergency hotline they can call whenever there's damage done to the vehicle, with side mirrors and windshield wipers the most frequent targets when drunk people become determined to scale the Wienermobile. That's not what Lauren wants to tell me about.

"Sometimes people follow us," she says, and explains how

she often needs to park the Wienermobile around the corner from where they're staying to protect them from being followed home. This has become second nature, she explains, but she's extremely careful not to forget anything in the Wienermobile after the sun goes down. She keeps looking at me apologetically, like I'm going to tell her she's overreacting.

"Let's say I leave a bag in the Wienermobile, so I mosey on out at eleven at night," she says, returning to a night where she forgot something and went to unlock the massive vehicle on her own, only to find that a man had followed her once she was inside. She closed the door, but the man was determined to get into the hot dog he had seen on television as a child, and started beating on the door violently.

She looks to me wildly. "And he was like, 'I saw you go in there!' Over and over, and that's why our hiding spot is right here." She points to the velveteen seat just like the others but out of sight from angry, drunk eyes that saw a young woman enter a Wienermobile alone at night.

"Does that happen often?" I ask her.

She nods solemnly, looking at me and then down at her lap.

"It's not, it's not as bad if you have a male partner that's very present, but I mean." She goes through a filing cabinet of examples and chooses one. "I've been at Walmart before and gotten stalkers and gotten love notes and it's been creepy. And then they start taking photos, and so my partner is like, 'Just go hide in the Wienermobile.'"

Once Lauren gives me one example they keep tumbling out—the time at a gas station someone didn't believe she could drive a hot dog, the time a man her father's age took a weenie whistle from her and then leaned against her and asked, "What else you have."

Nick approaches from the Del Taco beaming and pissless. Lauren sighs one last time and looks at me, resigned to a night of watching her Hotdogging brother present another girl with a Love Ornament.

"I guess," she says, "I guess I just wish I could do things without having bear spray in my pocket. You know?"

We say goodbye, and I walk to the train station with my keys between my fingers because I do know.

Alone but Not Alone,
Because Hot Dog

So not alone.

It's Christmas Eve and I'm alone and I'm telling myself it's because of the plague. The better part of the day was spent seeking out a COVID test the government said would be at my house at eleven in the morning yesterday, but it's four in the afternoon today and here I am. It arrives, I get the result I need, the Christmas tree I managed to find in the shed we used to share is sparsely decorated with ornaments that don't bring back a memory. It's a little lopsided but still glowing just enough to infuriate our (my?) cat into attacking it.

Hot dog.

No, not hot dog, Jamie, please not hot dog, Christmas is sad enough as it is. I'm rushing to make my deadline and have decided that I'm going to try juicing, something I would not recommend to anyone with an eating disorder but is fine when I do it. Sometimes I become possessed by the saddest thing I can think of in a given moment, and today it's this: what if I got a chili dog so wet it fell apart in my hands at midnight on fucking Christmas?

It's settled, and I put on four layers to look more masculine walking around at night by myself. Keys are in my hand, I am a human rectangle, I am walking to Original Tommy's World Famous Hamburgers fifteen minutes from where I live.

Hot dog.

Tommy's is open twenty-four hours a day, even when they shouldn't be, and I shuffle my way through the streets while the neighborhood fireworks thrown by kids remind me that either it's Christmas or New Year's Eve, or the Dodgers won tonight. My neighborhood is predominantly Latin and most of the celebrations have taken place on Christmas Eve for Nochebuena, a hybrid holiday that observes winter solstice Indigenous practices while still observing the aggressive Catholicism that Latin communities were indoctrinated into when the Spanish came a-colonizing in the 1800s. I pass a handful of families piling into the car to make it a few minutes late to a midnight mass and join a gnarly line around the corner at Tommy's.

Tommy's is most famous for its quarter-pound chili cheese-burger, a dish I could not finish with a gun to my head. It was founded in postwar Los Angeles by son of Greek immigrants Tom Koulax; I live closest to its original location with the red-and-yellow swiveling neon sign at the corner of Beverly and Rampart. Fools will wait in the drive-through line at Taco Bell across the street—real ones know that toughing it out at Tommy's back-to-back with your COVID-ridden peers is the nobler pursuit. The stand ran on the strength of its chili burgers and hot dogs then and still does now, with one of the most distinctive all-steel shit buckets full of chili in the entire country. It sits in repose next to a few sizzling patties that a rightfully annoyed employee is flipping, saying that his entire family is at church right now and what the fuck.

"This is church!" his coworker jokes. The first guy rolls his eyes.

The soupy chili here isn't the reason I come, although it does carry the highest risk-reward of any of the local options—it goes down easy, like a broth on top of a mostly decent dog that is best consumed in the smallest hours of the morning. I thought the Tommy's chili would force my period, but it set it back by a full forty-eight hours. It loves you as hard as it punishes you, and there's something about the pound of ground beef, chili powder, carrot, broth, and masa harina mixture in all its shit-bucket glory that demands your respect. The reason to come to Tommy's is the high drama that takes place in the line the moment the clock strikes eleven, and tonight I get a show.

"So I can't *vape* here?" a man in a silk Dodgers jacket with a tiny dog in a matching jacket yells at an elderly security guard. "On *Christmas?*"

The impossibly small guard, wearing a bright orange vest reading TOMMY'S SECURITY, holds her ground. "The sign says twenty-five feet, sir, you cannot smoke near the food." She points to the sign on the small red wooden shack where four employees are cooking shoulder to shoulder, wildly against plague protocols, as the mostly maskless line waits for their Christmas chili dogs.

The man in the Dodgers jacket is belligerent, reminding the elderly woman that America is still a free country, for *no-ow*. She rolls her eyes. There's an impossibly hot couple in front of me giggling at the whole thing, debating with each other.

"It's a public sidewalk, isn't it?" the boyfriend asks, grabbing her hand.

"I wouldn't want to cross her, though, shit," the girlfriend replies, nodding toward the increasingly agitated security guard. "She could kick both our asses."

The man in the Dodgers jacket pouts as he gets in line behind me, trying to get me involved. "That's bullshit, right?" he asks me. I make a gesture that is neither a nod nor a head shake, my noncommittal specialty, buying myself time that I don't need because *his* girlfriend, who has a jacket that matches both the dog's and the vapist's, bursts out of a parked car a few feet away.

"Are you fucking *kidding* me?" she asks, walking toward a

suddenly terrified Dodgers-jacket guy. "Yelling at a little old lady on Christmas? You're fucking serious right now?"

Her lover panics. "She wasn't letting me vape on a public sidewalk, did you see that?" The girlfriend swiftly apologizes to the security guard, who assures her it happens all the time, and the ugly jacket family is silently reunited. She takes his hand in a vise grip.

"That's the kind of thing that makes me not want you around my family, baby," she whines more softly, putting her head against his vape-scented silk chest. "You can't do shit like that, it's your temper."

He sighs but does not apologize. "Do you want one burger or two?"

She looks back up to him. "I'm serious, okay? No yelling at old ladies, it's Christmas."

He sighs but does not apologize. "Do you want *one* burger or *two*?"

The hot couple in front of me raise their perfectly manicured eyebrows. "That ain't us," he says to her softly, and sounds sure of it.

I elect for the chili dog, delivered hot into my hands with a bag of barbecue chips for me to walk home with. I'm a Partridge Family Christmas album purist and it blasts through the Air-Pods that were a gift from a man who now can't stand me, and I watch the top layer of the brownish-gray chili turn into a thin, brittle sheet while I walk past families debating who gets to sit shotbun. Finally home and just shy of Christmas, I slip past my cat, who's furious I had the nerve to leave him alone for forty-five minutes.

There is a snap to the Tommy's dog, but it's hard to focus on around all the goo that leaks from the wet bun onto my freezing hands. Still, it's good—my hands are covered in shit, my body is angry at me, my book is late, I am alone. My phone beeps to let me know it's Christmas, but I'm able to hold it together. I am processed meat held firmly inside of a casing that will only snap when you mercifully decide to bite my head off.

I open the fridge to store the other half of the hot dog for later, something absolutely disgusting I've managed to avoid telling you for nearly the whole book—the *for-later* fridge-crypt hot dog. Things are bleak in there these days—some salad dressing I bought when I was in love that doesn't go bad for another few weeks, that pornographic jar of mustard from Toledo, a Mike's Harder Lemonade.

Oh, right. Her.

The Mike's Harder sits in the vegetable crisper right where I left her in June. I haven't seen or thought about her since the first morning of Hot Dog Summer, when I held her in my palm and tried to remember how I was feeling. Six months later, it doesn't feel better, but it feels different. The plague is still here, but it's a new version; the emptiness is still here, but I've found a new and unhealthy way to fill it. I crack the Mike's and take a sip. Oh, disgusting. I wash it down with the rest of the hot dog. Oh, disgusting. Christ is Lord, hot dog is food, I am feeling a new and interesting pain.

And as for the question all you fuckos keep asking:

The best hot dog in the United States is at Rutt's Hut in Clifton, New Jersey. Everyone knows that.

Epilogue: On Bun Integrity

If you can't toast a bun to hold everything, stop putting wet shit on my hot dog. I don't care how interesting and regional it is. If your bun can't hold, then close the establishment because you are sick and you are lost. Goodnight!

RECOMMENDED READING

A lot of research went into *Raw Dog*—here are a few of the most important resources that aren't made of meat.

Bowen, Rich, and Richard R. Fay. *Hot Dog Chicago: A Native's Dining Guide.* Chicago: Chicago Review Press, 1983.

Douglas, Leah, and Georgia Gee. "A COVID Outbreak at a California Meatpacking Plant Started a Year Ago—and Never Went Away." *Mother Jones.* March 16, 2022, https://www.motherjones.com/food/2021 /03/a-covid-outbreak-at-a-california-meatpacking -plant-started-a-year-ago-and-never-went-away/.

Grabell, Michael. "The Plot to Keep Meatpacking Plants Open during COVID-19." *ProPublica.* May 13, 2022, https://www.propublica.org/article/documents-covid -meatpacking-tyson-smithfield-trump.

Grabell, Michael, and Bernice Yeung. "The Battle for Waterloo." *ProPublica.* December 21, 2020, https: //features.propublica.org/waterloo-meatpacking/as -covid-19-ravaged-this-iowa-city-officials-discovered -meatpacking-executives-were-the-ones-in-charge/.

Haimes, Nicole Lucas, dir. *The Good, the Bad, the Hungry.* Bristol, CT: ESPN Films, 2019.

How It's Made, season 10, episode 3, "Levels / Hot Dogs / Abrasive Grains / Sandpaper," created by Gabriel Hoss, aired September 3, 2008, on Science.

Kraig, Bruce. *Hot Dog: A Global History.* London: Reaktion Books, 2009.

Mercuri, Becky. *The Great American Hot Dog Book.* Layton, Utah: Gibbs Smith, 2007.

Schager, Nick. "Netflix Doc: CIA Flooded Black Communities with Crack." *The Daily Beast,* January 5, 2021, https://www.thedailybeast.com/netflix-doc-alleges-cia-flooded-black-communities-with-crack.

Schmidt, Samantha. "At Nathan's Hot Dog Contest, 15 Women Challenge the Gluttony Ceiling." *The New York Times,* July 4, 2016, https://www.nytimes.com/2016/07/05/nyregion/at-nathans-hot-dog-contest-15-women-challenge-the-gluttony-ceiling.html.

Segura, Melissa. "'How Am I Going to Survive?': A Costco Meatpacking Worker Speaks of Her Fears as She and Others Labor to Keep Chicken in Stores." *BuzzFeed News,* May 14, 2020, https://www.buzzfeednews.com/article/melissasegura/coronavirus-costco-meatpacking-workers-meat-shortage.

Sinclair, Upton. *The Jungle.* New York: Grosset & Dunlap, 1906.

Warrick, Jo. "'They Die Piece by Piece.'" *The Washington Post,* April 10, 2001, https://www.washingtonpost.com/archive/politics/2001/04/10/they-die-piece-by-piece/f172dd3c-0383-49f8-b6d8-347e04b68da1/.

RECOMMENDED EATING

And, if you're interested in this sort of thing, my top five hot dogs are found at:

Rutt's Hut in Clifton, New Jersey

Ruiz Hot Dogs Los Chipilones in Tucson, Arizona

Kim Jong Grillin in Portland, Oregon

The hot dog carts across the street from the Crypto .com Arena, or near Union Station in Los Angeles, California

Texas Tavern in Roanoke, Virginia

Flea cosplaying as a hot dog in Wisconsin.

ACKNOWLEDGMENTS

Huge and most important thanks goes to Ali Fisher at Tor for advocating for this book from the beginning—for her guidance through the objectively confusing world of publishing, for her friendship and her belief that hot dogs are worth it. Thank you for keeping me going throughout the (long) stretches of thinking maybe this was a bad idea. I wish I could be like her. She's so cool. It's fucked up! In the good way. She is the collaborator, friend, and advocate everyone deserves. I can't believe I got so lucky. Thank you so much, Ali. The whole Tor team has been so incredible throughout.

Thanks to former agent Meredith Miller at UTA and former manager Lisa Mierke for supporting this book. Free Palestine!

To Carolina, my perfect little skunk. I love love love you.

To you, asshole! I am so fortunate to have the support I've had over the years, and am so grateful to everyone who's said sure, I won't heckle this loser at the show, sure, I'll press play, sure, I can read, why not. Your kindness and willingness to give me a chance with your time and energy is deeply appreciated.

To Faye Orlove for the incredible hot dog illustrations for this book, I love and am in love with you. Thank you for watching fifteen whole minutes of *House of Gucci* before saying, "Okay, I'm taking my phone out now." Did you know Faye was pregnant when she worked on this book? Kind of incredible that I am reducing my friend to her body like this, and equally incredible that she is fostering life and making art whilst some of us are breaking off relationships left and right and have permanently damaged their reproductive organs thanks to eating too much processed meat.

My family is so important to me that it makes me want to die. Huge thanks to both my parents for being supportive of every unhinged idea I've ever pursued. To my mom, Jill, for giving me a love of performing and *Phantom of the Opera* and raising all ten of us as siblings and for choosing your own name and for the knowledge that you *have* your family and you *choose* your family too—I love you so much. To my dad, Mike, for teaching me to write and for Boston punk and for driving me to, oh jeez: *Pride and Prejudice* (2005) when it wasn't showing anywhere within an hour of us, to that poetry slam when I was twelve where I ended up chickening out, to that comedy show when I was twenty-one in Gloucester where the chairs were all dirty couches and I made disgusting jokes about you the entire time, to that Bright Eyes concert in 2007 when I was trying to impress a cool girl and told you to stand in the back and pretend you didn't know me and *you did,* and for bringing me to a strip club when I was underage so I could write a paper my freshman year of college. I think I need a ride to Tori's wedding next month, just a heads-up. Oh, and for not dying of cancer while I was writing as it would have been hugely inconvenient and self-centered of you. To my brother, Ben, for being the greatest person I know and the one I can trust with anything, you are kinder and funnier than me and I'll never get over it, bitch. Stop smoking cigarettes NOW!

My cousins Tamra and Chloe are my sisters, so I'm mentioning them here even though they're both vegetarians and were basically useless as it pertained to this process. Worthless!

To Bunny and Tom for bringing me food and being my second set of parents. To aunties Jane, Kate, and Julie and uncles Butch, Jack, and Craig.

On the hot dog front: I'd be remiss to ignore the works of Bruce Kraig (*Hot Dog: A History*), Rich Bowen and Dick Fay (*Hot Dog Chicago*), and Becky Mercuri (*The Great American Hot*

Dog Book) for laying the groundwork for this book. Same goes for the incredible work of Nicole Haimes, whose *30 for 30* about Joey Chestnut and Takeru Kobayashi were incredibly inspiring throughout, and the courageous reporting of Michael Grabell and Bernice Yeung at *ProPublica* for exposing the horrific abuses of power in American meatpacking throughout the pandemic.

Big thanks to the small business owners who were patient and kind with me, except for that one and you know who you are, and what was that all about? *No* thanks to you, you crusty old bitch.

Thank you to Isaac, for knowing me inside and out and for knowing the way. Thank you to Sunny for making me grateful that dogs cannot vote, and to Flea for making me grateful that cats can. Love forever.

It's very unlikely I'd have gotten to write this book without first having the support and love of my podcast family—to Caitlin, Sophie, Aristotle, Robert, Miles, Shereen, Anna, Beth Anne, Ian, Will, and my god Mister Jack O'Brien, this whole thing is your fault and I'm forever grateful. Thank you to Perry, Ellie, Dan, and all my pals at Allston Pudding for telling me that writing facts and writing chaotic horny aren't mutually exclusive. To the loser who fired me at *The Boston Globe,* how do you feel right now, Mr. Pee Pee?

To everyone who hosted us on this long slouch across the country: Sari, Tim, Mimi, Susan, Ben and Cole, Grace, Dad, Jake, Alex, Tammy, Carlos, Pierce, and Sarah for being so welcoming. To the Elysian Theater for letting me workshop an objectively nuts hot dog show to keep my mind on things (hi Paul), and to Leon, Sara, and Josiah for throwing up hot dogs into my mouth. To my best buds Caitlin, Bryant, and Julia for listening ad nauseum and always making the time. To Jess and John for reading this manuscript when it was still a trash fire. To Nick and Lauren for being so generous with your time and access to the motherfucking Wienermobile. To everyone who let me leave half a hot dog in your refrigerator in case I needed to taste-reference it later, that is fully disgusting.

Huge thank you to the mutual aid and leftist organizers in Los Angeles who have shaped my brain so I could attempt this book in the first place, and all the organizers and individuals who are doing the work day to day.

Thank you to the friends who ate hot dogs with me, reminded me to eat something that wasn't hot dogs, read early drafts and gave encouragement—Julia, Caitlin, Bryant, Meli, Maggie, Sarah, Rose, Jess, Jonny, Faye, Joshy, Abby, Michaela, Corie, Sophie, Christina, Alissa, Ember, Hannah, Molly, Lindsay, Will, Alex, Carolyn, Robert, Kate, Emily, Haley, Ben, Sara, Alissa, Cathy, Sam, Jake, Alex, Grace, Devon, David, and Miss Nina. To Steven for taking my virginity on August 15, 2010, God bless America.

To Al Freni, who I am too shy to contact but think about what you told me every day. To my pet rock, Bert, who I wish I'd told you about. To Freddy and Betty. To whoever I end up marrying who's reading this and being like, hell yeah, that's me, unless you're not reading this, in which case, what the fuck.

To the team at Tor, who somehow let me write this: Dianna Vega, Alexis Saarela, Libby Collins, Jennifer McClelland-Smith, Jamie Stafford-Hill, Dakota Griffin, Steven Bucsok, Linda Quinton, Devi Pillai, and the amazing Melanie Sanders, who correctly pointed out that Radiator Springs is a fictional American town and *not* a part of the *Cars* multiverse as I suspected. To Kavelina Torres—Yup'ik, Inupiaq, and Dene; filmmaker and storyteller; and Indigenous media professor, whose people come from the Yukon River, Kuskokwim River, and the Eastern Seaboard—for a thoughtful and empathetic sensitivity read. I am so grateful. Thank you all for your patience and support. I hope we can do it again.

And of course, thank you to Joseph Chestnut and the GOAT, Sonya Thomas.

Sunny trying the special at JJ's Red Hots in Charlotte, North Carolina.

ABOUT THE AUTHOR

Andrew Max Levy

JAMIE LOFTUS is a comedian, Emmy Award–nominated TV writer, and podcaster. She's worked as a staff writer on *Teenage Euthanasia, Robot Chicken,* and *Star Trek: Lower Decks,* and wrote and starred in her own web series for Comedy Central. She writes and hosts popular limited-run podcasts—*My Year in Mensa* (2019), *Lolita Podcast* (2020), *Aack Cast* (2021), and *Ghost Church* (2022)—and she cohosts, with screenwriter Caitlin Durante, a podcast on the iHeart Podcast Network called *The Bechdel Cast.* She has her baby teeth bronzed and loaded into a slingshot.